It's only the dirty ones we don't want

Philip Wilkinson

https://www.itsonlythedirtyoneswedontwant.co.uk

About the author:

© Author

During my childhood in Headingley, Leeds, in the 1970s, I was the oldest of five children. Our district was rapidly transforming into student accommodations, reflecting the changing times. Unfortunately, our family faced financial hardships, which compelled us to rent out the largest bedroom in our modest four-bedroom terrace house to two students. This arrangement helped us make ends meet, but it also meant we had to make do with limited space.

Our home had a cellar where we had a copper boiler and mangle for washing our clothes. Coal fires provided warmth in the two main rooms, as insulation was absent from the attic bedroom conversions (installed with the available funds from a grant scheme). The lack of insulation made those rooms very uncomfortable, especially during harsh weather.

In addition to the financial constraints, we didn't have a television or a car, which was not uncommon for families in similar circumstances at the time. However, our parents, who were actively involved in the evangelical Christian community, ensured that our entertainment revolved around our faith. We held Sunday school meetings in our lounge, fostering a sense of community within our own home. Another memorable experience was attending the televised Billy Graham rallies, which took place in marquees on Woodhouse Moor. These events provided spiritual nourishment and a sense of connection with a larger religious community.

Despite the challenges, we considered ourselves fortunate in one respect: we had an indoor bathroom and toilet. It was a small but significant comfort that set us apart from some others in similar situations.

Reflecting on those years, I realise that our upbringing taught us resilience and an appreciation for the simpler aspects of life. The contrast between those times and the conveniences and technologies we enjoy today is striking, but the memories and lessons from that period continue to shape who we are.

CONTENTS

About the author

Chapter 1 – 1970

A new school

Image of Rawcliffe's on Duncan Street Leeds   © Yorkshire Post Newspapers

Rawcliffe's

In the summer of 1970, at the tender age of eleven, I found myself at a pivotal moment in my life. It was a time of transition, as I was the last of a generation to sit the eleven plus exam and embark on a new chapter at a different school. Little did I know that this experience would shape my understanding of the world and leave an indelible mark on my memory.

With my mother by my side, we ventured into Rawcliffe's, a rather posh shop in Leeds that catered to all the needs of schoolchildren. As we entered, a sales assistant, a gentleman nearing retirement age, greeted us. He wore glasses and sported a distinguished large moustache. With a gentle touch, standing behind me he placed his hands on my shoulders and inquired about the school I would be attending. My

mother proudly stated, "Abbey Grange CofE." Very nice, came the reply, the assistant disappeared momentarily into the storeroom, only to return with a complete set of school uniform in hand.

Suddenly, in the middle of the shop, amidst other boys and girls going through the same process, I found myself being stripped down to my underwear. The assistant then presented me with a crisp white cotton shirt, a blue and grey silk tie in the school's colours, neat black cotton trousers, and a grey blazer with pale blue piping and the school crest on the pocket. All that remained was to find some nice shoes and a cap, as the salesman suggested. Promptly, he returned with three more shirts, socks, a pair of smart black leather shoes, and a cap matching the school colours. I felt very smart and proud dressed in the uniform, having never owned clothes of this quality before.

As we approached the counter, my mother retrieved the state-issued free school uniform vouchers. Instantly, the salesman's complexion turned pale. He practically dragged me to a corner of the shop, muttering under his breath about "bloody customers with free uniform vouchers." In a rush, he stripped me of everything except my underpants. Disappearing into the storeroom once again, he emerged with a pair of crimplene trousers that were a dull grey, a lacklustre off-white nylon shirt, and a blazer that seemed to be made from flimsy cardboard and was a different shade of grey to the previous offering, adorned with shoddy blue piping. "This, madame," he declared, "is the free school uniform entitlement."

My mother, visibly upset, inquired about the tie and cap. However, the salesman informed her that those items were not included with the vouchers. Having no money to buy the tie or cap, we left the store with the cheap and inferior uniform, disappointment weighing heavily on my mother's heart. It was only later, when my grandmother intervened and purchased the tie for me to complete the set. As for the cap, I simply decided it wasn't worth pursuing.

That experience at Rawcliffe's was a stark reminder of the disparities that existed between those who could afford the finer things and those who relied on the state's provision. It was an early lesson in the segregation and unjust treatment that can befall those from less privileged backgrounds. Despite the disappointment, I wore that subpar uniform with a sense of resilience and determination, knowing that my worth as a student was not defined by the clothes, I wore but by my character and potential.

As I entered Abbey Grange on my first day of school in Horsforth, a wave of unease washed over me. The sight of my new uniform immediately highlighted the social divisions among the students, leaving those of us from less privileged backgrounds feeling isolated and excluded.

Looking back, I can't help but attribute part of this situation to Rawcliffe's, in addition to the Government. As a prominent and influential supplier of school uniforms at the time, Rawcliffe's played a significant role in shaping uniform policies across the country. Each summer, they would sell an astonishing number of school uniforms, reaching up to half a million. However, it became evident that the system favoured wealthier families. They would frequently order multiple items and readily replace any older, soiled, or worn-out pieces throughout the year. Conversely, poor students like me received only one voucher per year, which fell short of addressing the challenges we faced.

It seems to me that Rawcliffe's could have implemented simple measures to address this disparity. One option would have been to eliminate the discrepancy entirely by providing all students with an affordable uniform of the same quality. Alternatively, they could have bridged the cost gap by offering higher-quality uniforms for the value of the vouchers given to less privileged students. Such practices could have fostered a more inclusive environment, where students were not judged or ostracized based on their financial circumstances.

By acknowledging their role in perpetuating the disparities in school uniforms, Rawcliffe's could have taken steps toward creating a fairer and more equitable educational experience for all students, regardless of their financial backgrounds.

A new school – a new start   © Pixababy

Abbey Grange CofE school, originally designed to accommodate a maximum of 500 pupils, was bursting at the seams with an intake year of 128 students, pushing the total student population to over 1,100. It was a stark contrast to my previous school, which had fewer than 100 students spread across just four classrooms. In that small and close-knit community, each subject was taught by the same teacher in the same classroom for an entire year. The new school, in comparison, was over 11 times its size, and that was just the beginning of the significant differences I would encounter.

One of the immediate challenges I faced was the issue of my uniform. Among a sea of students, there were twelve boys who stood out as poor. We became constant targets of bullying, manipulation, and mistreatment. Being from a very poor background, my parents couldn't afford a car, a radio, or a television set. This information, once discovered by the bullies, became ammunition for their cruel jokes. They would innocently inquire about my family, asking questions like, "How many brothers and sisters do you have?" Naively, I would reply, "Two of each." That's when they would pounce, sneering, "Don't your parents have a TV?" It took months for me to realise the true nature of their hurtful remarks and understand that it was all part of a malicious game. The contrast between my previous school and Abbey Grange was not just in terms of size but also in the treatment I received as a student from a disadvantaged background. The early days at this new school were marked by a harsh reality, where bullies took pleasure in preying on our vulnerabilities. It was a painful introduction to the disparities that existed among the student body, a stark reminder that not everyone's journey through education would be fair or equitable. To maintain a clear distinction between students who paid for their school dinners and those on free meals, the school implemented a double queue system. The paying students formed one line and were served their meals first, while the students receiving free meals had to wait. This segregation ensured that even those who had not noticed the poor free school uniform were aware of our status.

Unfortunately, this division between the two queues often led to unpleasant encounters. As the paying students sat at their tables enjoying their meals, some would take advantage of the situation and engage in disrespectful behaviour. They would taunt and belittle the students in the other queue, tossing chips their way and making derogatory remarks, insinuating that they were somehow inferior. These hurtful actions were accompanied by sarcastic comments like, "Here, poor boy, you need this more than me."

The double queue system, meant to provide order and fairness, inadvertently became a platform for mockery and humiliation. For those in the free meal queue, it was a disheartening experience, as they were reminded of their economic circumstances and made to feel lesser by their peers.

Government education policies – and their consequences   © Pixababy

The introduction of government policies aimed at addressing uniform affordability had unintended consequences that exacerbated the divisions among students. While schools advocating for uniform requirements argued that such policies created a sense of equality and unity, the reality on the ground told a different story.

It's only the dirty ones we don't want - Philip Wilkinson

For those students who qualified for free uniforms, the materials provided were far from ideal. The cheap nylon shirts and rayon trousers proved uncomfortable, particularly during warmer weather when they caused excessive sweating. The resulting body odours and discomfort became a source of ridicule and discrimination, further isolating these students. They were unfairly branded as "dirty" or "unhygienic" by their peers, deepening the sense of segregation based on economic circumstances.

Meanwhile, the government's broader changes to education policy brought about another challenge. Faith schools were now required to allocate 10% of their admissions to students from non-faith backgrounds, creating a need to vet candidates who lacked the usual church connections. This process led to the inclusion of approximately 12 students who, in the context of this narrative, came to be known as "the morons."

From the very first day, the presence of the morons sparked a series of disturbances. The situation escalated to the point where police intervention became necessary. On one occasion, the police were called to clear students off the school roof, disrupting the normal flow of education and safety within the premises. Another incident involved a thorough investigation into the staff car park, as every vehicle had suffered at least one broken window. The morons had caused widespread damage and chaos, leaving a lasting impact on the school community.

This combination of factors - the inadequate quality of free uniforms and the disruptive presence of the morons - created an environment of tension and discord. Instead of fostering unity and equality, the school experienced heightened divisions and unrest, leaving both students and staff grappling with the consequences of these unfortunate circumstances.

School bureaucracy at its worst　　　　　　　　　　　　　© Pixababy

The school's decision to adopt a six-day week timetable added an unnecessary extra layer of complexity to an already demanding academic environment. Understanding the schedule was no easy feat for overwhelmed schoolchildren grappling with a new regime and increased workload. During the first week, Monday was designated as day 1, while Friday was day 5. The following week, Monday would become day 6, and Friday would be day 4. This pattern continued, with the days aligning with their corresponding numbers until week 6, when the days and numbers finally matched, this was then repeated on a loop.

The ever-changing day numbering system proved to be a constant source of headaches. Students frequently found themselves mixing up the weeks and arriving at classes with the wrong books or materials. The confusion was amplified by the fact that most subjects were divided into five sets. For example, one would spend approximately four weeks studying algebra before taking a test and being reassigned to a new teacher, classroom and even a new set for the next subject, this was typical of all the set subjects taught. As someone who consistently ranked towards the bottom of the top set, I frequently moved between the first and second sets. This meant that I would often enter a classroom, standing among familiar faces from the previous days lesson, only to realise that I was now in a different set, in a different classroom, with a different teacher.

Adding to the bewildering nature of the school's layout and organizational system, the classrooms themselves presented their own challenges. They were numbered identically on different floors, creating a puzzling situation. For instance, there would be classrooms 1 to 9A on the ground floor, classrooms 1 to 9B on the middle floor, and classrooms 1 to 9C on the top floor. The levels and classrooms were indistinguishable from one another, leading to potential confusion and disorientation for students trying to find their assigned rooms.

Compounding this already complex situation was the issue of overcrowding. With the school accommodating significantly more students than it was designed for, it became a common occurrence to find two classes of pupils eagerly waiting outside a classroom. However, to everyone's surprise, a teacher would often arrive and announce, "Those of you with me, we will be in the gym today," prompting the assembled students to march off to an alternative location for their lesson. These impromptu relocations could take place in the gymnasium, the main hall, a corridor, a changing room, or even on the stage. Any available empty space was fair game for transforming into a temporary classroom.

For those unfortunates arriving just after the relocation announcement, or to have been taught in that classroom earlier in the week, but not today due to re setting, confusion reigned supreme. Without any knowledge of the new location, students would be left in a state of uncertainty, desperately searching for their class, and hoping to stumble upon their peers and teacher. Navigating the labyrinthine corridors, deciphering the cryptic classroom numbering, and adapting to the ever-changing locations for lessons became a test of resilience and adaptability for the students. It was a constant juggling act to stay informed, keep track of changes, and avoid being left behind in the chaos that pervaded the overcrowded school.

The school campus consisted primarily of three distinct buildings, each serving its own purpose. The two-story science and art block housed specialised rooms such as laboratories, while the three-story classroom block accommodated traditional subjects like mathematics, English, and technical drawing. Connecting these two buildings was the main hall, which led to the changing rooms and gymnasium. Positioned between all three of these structures stood the administration block, a central hub housing various facilities including the teachers' rest area, the headmaster's and deputy headmaster's offices, and the nurse's office for first aid.

Despite the administration block serving as the sole link between the three main buildings, pupils were strictly prohibited from entering this area. Our access was restricted solely to "the bridge," an open mezzanine level bridging the gap between the science block first floor and the classroom block second floor. There was no access to the hall, changing rooms or gym except to go out of the building and walk around. To manage the campus effectively, a master timetable was prominently displayed in the office administration corridor. Should a student find themselves disoriented or lost, they were instructed to consult this timetable for guidance. However, this instruction presented us with a perplexing catch-22 situation. As pupils, we were not permitted to access the office corridor, rendering the very solution to our navigational quandaries inaccessible.

This bureaucratic conundrum only added to the peculiarities of the school's layout and rules, leaving us to rely on alternative means to find our way, often seeking assistance from fellow students or discreetly observing the movements of staff members. Navigating the campus became a game of ingenuity and resourcefulness, as we strived to avoid the forbidden territories while making our way between classes and other areas of the school.

Fountain pens   © Pixababy

At the outset of our first week at school, an unexpected rule was imposed upon us: a complete ban on ballpoint pens. The administration insisted that every student must use a fountain pen, and we were given until the following Monday to comply. No exceptions were to be made, even for those receiving free school uniforms and lunches. Thankfully, my grandfather came to my rescue, presenting me with a cherished fountain pen and a bottle of ink to meet this newly enforced requirement. Little did I know that this would mark the beginning of a series of tribulations.

It's only the dirty ones we don't want - Philip Wilkinson

Adjusting to writing with a fountain pen proved to be quite challenging. As I diligently crafted my words on paper, my right hand gradually took on a permanent blue hue due to constant contact with the ink. The pen had an unfortunate tendency to occasionally leak, leaving unsightly blotches and smears on my work. Moreover, the ink stains stubbornly clung to the cuffs of my pristine white nylon shirt, presenting quite the obstacle when it came to washing them out.

Adding to the frustrations of this new writing instrument were a group of mischievous individuals who saw fit to turn their fountain pens into impromptu ink-firing water pistols. Within the first two weeks of the term, I found myself twice falling victim to their pranks, drenched in ink, and left to deal with the consequences. Removing the stubborn stains proved to be an arduous and often impossible task. Since replacing the uniform was not an option, I was left with no choice but to wear the soiled and damaged clothes for another year, once again singling me out as different.

Amidst the usual classroom chatter one day, a mischievous pupil seized an opportunity for a prank. Swiftly snatching another student's pen from their grasp as they were during writing, the scene erupted into a brief commotion, with some pushing and shoving as the victim sought to reclaim their stolen pen. As the tensions escalated, a towering student emerged triumphant, clutching the pen at a considerable distance from the victim.

In an unfortunate twist of fate, a teacher entered the room, catching the scene in its delicate equilibrium. Seizing the moment, the mischievous protagonist hurled the pen towards the victim, and with an unintended stroke of precision, the nib struck her forehead, leaving behind a conspicuous blue dot, a peculiar and unwanted tattoo. Understandably, the victim's expression conveyed a profound sense of displeasure and frustration.

The transition to using fountain pens came with unforeseen consequences. What was intended as a measure to encourage better penmanship instead became a source of daily challenges, leaving me with perpetually stained hands, ruined assignments, and a continuous battle against ink-related mishaps, including inadvertently marking a fellow student with an unwanted tattoo akin to a borstal mark.

The issue of fountain pens, with their tendency to leak, compounded the segregation of children from less privileged backgrounds. The financial limitations that prevented us from replacing expensive school uniforms, except once a year with the provided vouchers, meant we had to continue wearing stained, dirty, or even torn clothing. The light grey blazer, with its delicate pale blue edge piping and dry-clean-only care instructions, proved to be a nightmare to keep clean. After just a few weeks, those of us wearing these soiled garments once again became targets for bullying, exclusion, and disdain.

The treatment I and others received from our peers during this time at school reinforced the painful realisation that cleanliness and uniformity determined our social status and acceptance among classmates. As the title of my book (which came from a much later encounter) suggests, my peers' treatment of those in this predicament could be summed up in a sentence: "It's only the dirty ones we don't want...

It's only the dirty ones we don't want - Philip Wilkinson

Dinnertime   © Pixababy

One Monday dinnertime we dashed out of school and the whole back playground, sports field and gym were out of bounds, the morons, pupils from the school, over the weekend had driven a stolen car around the school grounds, crashing it into the back wall of the gym, then setting it on fire, it turned out to be the car of one of the parents of the morons from the nearby estate, to give him his dues he reported his son as having taken the car without his consent, and to having witnessed his own car being driven by three pupils from the school.

The resonating sound of the dinner bell would signal a remarkable spectacle, a stampede of students vying to be the first in line for their midday meal. The main classroom building, a towering three-story structure, featured a large open staircase and a spacious stairwell. As the pupils converged upon this central point, the scene resembled those captivating videos of wildebeest herds crossing canyons in the vast Serengeti plains. Upon reaching the staircase, students would hastily deposit their bags over the handrails, creating a mountainous heap within the depths of the stairwell. This practice served two purposes: to unburden themselves during the lunch break and to expedite their ascent on the staircase, ultimately leading to the bustling crush at the double doors that spilled out onto the playground.

However, my little cohort of free school dinner recipients followed a different routine. Obliged to queue separately and wait until the rest of the school had been served, we saw no sense in joining the frenzied rush. Instead, we would linger for a moment, observing the chaotic flood until it gradually subsided. Unfortunately, some thoughtless individuals perceived this moment as an opportunity for bullying, capitalising on the mayhem to target us. Seizing our bags, they callously hurled them from the top floor, with two incidents resulting in my ink bottle shattering upon impact. They even tossed poor Bog from the second floor onto the burgeoning mound of bags. However, the most malicious act unfolded when they cornered Lanky in the restroom a few minutes before the stampede. Utilising his tie and bag straps, they callously bound his limbs together, leaving him helplessly sprawled on the stairwell floor. Completely concealed beneath the cascade of bags, he remained immobile and undiscovered until after the lunch break when fellow pupils collected their belongings.

These distressing incidents served as reminders of the callousness that lurked within some individuals amidst the lunchtime rush. The repercussions of their actions extended far beyond the physical damage inflicted upon our possessions, leaving lasting impressions of fear and vulnerability etched in our minds.

A Victorian approach to discipline   © Pixababy

Mr. Slack, the headmaster, embodied the kind of leader who regarded teaching and schoolchildren as nothing more than an inconvenience. He actively sought to minimize his involvement with them, displaying a complete lack of familiarity with the names of any of the students in the school. This indifference extended to the teachers and staff as well.

The school's disciplinary approach harked back to the strict ways of the Victorian era. Every transgression committed by a student resulted in either capital punishment or the assignment of a punishment essay and sometimes both, the teacher would specify both the topic and the required number of pages. It was not uncommon to hear a teacher summon a pupil with a pointed finger, commanding them to write a four-page essay on the perils of running in school. The teacher would then deposit a slip detailing the punishment into the essay's designated box in the hallway.

The completed essay had to be dutifully submitted by 9:00 AM the following day. For every four essays assigned, the headmaster would administer two strokes of the cane upon the student's hand, a consequence seemingly fitting at first glance. However, some teachers took a vindictive approach when issuing these essays.

In Mathematics, for instance, Mr. Manri, with every new class, would intentionally allow the chatter to escalate before abruptly demanding that the entire class write four pages on the topic of avoiding distractions during lessons. Such essays were frequently doled out for seemingly trivial reasons like a loosely tied tie, a shirttail escaping its proper place, or trousers not pulled up to the expected height.

Another maths teacher had a wood test tube rack on his desk at all times, we wondered why he needed scientific equipment in the maths lessons, it became apparent when one of our number got out of line one day, the teacher told him to put the rack on his fingers, then to stand in front of the class and hold his hand in the air, after a while fatigue set in and it became increasingly difficult and painful to hold your hand up, every time he saw your arm drop, or you use the other hand to support your arm, he would slap you with a ruler, this became known as being put on the rack. These additional punishments compounded the chaos that plagued the overcrowded school, burdened by a demanding six-day timetable and a shortage of suitable classrooms. Failures of any kind, no matter how minor, were met with swift retribution.

© Pixababy

I, too, fell victim to the cane, for exceeding the allotted number of essays on three separate occasions. As an eleven-year-old, the experience of awaiting the headmaster's readiness to deliver this dreaded punishment was far from pleasant. The headmaster, a towering, athletic figure, cast an intimidating shadow. The aftermath of such chastisement left one unable to hold a pen, or even write, for a torturous period of approximately two hours.

It's only the dirty ones we don't want - Philip Wilkinson

Mr. Sherwood, a senior math teacher nearing retirement, had a unique passion for cricket, as well as a captivating model of the HMS Ark Royal aircraft carrier prominently displayed atop his blackboard. The school boasted a special connection with this illustrious vessel. However, Mr. Sherwood's classes were notorious for descending into utter chaos, reaching such levels of commotion that neighbouring teachers would send a student to verify his presence in the classroom.

Rather than managing the unruly atmosphere, Mr. Sherwood would simply abandon his attempts at teaching, opting instead to retreat to his desk, engrossed in a book. This disarray had a significant impact on my academic trajectory. Since our math sets were rotated among different teachers, each time my class was assigned to Mr. Sherwood for a few weeks, we would regress from the top set to the third set, only to regain our position after being taught by a different instructor. Consequently, gaps in my mathematical education persist to this day due to his ineffective teaching methods. Remarkably, Mr. Sherwood's poor instruction extended beyond my experience.

He later taught a girl, C, who was two years junior to our class. This cohort was part of an experimental middle school program that introduced students to middle school from 9 to 13 and then to high school at the age of 13, aiming for them to select their GCE/CSE subjects right from the beginning. By this time, the system had undergone changes, retained the six-day week but assigned a single teacher to each subject's set. Unfortunately, C was under Mr. Sherwood's tutelage for most of her three years at the school. The repercussions were dire, with his entire class performing abysmally in the mock exams.

Consequently, an oversight committee intervened, scrutinizing Mr. Sherwood's teaching practices and determining him to be unfit. A replacement teacher was swiftly brought in, tasked with compressing three years' worth of maths curriculum into a mere five months. Despite the immense challenge, C managed to achieve a grade 5 CSE in maths, while her other subjects hovered around grade 2 GCE. These shared experiences with C, who would later become my girlfriend and ultimately my wife, shed light on the profound impact Mr. Sherwood had on countless students' academic journeys.

It's only the dirty ones we don't want - Philip Wilkinson

© Pixababy

Another stupid stunt by the dozen or so intake of unruly kids was to take a brand-new razor blade, then, walking down the corridor at busy times, they would cut the back of your hand as they passed by, you did not feel anything except for some itching causing you to scratch the back of your hand, but later noted that you were bleeding profusely.

© Pixababy

Razor blades were banned in school. So the bullies moved on, bringing a Gat pop out air pistol to school, which they concealed in a rucksack, carrying the sack, they would shoot you as you passed by in a crowd, I can assure you, having been a victim to both types of assault, the dart gun was the worst as it typically required a trip to the medical room for the dart to be dug out of your body, an iodine wipe, plaster and even stitches.

It's only the dirty ones we don't want - Philip Wilkinson

Holy Communion © Pixababy

Within the confines of the Church of England-affiliated school, a unique tradition unfolded three times each year: the observance of Holy Communion, a sacrament shared by the entire student body.

However, my participation was denied on account of my Evangelical beliefs, which aligned more closely with the Baptist denomination than with the high church practices upheld by the school.

This exclusion only served to accentuate my sense of otherness among my peers. The transformation of the school hall into a grand high church chapel was a sight both intriguing and alien. Adorned with an elaborate altar, flickering candles, and a cross bearing the inscription "INRI" (Jesus, King of the Jews), the scene was complete with a Deacon and assisting Priest draped in resplendent vestments.

For hours on end, I watched from the back as fellow pupils filed by, receiving the solemn offering of the wafer and wine. The repetitive nature of the ceremony often left me yearning for more engaging pursuits, and on one occasion, the weariness overwhelmed me, lulling me into a deep slumber.

My respite, however, was abruptly shattered by the headmaster himself, who seized my ear with an unwarranted force, yanking me awake from my blissful ignorance. Without a word, he forcefully escorted me out of the chapel, relegating me to the desolate confines of the hall outside his office for the remainder of the day. The message was clear, I was to bear the consequences of my unintended transgression and conform to the customs that set me apart.

However, in RE lessons, held by Miss Brent, a frustrated spinster in her forties, I used to enjoy asking difficult questions, such as where did Mrs Cain come from?, What happens to people from other religions when they die? and "If God created the world, where do dinosaurs fit in?", If Jesus turned water into wine, does that mean it's okay for us to drink alcohol? and the like.

Classroom distractions © Author

It was an era where teachers resorted to various tactics to awaken sleepy or distracted pupils during class, sometimes sneaking up and hitting the pupil with a ruler, other times throwing the stick of chalk.

One such common practice involved launching the blackboard eraser with pinpoint accuracy, aiming to strike the desk or wall near the inattentive student. The impact of the eraser hitting its target was usually enough to startle them awake and re-engage with the lesson. However, there were instances when misfortune intervened. The eraser, propelled with unintended force, found its mark on the student's unsuspecting head, causing them to lose consciousness. It was a rare occurrence, but one that left an indelible impression on all who witnessed it. Today's students, living in an era of evolving educational methods and practices, can scarcely fathom the magnitude of such experiences that were once commonplace in classrooms.

On a day that seemed to drag on with monotonous lessons, a sudden disruption shattered the quiet ambiance of the school. A deafening explosion reverberated through the corridors, accompanied by the blaring sound of the fire alarm. Startled, we stepped out of the classroom to investigate the commotion. What I witnessed was both alarming and puzzling.

At the end of the corridor, lodged in the plaster, was a spent air bomb firework. Its distinctive shape and appearance were unmistakable. The fire doors, designed to keep us safe, had been maliciously propped open, allowing acrid smoke to billow throughout the corridor. It was clear that someone, one of the bullies no doubt, had orchestrated this dangerous prank and then vanished into thin air.

In response to the emergency, the entire school was swiftly evacuated to the designated fire muster points. The incident had injected a jolt of excitement into an otherwise dreary afternoon. However, as time passed and the adrenaline subsided, a chilling realization crept into my mind. What if a student had been compelled to leave the classroom during the lesson? The air bomb, with its explosive force, could have caused serious harm in the enclosed space, leaving them with no safe place to seek refuge.

The incident served as a sobering reminder of the potential consequences of such reckless actions. It underscored the importance of maintaining a secure and respectful learning environment for all students. From that day forward, I couldn't help but feel a heightened sense of vigilance, always aware of the lurking hazards that could disrupt our education and put lives at risk. It was a lesson learned not

only through the startling explosion but also through the realization of what could have been a far more devastating outcome.

Rivalries with other schools   © Pixababy

Another high school nearby, Moor Grange, had resulted in many incidents during school arrival and leaving times, kids from both schools would clash on a regular basis, especially on the No. 72 public service bus service used by many pupils from both schools, one clash had resulted in a pupil from Moor Grange, trying to evade capture, being run over near to the bus stop.,

Another incident I witnessed involved a pupil from each school, having stolen a motorcycle, they proceeded to ride it up and down the road where the other pupils were walking to the bus.

On one pass they suffered a tumble and the bike rolled over, picking it up and restarting the bike was their downfall, the bike suddenly caught fire from the spilled fuel, and both were badly burned requiring an ambulance and hospital treatment.

After this the schools changed their timetable to start and finish at different times, this did result in a reduction of incidents, but was not perfect, as Moor Grange finished half an hour before Abbey Grange, it gave their pupils time to plan ambushes either at the school gates, or commonly used bus stops etc.

Chapter 2 – 1971

Wakeup call

A pump like that at Birkby Grange farm   © Pixababy

Staying with Reg Umpleby

During the summer, our entire family had the privilege of spending several weeks on Birkby Grange farm in Thorner. The farmer, Reg Umpleby, was a friend of my father and had a quintessentially Yorkshire name associated with East Yorkshire.

The farmhouse itself was incredibly basic, with open fires, a large table, and an Aga cooker in the kitchen. There was no running water, as we had to draw water from a well in the front garden. The absence of carpets, minimal furniture, and lack of curtains did not diminish the warm and inviting atmosphere of the place.

To accommodate everyone, we filled palliasses with straw and used them as beds, placing them on the wooden floors. Our daily routine began withdrawing water from the well into buckets and jugs. We would then assist with the farm animals, followed by fruit and berry picking throughout the day. In the evenings, our time was occupied with breadmaking, preserving and jam making. On several days of the week, we would cut firewood, a task that we found enjoyable using a chainsaw and an axe. This experience was a world away from our usual environment in the terraced houses of Headingley.

After completing preparations such as cutting the hay and setting up a marquee, several hundred Evangelical Christians from the region gathered for a day of prayer and Bible meetings. The highlight of the event was an enormous barbecue held in the evening. Though mainly consisting of hot dogs and burgers, it felt like an extraordinary treat, and we were allowed to have as much as we desired.

In a twist of fate, Reg Umpleby's Birkby Grange farm, Thorner, in about 1998, was converted into a house, now valued at £1.35Million in 2023, along with the barns and outbuildings, now known as Grange House, Hillside Cottage and Grange Barn, all worth considerably over £1Million each, all are residential, one of the occupiers on the estate in 1998 was Gina Campbell daughter of Donald Campbell, of Bluebird fame. My company installed the intruder alarm systems for several of the properties created from the farm buildings, it was a trip down memory lane for me personally, and the new residents were amazed that I had stayed on the farm as a youngster.

Birkby Grange farm now

Imagery ©2023 Google, Imagery ©2023 Airbus, Infoterra Ltd & Bluesky, The GeoInformation Group, Map data ©2023 5 m

New year at school – same old bureaucracy

As the new school year began, I couldn't help but feel a sense of resignation. The notion of a fresh start, a new era, was quickly shattered as the familiar patterns of the previous year emerged once again.

The dreaded six-day week had come to an end on day 3, and now, on the first day back, it was a Tuesday, this could have been day 1 following a reset for the new year, or day 5 if we took the last day from the previous year and allowed for Monday that week, but as it turned out it was day 4 on the 6 day timetable. It seemed almost intentional, as if they wanted to maximise the potential for punishment and mistakes right from the start.

And true to form, the onslaught began immediately. Three punishment essays were assigned on that very first day as I had misunderstood how the 6-day week timetable would run continuously, even into the next year, setting a dubious record that still stands as one of the most overwhelming challenges I faced during my time at the school. It felt like a deliberate ploy to test our endurance and resilience right from the get-go, a stark reminder that there would be no respite from the demanding workload and high expectations.

The weight of those three essays hung over me like a dark cloud, casting a shadow on what should have been a fresh start. It was disheartening to realise that the cycle of excessive assignments and gruelling deadlines would continue unabated. The school seemed determined to maintain its reputation for rigorous academic standards, even if it meant pushing its students to the brink.

It's only the dirty ones we don't want - Philip Wilkinson

© Pixababy

A sniper in the playground

During the first week of the new term, a shocking incident unfolded at the school. It was a day like any other, with students enjoying their lunch break and taking a moment to relax. Little did we know that a group of troublemakers, known as the morons, had plotted an alarming act of cruelty.

Hidden in the dense grass and weeds at the far end of the playing field, the morons had positioned themselves with an air rifle equipped with telescopic sights. From their concealed vantage point, they began targeting unsuspecting pupils with sniper-like precision. Chaos and panic ensued as students found themselves under fire, unaware of the source of this sudden danger.

The severity of the situation quickly became apparent, and the school authorities wasted no time in acting. The police were immediately called to respond to this alarming armed incident. With the help of their expertise, they strategically approached the area where the morons were hiding. Employing a pincer movement from outside the school boundaries, the police closed in on the trio's location.

The gravity of their actions became clear as the morons were apprehended by the police. This was a serious offence that threatened the safety and well-being of the entire school community. In the aftermath of the incident and the suspensions imposed on these morons, we experienced a period of respite from their presence. For several months, the school was free from their disruptive behaviour, and we were able to focus on our studies and enjoy a more peaceful environment.

It's only the dirty ones we don't want - Philip Wilkinson

A cycling trip in the dales   © Pixababy

In the early days of our school friendship, Lanky, Dodge, Bog, and I decided to embark on a cycling adventure through the picturesque Yorkshire Dales. With February marked on our calendars, we eagerly anticipated the journey ahead. I borrowed my parents' old single-speed road cycle, which was far from ideal for such an excursion.

Setting off from Headingley towards Otley, our enthusiasm was quickly tested when my cycle's chain refused to cooperate. Thankfully, an elderly cycle enthusiast at a repair shop in far Headingley came to our aid, inspecting and fixing my bike without charging a penny.

Dunnies (Wharfedale) Café   © iStock

Image curtesy of Wharfedale observer https://www.wharfedaleobserver.co.uk/news/10976365.iconic-otley-cafe-dunnies-to-close-its-doors-for-the-last-time/

Our spirits lifted as we arrived at The Dunnies, a renowned cyclists' café on Bridge Street in Otley. It was mid-morning when we sat down to a sumptuous breakfast, indulging in generous portions of bacon, sausages, eggs, beans, tomatoes, fried bread, toast, and even a few chips. To our surprise, as we left the café, nobody asked us for payment, so we silently relished our good fortune and continued our way.

The next stop on our journey was The Sun Inn in Fewston. However, along the way, mishaps befell us. Two punctures, a broken brake lever, and a sprained wrist from a fall plagued our progress. Nonetheless, the gracious innkeeper served us bitter shandy, three-quarters of a pint topped with lemonade, if we enjoyed our drinks outside. Savouring the taste of alcohol for the first time, we repaired our bikes while relishing the moment.

Unfortunately, our attempts at repairs proved inadequate, prompting Bog to suggest seeking help at a cycle repair shop in Summerbridge rather than calling it a day and heading home. Determined to press on, we embarked on a slow journey to Summerbridge. Arriving just as the shop was closing, we managed to procure a puncture repair kit and batteries for our lights as darkness had descended upon us. It was then that Lanky, a member of the Youth Hostel Association, proposed riding a bit further to a nearby hostel where we could spend the night before returning home.

Image © Geograoh.org https://www.geograph.org.uk/photo/6895637

The former YHA building, Dacre Banks

Little did we know that the hostel Lanky remembered was much farther away, at Dacre Banks. Exhausted and chilled to the bone after a twenty-plus-mile ride, we arrived around 7:00 pm, hoping for respite. Unfortunately, our hopes were dashed as the hostel refused us entry, citing that it was reserved for hikers, not cyclists, regardless of our ages and the late hour. Faced with this setback.

It's only the dirty ones we don't want - Philip Wilkinson

Dodge then mentioned his parents' caravan at a campsite in How Stean which he thought was not very far, however it turned out to be 12 miles and a challenging distance of 31 miles from our starting point in Headingley. With determination and a touch of desperation, we pleaded with the caravan site owner to contact Dodge's parents for permission and provide us with the keys to the van.

A tired old caravan similar to the one we stayed the night in   © Pixababy

Our night at the campsite was far from comfortable, lacking food, bedding, and heating. Shivering and fatigued, we endured the cold until morning arrived. Realising the extent of our exhaustion, I called my father, who graciously agreed to come and collect us. However, due to limited space in his Mini Clubman car, the bikes had to be left behind in the caravan until summer, when our friends' parents returned and brought them home.

Before we left, Dodge took us to the other end to the caravan site, through the camp site, which was eerily quiet and across a tiny bridge, to our amazement we could see down into Howstean Gorge, a limestone cave that had collapsed thousands of years earlier, water had then removed the debris leaving a crystal-clear stream in the bottom of a deep, vertical sided gorge, nicknamed little Switzerland. What an unusual place, I had never encountered anything like it and determined I would return in better weather to explore…

It's only the dirty ones we don't want - Philip Wilkinson

© Author

The view from the bridge at Howstean Gorge.

An intriguing location, Howstean Gorge cuts through the limestone and has at one time been a cave, the roof has collapsed into the underground stream and been eroded away, so what remains is a cave, but open to the air, I recommend a visit if you fancied seeing down a cave, but cannot bear crawling through small dark spaces

It's only the dirty ones we don't want - Philip Wilkinson

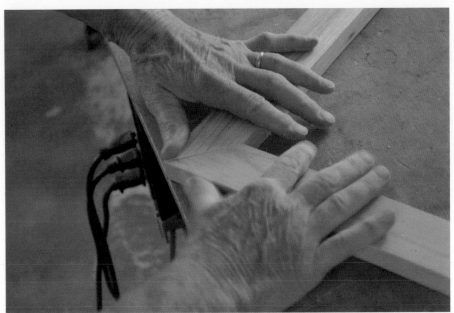

Changing the odds   © Pixababy

Returning to school on a Monday, our afternoon session commenced with woodwork class. Our teacher, always clad in a light brown knee-length "lab coat," expected us to don the same attire which we had to buy in addition to school uniform. Positioned at his workbench,

he would demonstrate woodworking techniques while we gathered around him, eager to learn. A half-inch wood dowel, approximately two feet in length, rested on the bench. Any unwary hands that dared to intrude upon his workspace would receive a sharp rap from this dowel. It didn't take long for us to realise the consequences of placing our hands on his bench.

However, on this day, we discovered during the lunch break that the woodworking block was left unlocked. Seizing the opportunity, we clandestinely entered the workshop and proceeded to carefully cut three-quarters of the way through the teacher's dowel in three strategic locations. Following his teachings, we filled the incisions with sawdust and a tiny amount of wood glue. Anticipation filled the air as we eagerly awaited the commencement of the demonstration. Three of us deliberately placed our hands on the table, bracing ourselves for what was to come.

With a resounding strike, the dowel snapped into three separate pieces, much to the delight and applause of the entire class. Our teacher, a genuinely good-natured man, saw the humour in the situation and shared in our laughter for a change. However, he calmly walked over to the bits box and selected a new dowel, this time a sturdy two inches in thickness. We wisely kept a safe distance as he resumed his demonstration.

It's only the dirty ones we don't want - Philip Wilkinson

School sports

The challenges at school continued to plague me, with my severe asthma being a constant obstacle. I found myself frequently needing to take days off due to illness, and even simple tasks like running to catch a bus were beyond my capabilities. These circumstances had several repercussions in the school environment.

My permanent exemption from school sports did not grant me any reprieve from the PE instructor's discontent. He was a typical sports instructor of the era, stocky, short haircut, never seen unless wearing sports kit for rugby, football or cricket and the type who simply could not understand why anyone would not be able to fully participate.

Despite my inability to participate due to my asthma, he insisted that I come prepared with the appropriate sports kit for every PE lesson, again a requirement to purchase clothing beyond school uniform, and a pointless purchase for me. I was expected to change alongside my classmates, then desperately attempt to keep pace with their hurried run to the sports field, all the while dreading the physical and verbal punishment that awaited me if I fell behind. Often, my efforts would leave me gasping for breath, lagging far behind the rest, and earning nothing but disdain and disgust from the teacher. Once we reached the field, I was left to sit and watch, regardless of the weather conditions. It was a miserable experience, and to add insult to injury, I was still required to change and shower with the rest of the students, despite not having participated in any physical activity.

Often my asthma would be much worse after 2 hours sitting at the touchline of a sports pitch in winter, at this time, there were no inhalers or steroids available, asthma sufferers just had to suffer. On one occasion I needed a week of school to recover.

These experiences left a lasting impact on me. To this day, I have no interest in sports whatsoever. I struggle to name more than a handful of football clubs or recognise any footballers, cricketers, rugby players, and so on. When I find myself in social gatherings where the conversation shifts to recent sports events, I often feel socially isolated, unable to contribute or engage in discussions on the topic.

It's only the dirty ones we don't want - Philip Wilkinson

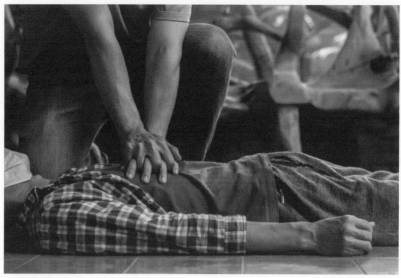

Unrecorded drowning   © shutterstock

During a school day, an unimaginable act unfolded as the morons, fuelled by their cruelty, targeted Bog with a vicious assault. They dragged him forcefully into the nearby toilets. With no regard for the consequences, they subjected him to an unspeakable torment, holding his head beneath the rushing water as the toilet flushed repeatedly, drowning out his desperate cries for help.

Witnessing this horrifying scene, I knew that immediate action was imperative. I summoned the courage to alert a teacher, desperately hoping they would intervene and bring an end to Bog's torment. But time was not on our side. The teacher arrived, their presence a mere heartbeat too late to prevent the unthinkable. Bog lay on the toilet floor soaking wet, unresponsive, and lifeless, a haunting silence replacing his screams of anguish.

Fortunately, the teacher leaped into action, their hands pressing against Bog's chest in a frantic rhythm. With every compression, they willed life back into his fragile body. The seconds stretched like eternity until, against all odds, a flicker of hope emerged, Bog sputtered and started to breath. The distant wail of an ambulance pierced the air, heralding the arrival of salvation.

Medical professionals took charge, their expertise combined with a glimmer of fortune reviving Bog's fading pulse. In the face of such a grave incident, one would expect an immediate and thorough investigation, led by the authorities responsible for the well-being of students in those times. Yet, inexplicably, silence prevailed. No official record was made, no questions were asked.

It was as if the incident had been erased from existence, leaving only the scars etched deep within Bog's spirit and the unspoken trauma eternally imprinted on our souls. In the absence of justice, we were left to grapple with the haunting echoes of that day, a reminder of the profound failures that allowed such darkness to flourish unchecked within our educational system.

It's only the dirty ones we don't want - Philip Wilkinson

Fireworks © https://www.thestar.co.uk/heritage-and-retro/retro/sheffield-retro-15-photos-showing-bonfire-night-celebrations-and-fireworks-displays-over-the-years-3901374

Alongside my growing passion for cycling and camping, I developed another fervour that ignited my imagination, fireworks. Bonfire night held a special place in my heart as the most anticipated night of the year. The narrow-cobbled back streets of our neighbourhood engaged in a friendly competition to create the most impressive bonfires, tantalizing feasts, and dazzling displays of pyrotechnics. With my siblings and friends in tow, we eagerly set out to gather firewood, and to add to the excitement, we dressed my younger brother Stephen as a "guy" and placed him in a pram to collect "penny for the guy" donations from the public. Even though my parents accompanied me to purchase the fireworks, I relished the opportunity to handpick each one from the open boxes in the shop's glass cabinet. The shopkeeper carefully packed my chosen fireworks into a brown paper bag, and I carried them home with great anticipation.

The fireworks on general sale were only on view for about two weeks before November 5th, these included many manufacturers such as Black Cat, Standard, Epic, Wilders, Brock's, Pain's, Astra, Excelsior, TNT, Lion and Apollo.

When November 5th finally arrived, the entire street came alive with an atmosphere of celebration. Every kitchen door stood open, welcoming anyone to help themselves to an array of delectable treats. Jacket potatoes, pies with mushy peas and mint sauce, Parkin cake, sticky treacle plot toffee, hot dogs, burgers—the street transformed into a culinary delight.

In those days, the fireworks available were smaller but possessed an element of danger that is unimaginable by today's standards. There were jumping jacks that, when ignited and dropped among a crowd, exploded every 15 seconds, leaping into the air around people and occasionally landing amidst open boxes of fireworks with explosive results. Some mischievous individuals even dared to place them in hoods or pockets for maximum fright. Bangers, small cardboard tubes with fuses, were notorious for causing finger injuries and countless fires. They were responsible for wreaking havoc on mailboxes, terrifying girls on the street, and generally inciting mischief when wielded irresponsibly. And then there were air bombs—cardboard tubes with plastic spikes to anchor them into the ground. Once lit, they shot balls into the air, exploding with a resounding bang. These were often fired at unsuspecting targets like people or cars. It was no wonder that air bombs were eventually banned, although they undeniably provided great amusement in their time.

In this realm of pyrotechnic fascination, my mother, who happened to be named on a Nobel Prize for her contributions to Chemistry as a junior chemist with the WIRA, encouraged my explorations in our basement chemistry lab. Equipped with a workbench, a Bunsen burner connected to a gas tap, and a Yorkshire Range fireplace with a chimney, our basement proved to be an ideal laboratory for my experiments. It also acted as a gas chamber of sorts, providing ample ventilation for our ventures.

© Pixababy

As a curious 12-year-old, armed with a chemistry set, my natural inclination led me to create explosives and fireworks. On one occasion, while standing at the local chemist's shop, bags of saltpetre, charcoal, and sulphur laid out before me on the counter, the chemist, peering over his spectacles, recognised the ingredients as gunpowder components. He leaned in and asked, "Does your mother know you're buying this?" I confidently replied in the affirmative, and he proceeded to bag the order, saying, "Oh, alright then."

From crafting bangers, we progressed to constructing pipe bombs, which provided even more exhilarating thrills.

Our ambitious curiosity led us to discover an explosive concoction using weed killer and sugar. With this newfound knowledge, we embarked on building our most audacious device yet, a bazooka. Dodge had a three-inch diameter ball bearing, and Bog possessed a six-foot length of cast-iron drainpipe.

We combined these elements with two pounds of explosive material and made our way to a disused railway line. Bog, with the bazooka on his shoulder, eagerly contemplated the target, but we quickly realised that holding the device might not be the wisest choice. Instead, we decided to rest the bazooka against the brickwork of an old railway bridge, shoring it up with bricks, soil, sand, and any other materials we could find. As a final touch, we even placed an old glass fish tank on top. Our intended target was a tree located approximately half a mile down the track. We crouched on the other side of the brick bridge stanchion, ignited the explosives using a modified piezo gas lighter as a remote detonator, and unleashed a massive explosion. Bricks, stones, and soil seemed to rain down from the sky for minutes afterward, leaving us staggering around, deafened, and dizzy. The embankment caught fire, and concerned locals promptly called the police and fire brigade. Thankfully, they arrived too late to apprehend us. The fate of the three-inch ball bearing remains a mystery, and our limited understanding of metallurgy was evident in the utter destruction of the cast-iron pipe. It was a stroke of luck that we had managed to dissuade Bog from shouldering the device, sparing us from potential catastrophe.

Over a span of two years, during our prolific explosive-making phase, we managed to summon the fire brigade no less than five times, including one instance where we accidentally caused a fire in the basement range chimney. Our experiments, while fraught with risk and mischief, instilled in me a profound appreciation for the power and beauty of fireworks.

Looking back, those formative years of explosive adventures intertwined with my love for cycling, camping, and the vibrant festivities of Bonfire night. They served as steppingstones in my journey toward self-discovery and provided a much-needed escape from the pressures of school and the troubles that beset my younger self. To this day, my passion for fireworks continues to burn brightly. The joy and excitement of creating magical displays have become a cherished part of my life. Over the years, I have had the privilege of running numerous garden displays around Bonfire Night, sharing the exhilaration with my neighbours and their families.

However, it was on New Year's Eve of 1999 that my fireworks hobby reached its pinnacle. With the looming anticipation of the new millennium and the infamous Y2K bug, which turned out to be much a damp squib, many people chose to stay home that night rather than travel. Restaurants, bars, and hotels took advantage of the situation by tripling their rates. Sensing an opportunity for a memorable celebration, my friends and I decided to ring in the new year together in the comfort of our own homes. To make the evening even more special, I had requested home videos and a list of favourite clips from everyone attending. I meticulously edited these videos onto a four-hour tape, ensuring it would provide non-stop entertainment throughout the evening. The tape played simultaneously on both television sets inside the house and on a large screen with accompanying speakers set up on the patio. A discreetly placed projector in the bedroom window illuminated the outdoor screen. At precisely 8:30 p.m., the tape began playing, captivating our guests with a montage of cherished memories and beloved moments. As the clock ticked closer to midnight, the recording seamlessly transitioned to Phil Collins' "In the Air Tonight," signalling the culmination of the old year. With everyone now outside, the countdown underway, the screen was dramatically pulled aside, revealing an array of fireworks equipped with electric detonators and connected to a homemade firing desk.

It's only the dirty ones we don't want - Philip Wilkinson

A firework electronic control centre

Synchronised to the enchanting soundtrack there could be miracles, from the film "Prince of Egypt," the night sky erupted in a dazzling spectacle of colour and light. As the opening sequence , four monumental 100mm ground mines and a breath-taking 1,000-shot, 25-second Roman candle illuminated the darkness, accompanied by a symphony of explosions and colour. Our families and friends stood in awe, captivated by the mesmerising display that seemed to defy the boundaries between heaven and earth.

The show continued with an array of magnificent fireworks, carefully choreographed to ignite wonder and joy in the hearts of all those in attendance. Laughter, cheers, and applause filled the air as each dazzling burst painted the sky with its ephemeral beauty.

Days later, the postman made a special visit to the house where the party had taken place. He sought out my friend's wife to relay his astonishment at having heard about the most extraordinary firework display in the entire area. News of our awe-inspiring celebration had spread, leaving a lasting impression on those who had witnessed the event, and even those who had only heard about it.

Our firework counter in Stephen Smith's Garden centre, Otley   © Author

Inspired by the resounding success of that memorable night, my friend approached me with a proposal. He suggested that we consider starting a firework company, as he believed that if we could create such an extraordinary display for ourselves, we could do the same for others. After several meetings and careful consideration, we established our own company. We secured a franchise in one of the largest garden centres in the north of England, obtained and registered a licensed explosive store, and gained access to professional-grade fireworks from exclusive catalogues not available to the public.

For over a decade, we ran the company with passion and dedication, delighting customers across Yorkshire with our vast selection of high quality, hand selected fireworks. We organised numerous professional displays, spreading joy and wonder on special occasions throughout the region. The journey was filled with unforgettable experiences, laughter, and the joy of igniting sparks of happiness in the hearts of others.

Looking back, I am grateful for that New Year's Eve celebration, which became the catalyst for a remarkable chapter in my life. It ignited a passion that would not only bring me immense joy but also allow me to share the magic and beauty of fireworks with countless others. And though the years have passed, my love for fireworks continues to burn brightly, lighting up the sky and filling hearts with awe and wonder, one explosion of colour at a time.

It's only the dirty ones we don't want - Philip Wilkinson

School bullying out of control © Pixababy

One dreary afternoon during a wet dinner break. Without uttering a single word, a lad entered my form room, his eyes brimming with malice. In a swift and violent motion, he seized a chair and shattered it against my defenceless back. The agonizing pain coursed through my body, a haunting reminder of the depths of cruelty to which my fellow students would stoop. The relentless assailant found himself in the custody of the police and questioned for his assault against me.

That was not the end of the brutality I endured. On another occasion, fuelled by an insidious darkness and a desire for revenge for the trouble I had caused him, he fostered a sinister desire for my demise. He orchestrated a horrifying plan, one that would unfold within the confines of the No. 72 public service bus that ferried me home from school.

With a grip tightened upon my hair, he callously dragged me towards the rear of the bus, opening the emergency exit door and propelling me through. Though the vehicle had slowed to a meagre 20 miles per hour, the design peculiarities of this bus model would thrust me into a perilous dance with fate. The emergency exit door, positioned on the opposite side of the entrance, swung open into

oncoming traffic. As I tumbled across the road, cars hurtled toward me, their drivers swerving and braking in desperate attempts to evade the impending catastrophe.

The gravity of the situation weighed heavily upon my mother's heart. Driven by an unwavering determination to protect me, she confronted the headmaster, Mr. Slack, seeking justice and solace. To ensure her voice resonated and to serve as an irrefutable witness, my grandfather, a BSc in Physics and revered head of the mathematics and physics departments at Roundhay School (retired), accompanied her to the meeting.

It's only the dirty ones we don't want - Philip Wilkinson

However, the scales of justice seemed tipped against me. Mr. Slack, far from an impartial arbiter, delved into my past with an ulterior motive. He unearthed every record of scuffles, bullying incidents, and any other misdemeanours, intent on weaving a narrative that painted me as the provocateur, a troublemaker instead of a victim. My grandfather, an astute observer of character, left that encounter with an indelible impression. In his esteemed opinion, Mr. Slack proved unworthy of the title of headmaster, a guardian of students' well-being.

© Pixababy

One day, whilst waiting in the poor kids dinner queue, one of the school morons suddenly said to me, bet you 20p I can hit that kid on the top playground in the nuts from here with this, showing me a lethal looking catapult, before I had chance to say anything, he had loaded a marble into the cup, drawn, aimed and fired, the kid, over 70 yards away, creased up and collapsed onto the floor in pain, the bully looked at me grinning, I said I suppose I owe you 20p now, he said, nah I missed his nuts, just got him on the top of his leg. This was the start of the moron's use of catapults to bring pain and destruction whilst remaining at a distance.

In the ever-present queue for dinner, I stood witness to a scene both troubling and intriguing. Half a dozen pupils, the morons, armed with catapults and bags brimming with marbles, had discovered a peculiar phenomenon. When propelled with sufficient force, they pierced through glass windows, leaving behind bullet-like holes. What a discovery, however rather than one of two shots, they took it to another level and fired hundreds of marbles in a matter of a few minutes.

Their targets of choice became the windows of the gymnasium changing rooms. Oblivious to the consequences that lurked beyond their sights, they unleashed their marbles upon the fragile panes, their shots true and unrelenting. Yet, they failed to anticipate the unwavering trajectory of these projectiles. Once through the initial barrier, the marbles continued their journey, wreaking havoc upon the windows on the other side.

Fate, in its peculiar manner, intervened in the form of the deputy headmaster. As he strolled by the gymnasium, a window erupted, showering him in a cascade of broken glass. Startled, he glanced around, searching for the source of this

unexpected assault. Another marble, propelled by an unseen force, crashed through one of the windows and whizzed across the back playground and it became obvious that he was witnessing vandalism on a scale he had not encountered previously.

Witnesses described a flurry of motion, the deputy headmaster driven by instinct, his pursuit fuelled by righteous fury. Racing around the gym, he apprehended the young perpetrators, catching them red-handed. The cost of their folly was not only measured in shattered glass but also in the substantial repairs that now burdened the school's budget.

It's only the dirty ones we don't want - Philip Wilkinson

A curious gift for a 12-year-old   © Shutterstock

One day on our terraced street, one of the neighbours announced he was moving out, he recruited myself and my siblings to help him with a promise of pop and biscuits, we moved many items from the house into a van, but one item intrigued me in his attic, a long heavy package wrapped in oiled cloth, I asked the neighbour what it contained and he put his finger to his nose and said, if you help me the rest of the day, you can have that, it's a surprise.

Surprise was the correct word, when opened the package contained a 1942 German bolt action single shot rifle, this was great, I now had the best weapon among my friends for cowboys and Indians, gangsters and any other roll play using weapons,

we quickly found that loading the bolt allowed a cap to be inserted into the gap, so when fired it made a bang, flash, and smoke, what a great toy, I was the envy of my friends on the street.

© Author

35

It's only the dirty ones we don't want - Philip Wilkinson

To add to the arsenal, we discovered a curious toy, a cap-fired spud gun, designed to resemble a miniature derringer gun from the Wild West. On sale in toy stores, and still on sale today this tiny gun was simple to operate. By opening the side, we could access a metal "bullet" with a triangular tube on one end and a flat surface with a small hole on the other. To load it, we inserted the triangular end into a piece of potato breaking off a small piece, then attached a cap to the back of the bullet before placing it into the gun. When fired, the cap would create a loud bang and explosion, propelling the potato fragment out of the barrel.

However, some of us decided to experiment further, replacing the potato with a mixture of match heads and sulphur. This modification made the experience more thrilling but also significantly more dangerous.

Fishing trip disaster   © Pixababy

On a fishing trip to the river at Pool in Wharfedale, I found myself in an unfortunate mishap. After spending hours without any success, my companions and I decided to cross the river via the bridge and explore the other side. Balancing my fishing rod in one hand while riding my dad's bike, an unexpected turn of events occurred.

Somehow, the rod became entangled in the front wheel spokes, causing the bike to come to an abrupt halt. The sudden stop propelled me over the bridge wall and into the river, much to the amusement of my friends, who burst into laughter. To add to the unfortunate turn of events, a passing lorry unintentionally ran over my bike. My parents were less than pleased with the outcome of this fishing excursion.

It's only the dirty ones we don't want - Philip Wilkinson

Meet the eccentrics   © Pixababy

At home, my parents' strong Christian beliefs attracted some rather eccentric individuals into our lives. One of them was Liz, a middle-aged woman with an unwavering obsession for cars and obtaining a driving licence. During a visit to her house one day, it became apparent that Liz was a hoarder. The rooms were cluttered with stacks of newspapers, magazines, boxes filled with various items, clothes, musical instruments, and cookware. The sheer number of possessions rendered three rooms completely inaccessible, leaving narrow corridors leading to and up the stairs, toilet, and bathroom.

Feeling bored in the living room while my parents engaged in conversation, I stumbled upon a tin box on the table and curiously opened it. To my surprise, it contained around 15 small books, meticulously filled with entries. Each page held about 15 entries on both sides, amounting to approximately 13,000 records over a span of 20 years. These were detailed records of driving lessons Liz had booked throughout her life to that point. It was a staggering number, and I couldn't help but marvel at the dedication and persistence she had shown. Eventually, Liz achieved her goal and passed her driving test, however only for an automatic. And then came the selection of her first purchase, a Land Rover Defender 110 she named Betsy.

One of our peculiar visitors was a neighbour used to visit our house regularly. His wife seemed troubled and sought a chance to discuss family matters with my parents. Unfortunately, her husband, an egotistical college lecturer, always dominated the conversation, steering it back to himself and his supposed greatness. Unbeknownst to us, the reason for his wife's desperation to talk was the disturbing truth that he was involved in inappropriate relationships with his students. It later came to light that he had even impregnated his youngest daughter, leading to the hurried marriage of the daughter and the

It's only the dirty ones we don't want - Philip Wilkinson

dissolution of their marriage, as far as I am aware. The discovery of such shocking revelations shed light on the dark side of someone we once considered a neighbour.

Another interesting character would babysit us whilst my parents went to bible readings, prayer meetings and the like, thin and gaunt, she was blind in one eye and hopeless at the tsk set for her, we ran riot when she was in charge, hide and seek was one such event, on this occasion we could not find my little brother, eventually he revealed his hiding place, he had climbed up the airing cupboard, then entered the water header tank, sitting in the cold water he had closed the cupboard door behind him.

On another occasion, I ran into the bedroom, leapt onto the bed into a handstand with my feet against the window, unfortunately my feet went through the glass with a huge crash as the broken glass fell into the back yard. Again, on her watch, my little brother had caused an issue worthy of sibling reprisals, running away from us, he made it to the toilet and locked the door, fearful that we would break the lock to gain access, he climbed out of the window with the intention of climbing back in through the bedroom window to escape, unfortunately he falls into the back yard, breaking the washing line as he passed.

Our babysitter, sitting in the room below, heard the commotion and looked out of the window, there was nothing to see, my brother, dressed in just his pants, had run around the block and re-entered by the front door, later my parents questioned the huge bruises on his back and bottom, and the long red wield across his side, we all denied any knowledge of course.

The morons are in the toilets   © Shutterstock

In the girls' restroom at school, a disturbing incident took place. Some students (the morons) had vandalised the facilities, tearing out the fixtures such as toilet pots and sinks, and hurling them through the glass windows. Tragically, the staff car park happened to be located below, resulting in significant damage to both the school property and the vehicles owned by the staff members. This act of vandalism caused great distress and inconvenience to the school community, and the girls could not use their toilets for some weeks.

It's only the dirty ones we don't want - Philip Wilkinson

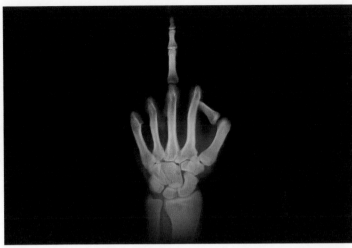

A broken arm   © Pixababy

Life has a peculiar way of teaching us lessons, sometimes in unexpected and painful ways. It was during a seemingly harmless school lunch break that fate intervened, causing me to stumble and fall on the grassy slope that encircled the playing fields. Little did I know that this unassuming accident would set in motion a chain of events that would test my resilience and expose the shortcomings of those entrusted with my well-being.

As the subsequent lesson unfolded, a discomfort began to grow. Recognizing the growing discomfort, I summoned the courage to seek out the school nurse's care. However, my timing proved to be unfortunate, for it was in that moment that the headmaster, Mr. Slack, happened to be occupying the sick room.

With a stern and callous demeanour, Mr. Slack disregarded the genuine concern of the nurse, his authoritarian voice overpowering any empathy that might have softened his response. "What is your next lesson?" he demanded. I mustered my voice, weak with pain and confusion, and replied, "Maths, sir." But his reply, void of compassion, only served to deepen my distress. "Get to your lesson, boy," he barked, dismissing my plea for care

That night, the invisible injury exacted its toll. My arm, once a mere source of discomfort, swelled and darkened now showing the severity of my condition. The pain became an unwelcome companion, relentless in its presence. Recognising the need for urgent medical attention, my parents took me to the hospital's A&E department.

Within the sterile confines of the hospital, an X-ray painted a vivid picture of my fractured right arm, a greenstick fracture, a testament to the impact of my fall. The medical professionals skilfully set the broken bones, encasing them in a protective plaster cast. Their advice was clear, I needed a week of rest and recovery, a respite from the school environment.

Upon my return, the school nurse greeted me with a mix of surprise and concern, her words laced with genuine remorse. She apologised on behalf of Mr. Slack, recognizing the gravity of my injury that had gone unacknowledged by the headmaster himself. Mr Slack chose not to comment.

It's only the dirty ones we don't want - Philip Wilkinson

School reports

Every term, the ritual of report cards unfolded, a tangible reflection of my academic journey. The carefully handwritten remarks from each subject's teacher adorned the pages, carrying both praise and critique, all to be scrutinised by my parents.

In a cruel fashion, these reports were handed to pupils to take home to their parents, they were not sealed and could be read by the individual to which the comments were describing. In these days, it was not uncommon for parents to beat children who failed, misbehaved, or brought the family into disrepute, I suspect many ended up mysteriously lost.

In subject after subject, the sentiments echoed a similar refrain. "Philip could truly excel if only he applied himself," read one teacher's assessment, awarding me an A-. Another comment spoke of missed opportunities, stating, "If Philip exhibited even a fraction of effort, his grades would soar," accompanied by a B+. And then there were the more candid remarks, filled with a mix of exasperation and belief: "If Philip would only embrace his capabilities and invest in his homework, the sky would be the limit," resulting in an A.

It's only the dirty ones we don't want - Philip Wilkinson

In stark contrast, my younger sister Judith, several years my junior, received reports that seemed to defy logic. Words of commendation and encouragement adorned her pages, painting a picture of a diligent and dedicated student. "Judith has exhibited admirable effort this term," proclaimed one teacher, though the final grade of D- failed to capture the essence of her perseverance. Another comment highlighted her unwavering commitment: "Judith is a shining example of a star pupil, always eager to contribute and with assignments that are impeccable in their presentation, and accuracy," accompanied by an exceptional E+.

The incongruity between our reports left me pondering the elusive nature of academic evaluations. How was it that my own potential seemed forever just beyond my grasp, while Judith effortlessly garnered praise and accolades for her unwavering dedication?

Cycling, camping, and caving in the dales   © Pixababy

Despite the harrowing incidents involving cycling and camping during my previous excursion, I found myself inexplicably drawn back to the allure of adventure. That summer, a different group of friends approached me with a proposal to embark on a seven-day camping trip to How Stean, all on our trusty bicycles. Though one would think my previous misadventure would have deterred me, I couldn't resist the temptation. Their plan was to delve into the depths of the How Stean Gorge and explore the surrounding potholes using the lamps of our bikes. Astonishingly, even with my parents fully aware of our intentions, they granted me permission to go.

And so, with a sense of both trepidation and excitement, we set off on our expedition. The days that followed were filled with unforgettable moments of exploration and discovery. We revelled in the rugged beauty of the gorge, fearlessly clambering in and out of the mysterious potholes that dotted the landscape. Our daring spirit even led us to coax a group of seasoned adult potholers into guiding us through a secured cave system, a hidden realm accessible only to the intrepid.

It's only the dirty ones we don't want - Philip Wilkinson

A view of How Stean beck gorge including paths and bridge © Author

It's only the dirty ones we don't want - Philip Wilkinson

How Stean is an unusual place, the main section was created by water as a cave system in the limestone, however the roof section has collapsed into the cave and the debris washed away over thousands of years leaving an open gorge, there are ladders, narrow bridges and difficult walkways for the public to traverse the length of the gorge with some safety and without getting wet, however using the open gorge as a playground we rode the river rapids through the gorge at speed and swam in the deeper pools.

During one lunchtime adventure, we decided to embark on a cycling expedition up the daunting and winding hill to Middlesmoor. It was a challenge that tested our endurance, and as expected, I found myself trailing behind the others, struggling to conquer the steep incline. Eventually, though, we all reached the top, where we were met with a small hamlet that marked the end of the road. And just as we were catching our breath, a welcoming sight appeared before us—the local pub.

© Author

Eager to replenish our energy, we entered the pub and promptly ordered a hearty pub dinner. To our surprise, the accommodating landlord informed us that we could enjoy a pint of beer alongside our meal. The condition was simple: if we were eating, we were welcome to indulge in some libations. With enthusiasm, we each requested a pint of beer to accompany our chosen meals.

As our food arrived, I couldn't help but marvel at the generous portions and the tantalizing aroma that wafted from the plates. My eyes widened in awe as I beheld a sight I had never seen before—a homemade steak in ale pie, perfectly golden-brown and adorned with a rich, savoury gravy. It was accompanied by a generous helping of chips, peas, potatoes, carrots, and even onion rings, all meticulously arranged on the same plate. This was a feast that

43

surpassed my mother's home-cooked meals in both size and presentation. The sight alone was a treat for the senses, and my anticipation grew with every passing moment.

We wasted no time in tucking into our meals, relishing each flavourful bite and savouring the mouthwatering combination of tender steak, flaky pastry, and rich gravy. The chips were perfectly crispy, the peas burst with freshness, and the accompanying vegetables added a delightful touch of colour and texture to the feast. We revelled in the Flavors that danced on our tongues, thoroughly enjoying the indulgence that the pub dinner provided.

With satisfied appetites and a newfound appreciation for the culinary delights that the countryside had to offer, we bid farewell to the pub and prepared ourselves for the journey back down the steep hill. The pints of beer we had savoured during the meal added a jovial spirit to the descent, as we glided down the winding road with a sense of adventure and contentment in our hearts. It was a memorable ride, etched in our minds as a unique experience that blended camaraderie, exploration, and the simple pleasures of good food and drink.

The memory of that day, cycling up the hill and enjoying a delectable pub dinner at the hamlet's welcoming pub, remains a cherished tale among our group. It serves as a reminder of the joy that can be found in unexpected moments, the beauty of the countryside, and the warmth of shared laughter and delicious food.

The gorge in our day had been rigged for public access, but was not commercialised other then a camp site and an honesty box in the farmhouse wall for donations, however it is now very popular, the campsite has been expanded and a visitor centre with a large café has been built which extends out over the gorge, with glass floors in sections, this it a fabulous way to enjoy the spectacular scenery from the comfort of the café, and hot coffee is a bonus.

On our return to the campsite, a team of cavers had arrived and offered to take us into one of the nearby closed cave systems, we followed their land rover down farm tracks and across a few fields to reach the entrance and having scrambled into our wetsuits, and helped to open the locked metal door installed to keep the curious at bay, we entered a large cave system for the first time

Exploring the cave was both thrilling and terrifying in equal measure, squeezing through sideways into smaller and tighter sections was nerve wracking, that feeling of getting stuck and being left was indescribable, in addition, there was the fear of flooding and losing our way, the cavers knew the pot well, so the biggest single fear was getting separated and lost.

Suddenly, after a particularly tight crawl, we were in a vast cavern, with hundreds of fine stalactites hanging from the ceiling and the reciprocal stalagmites on the floor, in the lights the stalactites looked like fine straw, pure white, with a dop of water at the tip making them translucent in parts, and transparent in others. There was a contend dripping of water and a small stream flowed lazily through the middle, one of the cavers said, come and look at this, so we moved over to him and could see a blind white newt in the water.

We felt incredibly privileged to have been invited and within weeks we started to plan our own excursions into caves, however, having almost boiled ourselves alive, we knew our 6mm wetsuits were completely unsuited to the task, new wetsuits were needed, and this time we chose 4mm material for the job.

Chapter 3 – 1972

The Scientific era

The scientific era   © Pixababy

With my newfound friends, the twins, Frodo, and Bilbo, I experienced a significant turning point in my school life. They were part of a group of budding scientists and explorers, their minds constantly brimming with curiosity and a thirst for knowledge. It was through their influence that my own passion for science and exploration began to take flight. Eager to keep pace with this intellectually stimulating group, I embarked on a personal quest to bridge the knowledge gap and immerse myself in their world of scientific discovery. I sought out various avenues that would provide me with the tools and understanding necessary to explore the realms of science and electrical engineering alongside them.

One such avenue that became an invaluable resource was my subscription to Practical Wireless magazine. Every month, a copy of this magazine would arrive, bearing a treasure trove of information within its pages. From articles on circuitry and electronics to practical experiments and innovative projects, it became my go-to source for technical knowledge.

With each issue, I delved into the captivating world of wireless communication, electronic circuits, and the intricate workings of various devices. I eagerly absorbed the practical tips, step-by-step instructions, and expert insights that the magazine offered. Through its pages,

It's only the dirty ones we don't want - Philip Wilkinson

I discovered new concepts, honed my understanding of electrical engineering principles, and learned about the latest advancements in the field.

Practical Wireless became more than just a magazine; it was a gateway to a vast realm of possibilities. Its articles and tutorials served as a foundation upon which I could build my own experiments and explorations. Armed with newfound knowledge, I began tinkering with electronic components, constructing circuits, and pushing the boundaries of my understanding.

The magazine not only provided technical guidance but also fostered a sense of community. Within its pages, I found letters from fellow enthusiasts sharing their own projects, insights, and challenges. This sense of camaraderie fuelled my enthusiasm and encouraged me to push further, to experiment and explore with greater fervour.

As I delved deeper into the world of science and electrical engineering, my friendship with Frodo, Bilbo, and their group blossomed. We became a tight-knit collective of young scientists, sharing ideas, conducting experiments, and embarking on thrilling adventures of discovery. Together, we would spend hours discussing the latest articles from Practical Wireless, dissecting their contents, and brainstorming ways to apply the newfound knowledge to our own projects.

Through my subscription to Practical Wireless and the friendships it helped foster, I not only expanded my understanding of science and electrical engineering but also developed a deep appreciation for the power of knowledge, curiosity, and collaboration. It became clear to me that the pursuit of scientific exploration was

not just a solitary endeavour, but a shared passion that could ignite imaginations, push boundaries, and unlock a world of endless possibilities.

In the years that followed, Practical Wireless continued to be a guiding light on my scientific journey. It remained a constant source of inspiration, providing me with the guidance, ideas, and motivation to continue exploring and pushing the boundaries of my understanding. The magazine became a trusted companion, accompanying me through my academic pursuits and shaping my career path in the field of science and technology.

Looking back, I am grateful for the role that Practical Wireless played in fuelling my passion for science and electrical engineering. It was more than just a subscription—it was a key that unlocked a world of knowledge, curiosity, and exploration. And as I reflect on those formative years, I am reminded of the power of a simple magazine to shape one's aspirations, connect kindred spirits, and ignite a lifelong love affair with the wonders of science.

However, it was not just my thirst for knowledge that fuelled my aspirations. A part-time job at Teleservicenter in Headingley became a gateway to an array of electronic components and equipment. The position bestowed upon me a unique advantage, as I could obtain these items at staff-discounted prices. This newfound ability to acquire and share the tools of the trade made me popular among my peers. No longer did my friends need to venture out to the store; instead, they could rely on me to provide them with a bag filled with resistors, capacitors, and other essential components, ready for their scientific endeavours.

It's only the dirty ones we don't want - Philip Wilkinson

With each passing day, my involvement in the world of electronics deepened. Armed with my bag of supplies, I eagerly shared my newfound resources with my friends, and together we embarked on a journey of exploration and innovation. We tackled challenges, brainstormed ideas, and collaborated on various scientific projects, all fuelled by our insatiable curiosity and collective passion for discovery.

In the company of Frodo, Bilbo, and the rest of our like-minded group, the boundaries of our knowledge expanded. We engaged in discussions, exchanged ideas, and challenged one another to reach greater heights. As we delved deeper into the realm of electrical engineering and many other science subjects, we realised that the pursuit of knowledge was not merely an individual endeavour; it was a collaborative effort that propelled us forward.

Our collective enthusiasm and shared experiences fostered an environment of joint support. We revelled in the joys of unravelling complex circuits, tinkering with electronic devices, and witnessing the marvels that science had to offer. Our shared passion for exploration served as the cornerstone of our friendship, binding us together in a common purpose.

Through our collaborative endeavours, we not only honed our technical skills but also developed lifelong bonds. The moments spent exchanging components, discussing circuit designs, and witnessing the fruits of our labour forged memories that would forever remain part of us. As the days turned into months and the months into years, our collective pursuit of scientific knowledge continued to shape our lives. The lessons learned, the challenges overcome, and the friendships forged became the pillars upon which we built our futures. Though our paths may have diverged in the years that followed, the shared experiences of our scientific exploration would forever connect us, serving as a reminder of the transformative power of curiosity and friendship.

And so, armed with a bag filled with resistors and capacitors, I embarked on a journey of discovery, forever indebted to the twins Frodo and Bilbo, and the remarkable group of young scientists who ignited the spark of curiosity within me.

Together, we embraced the wonders of electrical engineering, unravelling its mysteries one circuit at a time.

A valve radio chassis   © Author

Working at Teleservicenter proved to be an interesting and challenging experience, largely due to the peculiarities of the owner and the idiosyncrasies of the job. The owner, a rather eccentric middle-aged man, had a noticeable physical appearance and a propensity for anxiousness. Every small inconvenience seemed to weigh heavily on him, causing visible distress. The owner's stinginess was well known among the staff. He paid his employees by the hour, but the remuneration was meagre, calculated at one pence per year of age.

As a young worker, I earned a modest 13p per hour, a fact that the owner never failed to remind me of. He often compared my wage to that of a paper round, highlighting that working indoors offered the advantage of being sheltered from inclement weather.

Teleservicenter itself was filled with countless tiny drawers, each containing various electrical components such as resistors and capacitors. These components were sold to customers, who were primarily hobbyist electronic enthusiasts. I distinctly recall an incident involving my friend Bilbo, who purchased a resistor for 1p plus 1/2p VAT. The owner insisted that VAT must be rounded up to the nearest whole coin, completely disregarding the fact that the initial purchase had already been subjected to the VAT rounding up, effectively resulting in a 50% surcharge. When Bilbo decided to buy a capacitor as well, it cost him an additional 2p plus 1/2p VAT, further compounding the VAT rounding issue.

Hundreds of drawers full of components, all to be stock checked © Author

My role at Teleservicenter appeared straightforward at first glance. Each drawer contained a card indicating the required stock level and the quantity to be ordered. For example, a card might read "33ohm 1/4W metal film resistor, less than 50, order 100."

The task primarily involved emptying the drawer, counting the components, and placing them back accordingly. However, the monotonous nature of the job made it all too easy to make mistakes. Errors such as writing down "1/2W" or "330ohm" instead of the correct values could lead to incorrect orders being placed.

These mistakes became apparent when the stock was returned to the drawers. Each pound of error would cost the employee 1p from their hourly rate for a duration of three months.

There was one instance that exemplified the potential repercussions of such mistakes. One of the service engineers in the TV repair room mistakenly ordered an item worth £55, a significant amount considering his hourly wage of 37p. As a result, he ended up owing the company 18p per hour, leaving him in a difficult financial situation for a while.

Despite the challenges and peculiarities of the job, my time at Teleservicenter provided valuable insights and lessons. I learned the importance of attention to detail and the consequences of even minor errors. Additionally, I witnessed first-hand the impact of a penny-pinching mentality on both employees and customers.

Looking back, it was a unique experience working at Teleservicenter, one that shaped my understanding of the value of precision, the significance of fair remuneration, and the consequences of financial miscalculations.

British Association of Young Scientists   © Pixababy

My group of school friends had formed a habit of gathering during lunchtime and after school to engage in lively debates about the latest theories in physics, electronics, and other scientific topics.

Encouraged by their enthusiasm, I decided to join B.A.Y.S. (the British Association of Young Scientists), a club organised by Leeds University. The club held monthly meetings in one of the university's lecture theatres, where a scientist from the university would deliver a presentation on various subjects. Though some presentations went over our heads, they were intriguing enough to keep me attending for several years.

On one occasion, my sister Fiona expressed a desire to accompany me to a B.A.Y.S. meeting. While I suspected her interest lay more in being around my friends than in the scientific discussions, I agreed to let her come along. We arrived early, taking seats near the back of the lecture theatre, eagerly anticipating the start of the presentation. The topic of the day was volcanoes, and as the scientist began describing the different types of volcanic eruptions, an unexpected and embarrassing situation unfolded. Fiona started experiencing flatulence, and the uncomfortable wooden bench seats amplified the sound, making it impossible to ignore. Coincidentally, her gas emissions seemed to align perfectly with the lecturer's descriptions of long, slow eruptions and fast, powerful eruptions. The audience couldn't help but notice, and although some found it amusing, the situation left me feeling mortified. After the meeting, my friends jokingly advised me never to bring Fiona along to future gatherings.

While the incident was undoubtedly embarrassing at the time, it became a memorable anecdote shared among my friends. It serves as a reminder that unexpected and humorous moments can arise even in serious settings, creating lasting memories and laughter in the process.

Repairing valve radios   © Author

Inspired by my growing interest in physics and electronics, I stumbled upon a remarkable discovery during my walk home from school one day. I came across two discarded radios left near the bins of a student apartment, seemingly abandoned by their previous owners. Intrigued, I decided to take them apart and investigate their inner workings.

As I disassembled the radios, it became apparent that they relied on vacuum tubes, or valves, for various essential functions such as signal amplification, power amplification, rectification, and tuning. I was aware that valves often experienced failures, sometimes ceasing to work properly after a power cycle. However, these valves were conveniently fitted into bases, making them easy to remove and replace.

With the back panels removed from both radios, I noticed that they employed identical valves for the same tasks. An idea sparked in my mind, I could swap these valves between the sets and potentially create a fully functioning radio. Excitement filled the air as I carefully interchanged the valves.

To my delight, my experiment yielded successful results. Suddenly, I had a working radio in my hands. This marked a significant turning point for me and my family, as we had never owned a television or a radio until that moment. The repaired radio provided us with access to music and news, opening a whole new world of entertainment and information for all of us to enjoy.

At last, a TV set   © Author

After my successful venture with the repaired radio, again on my way home from school I stumbled upon a discarded TV set outside a grand house. Recognizing the potential hidden within its bulky frame, I sought assistance and a wheelbarrow to transport it back home. However, my parents were less enthusiastic about my newfound treasure. They expressed concerns about the dangers involved in dismantling and repairing the set as high voltages were utilised and potential need for a TV license and the perceived intrusion of the "devil" into our household.

Undeterred by their reservations, I eagerly examined the TV set. It was a hybrid of old and new technologies, still utilising valves for certain functions but also incorporating transistors, a relatively new and evolving component at the time. To restore this TV to its former glory, I invested some of my hard-earned wages and sought guidance from the service technicians at work.

Following their advice, I replaced one of the valves and two of the transistors, hoping to breathe new life into the television. To my delight, my efforts were rewarded as the TV came to life, gracing our home with its flickering screen. We were overjoyed to finally have our very first television.

Suddenly we had the facility to watch television, can you imaging how enthralling and yet disappointing in equal measures this would turn out to be, firstly there were only three channels, BBC1, BBC2 and ITV. Secondly, a test card was typically shown all day until children's TV started at about 4pm, then at 6pm it was time for the news and that marked the end of children's TV for that day.

Reading Practical Television magazine, it was intriguing to see reports on antennas that could pick up TV channels in Europe, and we did try to add a new larger arial pointed in the direction, but we were too far away in Yorkshire to stand any chance.

Sadly, our elation was short-lived. After approximately 15 months of nightly entertainment, disaster struck. One fateful evening, as my father was engrossed in a late-night program, he suddenly noticed that the flames on the screen appeared a bit too realistic. It dawned on him that the flames were not mere illusions but an actual fire engulfing the TV set. Swiftly, he extinguished the flames, but the damage was done. The fire had ravaged the TV beyond repair, leaving me and my siblings deeply disappointed.

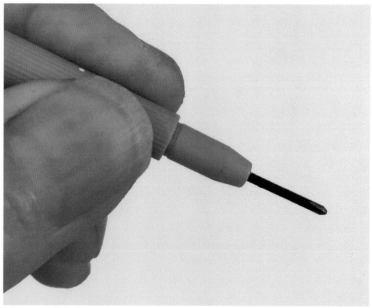

Screwdrivers in school   ©Author

At school, a mischievous game had taken hold, involving the removal of screws from various objects around the premises. Fire door hinges, desks, chairs, and even window hinges were targeted, causing unexpected collapses and breakages. The school community became increasingly cautious, testing everything before trusting its stability.

Frodo and Bilbo, being identical twins and part of the group interested in electronics, often played along with the game. When a teacher would ask, "Are you Frodo or Bilbo?", they would teasingly reply with, "Which one do you want?" and consistently present themselves as the other twin.

The headmaster was aware of these occurrences and knew in his mind that the twins were involved. He had received reports that one of them had been seen with a screwdriver, which further fuelled his suspicion.

© Pixababy

In response, the twins were summoned to the headmaster's office for a serious interrogation. Recollecting the encounter later, Frodo and Bilbo described Mr. Slack's intense anger. His face turned puce, and steam seemed to escape from his collar as he shouted and gestured at them both. He pointed his finger aggressively, banging it on the edge of the desk until it caused him pain. Mr. Slack expressed his outrage at the ongoing criminal damage being inflicted upon the school by someone wielding a screwdriver. He emphasised the severity of the situation, claiming that it was only a matter of time before someone would be seriously injured or even killed due to this reckless vandalism. He also mentioned involving the police.

During the heated confrontation, Mr. Slack was informed that one of the twins had a screwdriver in their possession. This detail served as the catalyst for his outburst. He demanded that the alleged screwdriver be produced and placed on his desk immediately. If it wasn't presented, both twins would face punishment in the form of caning and suspension from school.

In response, Bilbo reached into his blazer pocket and retrieved a small screwdriver. It was the kind typically provided as a gift with the previous month's Practical Wireless magazine, useful for repairing loose screws in glasses. Bilbo placed it on the desk as requested, but it became evident to everyone present that this innocuous screwdriver couldn't possibly be the one causing the school's havoc. Despite the realisation, Mr. Slack failed to find any humour in the situation. He simply pointed to the door and screamed, "Get out!"

It's only the dirty ones we don't want - Philip Wilkinson

A caning I suspect I deserved   © Pixababy

My enthusiasm for fireworks led me into a difficult situation. I had constructed a large air bomb-style firework and brought it to school to show my friends. Unfortunately, once word got out that I had the firework, some individuals with a lack of judgment confronted me at the end of lunch break. They forcibly took the firework from me and proceeded to set it off.

The explosion was powerful and resonated throughout the school and the neighbouring housing estate. Left alone to deal with the consequences, I found myself out of breath due to my asthma and on the ground. The elderly gentlemen employed to keep order at lunchtime (the dinner gimmers) had no difficulty in rounding me up, as I was next to the spent firework, I was correctly identified as the guilty party. I was later called in for an interview with Mr. Slack, the headmaster, and received a caning as a form of punishment. Despite the ordeal. Mr Slack was obviously not a firework aficionado, the home-made device with no labels or branding stood out as just that, homemade. I made the decision to keep quiet about the fact that I had constructed the firework using materials from my chemistry set at home.

Chapter 4 – 1973

Family Holidays

A trip to Grassington for the whole family and the Sunday school   Author

During the summer months, our family would eagerly anticipate the arrival of our mother's friends from Grassington, the Thompson's, They would collect us using their furniture removal van, which we would load with all our essentials, beds, mattresses, chests of drawers brimming with clothes. Excitement coursed through our veins as we prepared to embark on our journey, leaving behind the terraced streets and coal fires of the city. Grassington beckoned us, promising a glimpse of another world.

Upon our arrival, we were warmly welcomed by the Thompson family, who resided in Chapel Fold, a charming old chapel that had been partially converted into a home. The main meeting room, now mostly empty and re purposed as a gymnasium, with wall bars, hand grips on roof supports etc. an adventure ground for children had been created. This room would become our temporary haven. We transformed the space into a cosy retreat, setting up our beds and making ourselves at home. With four adults and nine children in the chapel, our visits were a joyful shared experience with endless adventure.

It's only the dirty ones we don't want - Philip Wilkinson

A furniture workshop similar to that of Mr Thomson's   © Pixababy

Mr. Thompson, a skilled furniture maker and restorer, operated his workshop just opposite the chapel. His craftsmanship was renowned, and he created exquisite pieces that stood as testaments to his dedication and expertise. But his talents extended beyond woodworking. In the community, he wore multiple hats. He served as the local preacher at the nearby church, his sermons resounding with conviction and faith. And he was also a licensed butcher, entrusted by local farmers for the personal use slaughter of their animals.

© Author

Image of Chapel Fold Grassington, the Chapel on the left was the Thomson's home, the smaller single storey building opposite was the furniture workshop

Our visits to Grassington were never short on surprises. Life in the countryside had a rhythm of its own, dictated by the whims of nature and the ebb and flow of daily existence. One day, we were greeted by the sight of a mother pig giving birth to a litter of fifteen piglets. Amidst the flurry of activity, two piglets required special care, necessitating early mornings and bottle rearing.

It's only the dirty ones we don't want - Philip Wilkinson

Another memorable day unfolded when a pig arrived for slaughter and butchering. The air crackled with purpose as Mr. Thompson readied himself for the task at hand. With humane precision, the pig's life was ended swiftly, followed by the meticulous removal of its bristles using boiling water. The butchering process commenced, guided by Mr. Thompson's practiced hands. From dawn till dusk, we witnessed the transformation of a humble animal into a bounty of nourishment.

© Pixababy

As the evening cast its shadow and the work ended, our families gathered around the fruits of our labour. Countless pork chops, sides of bacon, and savoury sausages lay before us, ready to be divided and shared. During this, Mr. Thompson's appetite suddenly awakened. "I'm feeling peckish," he declared, his eyes twinkling mischievously. My father said he could manage something to eat, sausages, replied to Mr Thompson with a knowing smile. "I think I'll go to bed," my father replied.

These interludes in Grassington gifted us with more than just a change of scenery. They were reminders of the inherent beauty in life's unexpected twists and turns, the harmonious blend of craftsmanship, community, and the joys of rural existence. And as we bid farewell to Grassington, its echoes lingered in our hearts, a cherished memory etched forever in our family's narrative. In the enchanting world of Grassington, where time seemed to slow down, Mrs. Thompson reigned as a culinary magician. Her kitchen, adorned with two full-size coal-fired Aga cookers, served as the stage for her culinary prowess. With boundless creativity and an unwavering passion for cooking and baking, she transformed simple ingredients into gastronomic masterpieces. Her reputation extended far beyond the walls of Chapel Fold, as she fearlessly entered local cooking competitions, capturing numerous prises along the way.

For our family, accustomed to humble meals and my mother's culinary misadventures, Mrs. Thompson's culinary mastery was a revelation. We gazed in awe as she effortlessly conjured delectable treats from scratch. In a household where the scent of freshly baked bread permeated the air, and the rhythmic crackling of coal-filled stoves provided a comforting soundtrack, we were transported to a realm of abundance and flavour.

57

It's only the dirty ones we don't want - Philip Wilkinson

© Pixababy

During this trip, following several previous years extended stays, our entourage had expanded, as the Sunday school held in our home had accompanied us. The kitchen now accommodated a gathering of seven adults and twenty-six children, a joyous assembly that filled the room with laughter and anticipation. Around the expansive kitchen table, we sat shoulder to shoulder, ready to partake in a feast fit for royalty.

Breakfast became a symphony of indulgence. Mrs. Thompson's table overflowed with delights that were previously unimaginable. We began our mornings with cornflakes, pouring them from a colossal box that seemed large enough to double as a playhouse. The milk, still frothy from the cow's udders, resided in a grand enamel jug, adding a touch of rustic charm to the table. Toast, lovingly crafted from homemade bread, awaited our eager fingers, its rich aroma beckoning us closer. And in lieu of margarine, which had become a casualty of governmental price manipulation, our taste buds revelled in the creamy goodness of real butter, churned right on the premises.

© Pixababy

But breakfast was just the prelude to the gastronomic symphony that awaited us. As the day unfolded, Mrs. Thompson orchestrated a culinary masterpiece that left us spellbound. Sunday lunch arrived on a grand scale, surpassing our wildest dreams. A magnificent platter of Yorkshire puddings, numbering close to a hundred, graced the table, their golden crusts glistening with savoury promise.

And then, a sizable side of beef emerged, cooked to perfection, its juices infused with a symphony of flavours. Alongside, the roast potatoes, resplendent in their golden coats, beckoned us to savour their crispy exteriors and fluffy interiors. With every bite, we were transported to a realm of unparalleled bliss.

Mrs. Thompson, her eyes dancing with delight, revelled in the sight of children, wide-eyed and content, savouring her creations. For a moment, the kitchen became a sanctuary of shared joy, where the simple act of nourishment became an expression of love and abundance.

© Author

Grassington currently is basking in the limelight if the new Channel 5 TV series, all creatures great and small, the second TV adaptation of the novels by Alf Wight under the name James Herriot, we happened upon the village when the shops etc. were dressed for filming and could not resist a few photographs.

It's only the dirty ones we don't want - Philip Wilkinson

© Author

The Devonshire on the square doubles for the Drovers in the adaptation, compare the changes with the similar image taken recently at the start of this section, the windows were converted to look like acid etched glass in the name Drovers, this detail has remained and looks to be permanent now.

© Author   © Author

Two more shops at the top of the square have been transformed, along with a house modified with double doors, and columns to become Skeldale House. Again these can be compared with the recent image at the start of this story, the double yellow lines all around the square have been covered over with bark chippings and straw, inconvenient things like intruder alarm sounders have been covered over and dressed to blend into the stone facades, streetlights have been added to look like gas lights, and even television aerials, overhead telephone lines etc. have been removed. It goes without saying that the cones and warning signs are collected up for a shoot.

Grassington was always an adventure and a very far cry from our cold, dark terraced house in Headingley, especially during the coal burning years where everything was black with soot particles all winter.

© Author

No. 15 Richmond Mount (centre) where we lived until I was thirteen, two students rented the large front bedroom with double windows, the boys had the front attic room, uninsulated, with the Dorma, the girls shared the back attic bedroom, and my parents had the back second bedroom. Unusually the house had two different addresses, it was No. 15 this side, and No. 30 Richmond Road on the other.

All are now student let HMO's (houses of multiple occupancy) and this was starting to happen as we lived there, coming home from primary school to students drunk and peeing in the street was entertaining, if not entirely acceptable in what had been a family area.

A cine film to remember   © Pixababy

Later that day, we embarked on a cinematic adventure, borrowing Mr. Thompson's 8mm cine camera to capture our youthful spirits and the timeless tale of the parable of the Good Samaritan.

Donned in shepherd's garb and other roles, created by wearing striped pyjama tops, and a tea towel on our heads, complete with bailing twine for both, we wove our narrative against the backdrop of a small path winding alongside a babbling stream.

The next day, Mr Thompson looked at the camera and determined we had only shot about 40 seconds of film, he said that this would not do, so we went back to the stream and re shot the story taking longer over each scene, and adding some dramatizations, including having a donkey provided by a family friend.

The presence of a real donkey lent an air of authenticity to our production, and as the camera rolled, we became the architects of our own magical world.

Many years later, I borrowed the original footage and converted it to video, then edited both days shoots together for a film now lasting about five minutes

A record player as a gift   © Author

During the summer months, a wonderful gift from my grandfather breathed new life into our home and opened the doors to a world of musical enchantment. He generously bestowed upon us his beloved Dansette mono portable record player, having recently acquired a new and sophisticated stereo system for himself. The moment that sleek, vintage device entered our lives, it became the centrepiece of our household, radiating a sense of nostalgia and anticipation.

Eager to explore the realms of music, my sister and I pooled our meagre pocket money together and set off on a mission to acquire our very first vinyl album. After careful consideration, we unanimously chose Simon & Garfunkel's timeless masterpiece, "Sounds of Silence." With the album safely in our possession, we returned home, brimming with excitement, eager to embark on a musical journey unlike anything we had experienced before.

As we placed the vinyl gently on the turntable and gingerly lowered the needle onto the groove, the room filled with the warm, crackling sounds of the opening track. The melodies of Simon & Garfunkel flowed through the air, captivating our senses, and transporting us to a realm of heartfelt emotions and profound storytelling. We were spellbound.

What made our Dansette record player even more special was a unique feature that allowed us to leave the arm raised, causing it to automatically repeat the side of the album it was playing. This feature became a constant companion, allowing us to lose ourselves in the music for hours on end. We would often find ourselves engrossed in the gentle strums of the guitar and the harmonious voices of Simon & Garfunkel, all the while mesmerized by the spinning vinyl and the comforting hum of the turntable.

While the music enveloped our ears and filled our hearts, I found myself immersed in the captivating world of literature. Thor Heyerdahl's remarkable book chronicling the Kon Tiki expedition became my literary companion during those enchanting musical sessions. As the melodies of Simon & Garfunkel enveloped the room, I would lose myself in the tales of adventure, bravery, and the insatiable human thirst for exploration. The combination of music and literature became a harmonious symphony, intertwining and evoking a sense of wonder and curiosity within me.

To this day, whenever I listen to "Sounds of Silence" or any track from that album, certain melodies and lyrics transport me back to that time, a time when the music and the written word intertwined, creating an indelible tapestry of memories. The sounds emanating from our cherished Dansette record player became the soundtrack of my formative years, igniting a passion for music that has persisted throughout my life.

That gift from my grandfather was not just a portable record player; it was a gateway to a world of melodies, emotions, and artistic expression. It awakened a profound appreciation for the power of music and its ability to evoke emotions, tell stories, and connect us to different eras and experiences. It became a catalyst for my lifelong love affair with music, shaping my tastes, expanding my horizons, and providing solace and joy during both the highs and lows of life.

In the years that followed, music became an inseparable part of my existence. It accompanied me through moments of celebration, offered solace during times of introspection, and provided a medium through which I could express my own creativity and emotions. From that humble Dansette record player to the modern streaming platforms of today, music has remained a constant companion, a trusted confidant, and a source of inspiration.

Looking back, I am grateful for the gift of music that entered my life through the portal of that Dansette record player. It instilled in me a profound appreciation for the power of melodies, lyrics, and harmonies to transcend time and touch the deepest recesses of our souls. That gift not only enriched my own existence but also connected me to a universal language, one that unites people across cultures, generations, and circumstances.

The memory of those early days, with the sounds of Simon & Garfunkel filling the air and the pages of Thor Heyerdahl's book at my side, will forever be etched in my heart. They serve as a reminder of the transformative power of music, literature, and the meaningful connections we forge with art forms that shape our lives. From that moment forward, music became more than just a collection of sounds, it became an integral part of my identity, a source of inspiration, and a lifelong companion.

Family holiday at Staithes © Shutterstock

In addition to enjoying the music on the record player, that summer our family went on a holiday to Staithes, a charming coastal town in North Yorkshire, located about 10 miles north of Whitby. All seven of us squeezed into a small two-bedroom cottage next to Captain Cook's cottage on Church Street. Although the rental listing claimed to have a sea view, it was a bit of an exaggeration. The only way we could glimpse the sea was by looking at a mirror positioned in the cottage's window.

Despite the misleading description, we had a fantastic holiday filled with both thrilling and healing experiences that would leave a lasting impact on each member of our family.

The picturesque town of Staithes greeted us with its quaint charm and idyllic coastal setting. As we settled into our cozy two-bedroom cottage on Church Street, nestled next to Captain Cook's cottage, we quickly realized that our accommodations were far from spacious. Nevertheless, the close quarters fostered a sense of togetherness and adventure, as all seven of us embraced the opportunity to create cherished memories in this seaside retreat.

While the rental listing had promised a sea view, we soon discovered that it was a slight exaggeration. The elusive sight of the sea required us to position a strategically placed mirror in the cottage's window, allowing us glimpses of the shimmering waters beyond. Although the view may not have matched the description, it added a touch of whimsy to our stay, transforming each glimpse into a treasured moment of anticipation and wonder.

The days in Staithes were filled with a delightful mix of exploration and relaxation. We embarked on scenic walks along the rugged coastline, tracing our steps along the winding paths that offered breathtaking vistas of the North Sea. The rhythmic crashing of the waves against the cliffs serenaded us as we ventured further, uncovering hidden coves and secluded beaches that invited us to dip our toes into the refreshing waters.

For me, the holiday held a special significance as I found solace and healing in the embrace of nature. The soothing sounds of the sea, the salty breeze caressing my face, and the vast expanse of the ocean before me provided a welcome respite from the challenges and uncertainties of daily life. It was a time of reflection and rejuvenation, where the beauty of nature acted as a balm for the soul.

The town itself was a treasure trove of experiences. We wandered through the charming streets, admiring the quaint cottages adorned with vibrant flowers and the inviting storefronts offering local crafts and delicacies. Staithes, with its rich maritime history, was a haven for artists, and we delighted in exploring the numerous art galleries, each showcasing unique works inspired by the coastal landscapes.

One of the highlights of our holiday was the opportunity to witness the vibrant fishing community in action. We observed fishermen returning from their daily catch, their boats filled with the bounties of the sea. The bustling fish market, alive with the sounds of lively banter and the aroma of freshly caught seafood, was a sensory delight. We savoured the Flavors of the coast, indulging in delicious fish and chips from the local eateries, relishing each bite as we soaked in the authentic seaside atmosphere.

Looking back on that summer holiday, it was not just the picturesque setting or the deceptive sea view that made it memorable. It was the collective spirit of adventure, the joy of discovery, and the bonds forged through shared experiences that transformed it into a truly unforgettable time for our family. Staithes became more than just a holiday destination—it became a place where we found solace, healing, and a renewed sense of togetherness.

One memorable incident occurred when we loaned our inflatable dinghy to another family. Their children hopped in, but a sudden gust of wind carried them far out to sea within minutes. About forty minutes later, a coble (a type of traditional fishing boat) returning from collecting crab pots spotted them and towed them back to shore.

The villagers, including several locals in Staithes bonnets knitting on the front, witnessed the dramatic rescue. As if not learning from the previous ordeal, three of us immediately set out in the same dinghy while the villagers and fishermen watched in disbelief. However, the circumstances were different this time.

It's only the dirty ones we don't want - Philip Wilkinson

The tide was high, the wind had calmed, and we were strong swimmers who could make it back to shore if necessary. At the time, Staithes had a significant fleet of cobbles, with around 70 in operation. Roughly 20 cobbles were moored in the harbour, while the rest were positioned up the river. It was an incredible sight to behold, fishermen in their Staithes-pattern knit jumpers and hats walking from boat to boat across the river and harbour.

The fishing villages on the coast had traditional knit patterns for their jumpers and hats, every village had a different pattern, this had nothing to do with fashion, village identity or technical skills, it had a gruesome practical reason, should a fisherman be lost at sea, as and when the body was eventually found, the unfortunate soul could be immediately identified to a single village by his knitwear.

Upon our arrival at the holiday let, I experienced an asthma attack triggered by the dust in the 400-year-old cottage. At this time there was no treatment available for asthma sufferers, there were however some dubious products available, see image of a lack of Kellogg's asthma cigarettes! I spent several days wheezing and unable to engage in much activity. On Wednesday evening, my parents wished to attend a prayer meeting in the church up the hill from our accommodation. They were reluctant to leave me behind given my condition. So, they helped me up to the church, and I struggled through the meeting, wheezing, and gasping.

The chaplain must have noticed my distress because during the prayers, he walked over to me and placed his hand on my head. He asked the congregation to pray for my recovery. As he stood silently in prayer, a remarkable thing happened—my symptoms began to fade away. Within a few minutes, my asthma attack subsided, and since that day, I have never experienced asthma again. This episode in Staithes became a significant turning point in my life, where faith and the power of prayer were intimately intertwined with my personal healing.

© Author

Chapter 5

A new school year

© Pixababy

School had started to show signs of improvement. I was no longer confined to wearing the cheap and uninspiring grey blazer that was provided for all students. As we entered the upper school in our third year, we were granted the privilege of

wearing a black blazer instead. This simple change in attire brought a sense of distinction and maturity. Additionally, we were granted the freedom to leave the school grounds during the lunch break, adding a newfound sense of independence to our daily routine. These small privileges made the school experience more enjoyable and marked a positive shift in my academic journey.

The school had reversed the free school meals segregated queuing system deployed for the previous three years, we could now all queue together, the free dinners qualifying students simply had a printed pass to present instead of cash, this did a better, if not complete, job of concealing those unfortunates needing the free service and reduced the chants, food throwing and taunting we had suffered.

The year brought a new intake of students, the first since I had started as the middle school system had caught up, around 120 new pupils started which meant that lessons in strange locations were back on the menu following a brief respite with no intake for two years, however, the school, having made grave errors of judgement in my intake year in their selection process of the 10% from non-faith backgrounds, had learned their lesson, this time they selected well and a repeat of the "morons" looked to have been avoided. If only the damn school would drop the hated and confusing 6-day timetable, things should and could be much better, however, after three years of the timetable, it was starting to become second nature now.

One of the boys at school, who happened to be a dear friend of mine, had gone through an unimaginable tragedy during the summer break. His father, a respected reverend, had tragically taken his own life, leaving a profound impact on my friend's life. He had discovered the heart-breaking scene, burdening him with a weight no child should bear. Physically, he was tall and slender, possessing a distinctive chin that unfortunately drew unwarranted attention from the bullies at school. They would seize any opportunity to mock him, taunting him with the hurtful nickname "Chinner," referencing his prominent chin. As a result, he became withdrawn, seeking solace in his own company and silently enduring the pain caused by their cruel actions.

During this challenging period, I remained a steadfast friend, offering my support and understanding as he navigated the grieving process. As the story progresses, you will witness how our bond strengthens, and eventually, we embark on our professional journeys together. We faced the trials of adolescence, the wounds of the past, and emerged resilient, proving that true friendship can overcome even the most profound hardships.

During the year of our mock exams, I found myself well-prepared thanks to the wisdom passed down from my grandfather and mother, both experienced educators. They had imparted valuable tips on exam strategies that would prove useful. During the physics mock exam, a challenging question worth 40% of the total marks awaited us: "Draw a schematic diagram of a nuclear power station." Taking a bold step, I decided to tackle this question head-on, even though no other student in my set dared to do so. With confidence, I sketched a hand-drawn block diagram, carefully including only the essential components: the reactor, turbine, generator, and the water system responsible for heat absorption, steam production, and powering the turbines. It was a concise representation of the complex system.

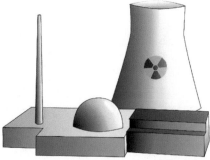
© Pixababy

To my delight, my approach proved successful. The deputy head, who happened to be our physics teacher, singled me out for praise. He commended my ability to handle such a demanding exam question with finesse. The full marks awarded to me validated the effectiveness of my approach, and I felt a sense of accomplishment. This experience served as a reminder that sometimes, taking a unique and confident approach to exams can yield remarkable results. The recognition I received from my teacher provided a boost of encouragement and reaffirmed the value of thinking outside the box.

Testing the punishment regime © Author

After yet another mix-up with classrooms and sets, I found myself feeling lost once again. Frustrated, I made the impulsive decision to hide out in the toilets for the duration of the period. Unfortunately, my attempt to evade detection was thwarted when a prefect discovered me and promptly escorted me to the headmaster's office.

There, the master timetable was consulted, and it was determined that I should attend a French lesson taking place in a science lab. As an additional consequence, I was assigned the task of writing a four-page essay on the importance of punctuality.

That evening, feeling mischievous, I decided to put my theory to the test. I questioned whether anyone read the punishment essays we were assigned.

The following morning, I submitted my essay, taking a risk by barely writing a paragraph before filling the remaining pages with the repetitive phrase "blah, blah, blah." I waited to see if anyone would approach me regarding the content of my essay. To my amusement, no one made any mention of it, solidifying my belief that these essays were going unnoticed and unread. This would be the last essay I received as a punishment as during my high school years.

It's only the dirty ones we don't want - Philip Wilkinson

No. 130 Town Street, Beeston the home of Bilbo, Frodo and Teddy

The Thursday Club

We had initiated a Thursday club at the twins' house, where a gathering of like-minded lads would convene to engage in stimulating discussions. Our topics ranged from scientific subjects to various outdoor activities such as cycling, camping trips, and even exploring caves. These gatherings provided us with a forum for fun and debate and allowed us to form strong bonds with one another. It was a remarkable feeling to have a group of friends who would support and stand by you when the need arose. The club consisted of myself, the twins Bilbo and Frodo, Richie, Marsbar, Teddy (the twins' younger brother, who was a lover of 50's rock n roll and a Ted), Erotic, LTJ, Eppie, and Jugsy, with occasional appearances from other siblings and casual girlfriends who tagged along. These meetings became cherished moments for our group, fostering lasting friendships and creating memorable experiences. During our gatherings, there were certainly some silly antics taking place. One of the tricks we played involved a coiled spring exercise bar, (popular at the time), which we would bend double and pass around, testing if someone would unwittingly take it without realising the force required to hold it. It was all in good fun.

The challenge of obtaining alcohol was also a part of our adventures. We would all try our luck, and some of us would succeed in procuring some drinks, which we would then share among the group.

Meanwhile, the twins had discovered their musical talents. Bilbo picked up the bass guitar, while Frodo became skilled on a Fender Telecaster. They formed a popular band called Last Orders, and they started playing cover songs at various venues, including the church hall, pubs, and working men's clubs in the area. Their favourite tracks to cover were by Queen, although they faced a challenge with reproducing a particular high note in the song "I'm in Love with My Car." It seemed that a special instrument or a specifically tuned string was used to achieve that note, which they couldn't replicate.

© Author

Around the same time, music was evolving to another level. Following the release of The Beatles' "Sgt. Pepper's Lonely Hearts Club Band" in 1967, considered the first concept album, other bands began releasing their own. Pink Floyd's "The Dark Side of the Moon" and Supertramp's "Crime of the Century" were among the notable albums that followed. Genesis also contributed with "The Lamb Lies Down on Broadway." These albums had a profound influence on my life, and I still regularly listen to all three of them, and yes, I admit, I was one of those bores walking around school with copies of the LPs.

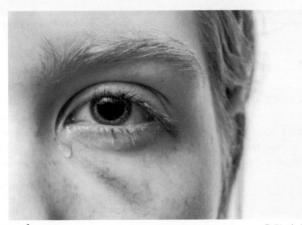

Unforeseen hazards   © Pixababy

As fate would have it, a seemingly ordinary day at school took a dramatic turn when a sudden downpour forced us to seek shelter indoors. In our haste to escape the deluge, an unexpected accident unfolded.

71

It's only the dirty ones we don't want - Philip Wilkinson

Amidst the flurry of students rushing past the hall, a fellow pupil unknowingly unleashed an unforeseen peril. In a cruel twist of fate, the out-swinging pivoted metal window opened just as I passed by, its corner aligning perfectly with the height of my head. With a force that seemed to defy logic, the unforgiving metal frame collided with the crown of my head, delivering a blow that sent shockwaves through my body.

The impact was severe, causing me to lose consciousness and crumple onto the wet ground beneath the pouring rain. During this unexpected calamity, a vigilant teacher bore witness to the distressing scene that unfolded before their eyes. Acting swiftly and, they dashed around the building. Bearing witness to the blood cascading down my face from the open wound, the teacher with swift and determined movements, cradled me in her arms and helped me to the sheltered sanctuary of the school's interior. The echo of concern resonated through the hallways as my fellow students watched. Recognizing the gravity of the situation, an ambulance was summoned, and I was swiftly transported to the A&E Department where medical professionals attended to my injuries, conducting thorough examinations to ascertain the extent of the trauma. The diagnosis revealed a slight concussion, a testament to the severity of the impact I had endured.

To their credit, the school acted promptly and responsibly in the aftermath of this unfortunate incident. In a gesture of accountability and concern for the well-being of its students, measures were taken to prevent a recurrence of such a distressing accident. The windows, once potential hazards, underwent modifications with the installation of limit stops, designed to prevent any re-occurrence.

Finally, a car for the family   © Car & Classic

Liz, the lady mentioned previously for requiring thousands of lessons, failing many driving tests, and owning a Land Rover named Betsy, had a divine vision one day. She believed that she was destined to help my parents buy a car. Out of the blue, she arrived and announced her mission. Taking my father along, she led him to a car dealership where they purchased a two-year-old Mini Clubman estate with an automatic transmission (Liz only had an auto licence, she believed this would be easier for my parents, and that she could act as the driver during their lessons).

This car was deemed perfect for our family of seven, with two adults in the front, three kids in the back, and two more fitting comfortably in the boot, which had double doors for easy access. Despite neither of my parents having a driving license at the time, Liz remained undeterred. They put L plates on the Mini, and driving lessons commenced with Liz in the passenger seat. After several weeks, my father successfully passed his driving test. However, my mother never quite got around to taking hers, yet she regularly drove the car anyway, one of her foibles, highly religious, never shopped on Sundays, always paid the tithe on my father income to the church, yet happy to break the law driving on a provisional licence.

We often enjoyed surprising my father. Before embarking on a trip in the car, we would make sure we were all ready and head out to the vehicle. While my father believed it was locked and secure, we would subtly slide the back window open just enough so that the plastic toggle locking it was not trapped by the sides of its frame. A gentle tap on the frame behind the toggle would cause it to drop into the unlocked position. With the window opened, we could then unlock the car and climb inside. When my father arrived, he would unlock the car, only to find us all seated inside, much to his surprise. We managed to keep this playful act going for weeks before he finally caught us in the act.

Moving house©   Author

That year, due to the increasing and inevitable advance and misbehaviour of students in our street in Headingley and the closure of the City Evangelical Church, located in a converted warehouse scheduled for demolition behind Burton's menswear on Boar Lane, we made the decision to move house. The church split into two groups, each setting up a new Evangelical church in different locations.

One group established their church in an old mission house in Garforth, while the other found a home in an old Baptist church in Beeston, (the 120-foot-long red sign reading "City Evangelical Church" sign written by my father in sections in our home can still be seen from the M621 link road).

It's only the dirty ones we don't want - Philip Wilkinson

City Evangelical Church Beeston   © Steve F

No. 15 Park Row, Beeston centre left, it did not have a Dorma in our day. ©Author

We moved during the late winter to a larger terraced house in Beeston, situated just behind the bowling green in the park. Despite costing almost the same as the house we sold in

Headingley, it provided us with more space, allowing each of us to have our own room. However, we were still one bedroom short, so my seven-year-old sister Judith improvised a tiny bed in the cupboard under the attic stairs, just as in the Harry Potter movies, whenever I went up to my attic room, I would deliberately stomp up or down the stairs dislodging dust and insects onto her in the cupboard below.

The new house boasted spacious basements, in addition to a coal store. These areas proved to be incredibly useful for repairing bicycles and engaging in various DIY projects. The only downside for me was the daily commute to school. I had to catch a bus into Leeds centre and then transfer to another bus that would take me to Horsforth, where the school was located. It was quite a lengthy journey. Fortunately, my newfound school friends Frodo, Bilbo, and Teddy lived just up the road, and we often found ourselves on the same bus, making the trip more enjoyable.

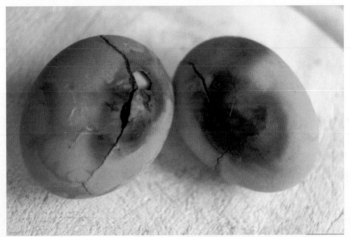

Culinary delights from the only woman who could burn water   © Pixababy

My mother's cooking skills were never the greatest, and as a result, our meals were often burnt, or consisted of cornflakes and sandwiches. It was not uncommon for her to serve up a meal, one item at a time, hence potatoes would arrive to the table, a long wait later some peas would turn up, another wait and sausages arrived, burned black, then pudding such as Swiss roll cut into slices with cream (top of the bottle of milk) poured over it, then she would stick her head through the serving hatch and announce, by the way I just found a pan full of carrots if anyone can eat more.

One day, Richie came over to my house, and my mother, being polite, asked if he had eaten. When he replied that he hadn't, she kindly offered to make him something to eat. After some time, she brought out a plate with a beefburger, chips, and peas. Richie started to cut into the burger, even with a stainless-steel knife with serrated edge, he found this surprisingly difficult, just them my mother leaned in through the serving hatch and casually mentioned, "Oh, by the way, the burger may be a little tough. It's been warmed up a few times." It was quite an interesting dining experience.

On another fateful day after school, we arrived home to smoke billowing out of the kitchen windows, an attempt to cook a chicken had proven a step too complex and the whole dinner was on fire, turns out my mother had expected the chicken to take longer to cook, but having set the oven to grill, rather than cook, the ribs caught fire whilst she was collecting my siblings.

Burnt pork ribs anyone   © Pixababy

My father blathered everything in brown sauce, this way he retained some degree of control over the food he ate and how it tasted, my brother decided that the only food he would eat was fried egg and chips, as he could make this for himself, he could control consistency.

© Author

My mother decided it would be nice to invite Erotic over for a family tea. Intrigued by the invitation, he accepted, not having a clue about what awaited him. You see, his own mother had a reputation for serving extravagant meals, piled high with pancakes, and followed by indulgent puddings. Little did Erotic know; he was in for a disappointment.

It's only the dirty ones we don't want - Philip Wilkinson

As we entered the dining room, my siblings and father were already seated, fully aware that I had invited a guest for tea. An extra chair had been squeezed in, and we all eagerly awaited the culinary spectacle. Suddenly, the serving hatch burst open, and my mother triumphantly passed bowls of cornflakes through to each person at the table, including herself. She then followed it up with two bottles of milk and the sacred sugar bowl.

Erotic glanced at the bowl of cornflakes, trying to decipher if this was some sort of avant-garde starter. Before he could ponder further, my father cleared his throat and began saying grace. Like obedient sheep, we all bowed our heads, and Erotic joined in, not wanting to stand out. And just like that, grace was over, leaving us famished souls to unleash our inner savages.

© Author

Eight hungry individuals around the table suddenly transformed into contestants on a game show, fighting tooth and spoon for the limited supply of milk, sugar, and spoons. Erotic, caught in the frenzy, devoured his cornflakes, trying to process the absurdity of the situation. He sat there, stomach still rumbling, waiting for the grand finale.

But to his utter astonishment, that was it. The cornflakes constituted the entire tea affair. Oh, how my mother had truly pushed the boat out! Fresh milk and crunchy cornflakes, a culinary masterpiece in her eyes.

While Erotic may not have experienced the grand feast he had anticipated, he couldn't help but chuckle at the sheer absurdity of the situation. At least my mother's cornflakes were a shining example of freshness, leaving us all with a bowlful of humour and a touch of confusion.

On one occasion, returning from school my father was home, my mother was incapacitated and had taken to her bed, at last we thought, tonight's tea might even be edible. We were wrong however, my father, struggling to find anything to eat in the house, had prepared a large stack of bread and dripping soldiers, placing these on a plate in the middle of the table.

It's only the dirty ones we don't want - Philip Wilkinson

As we waited for him to say grace, he made a large pot of tea, he poured me a cup first and then started to pour for the rest of the family, he then sat down, and we said grace. I was the first to take a mouthful of the tea, shocked by what I had imbibed and its taste, I immediately sprayed the contents from my mouth, soaking the plate of bread and dripping fingers.

My father understandably was annoyed at my destruction of the only food in the house in such a disgusting manner, then he tried the tea and had to spit it back out into the cup. It seems that in his search through the cupboards for a tea bag, he had discovered an item he had never encountered before, a bouquet garni, from which he had made tea. It was not just my mother who was a bit hopeless in the kitchen after all.

On another occasion, my sister found an unexpected item in one of the storage jars in the kitchen, a Mars bar, she could not sneak off and consume it as we had all seen what she had found and new our sweet tooths and peaked interest had been aroused. With five excited children pulling at her.

© Mars confectionary

My mother needed to provide us with a fair portion of the sweet treat, but how do you make a single chocolate bar go around so many, in a scene reminiscent of the loaves and fishes story from the bible, my mother cut the bar into very fine slices, then taking a loaf of sliced bread, she made five sandwiches with a few slices in each, to make the treat spread further, she took apple sauce and added a layer to each and we had sliced Mars bar and apple sandwiches. A new culinary delight and unexpected treat.

It's only the dirty ones we don't want - Philip Wilkinson

A Colour TV

After the unfortunate demise of my previous TV set, my brother shared an intriguing discovery with me. He had spotted a discarded television in the nearby graveyard. Curiosity piqued, I decided to accompany him on an investigative expedition. As it turned out, he was right. There, nestled amidst the headstones, lay a colour TV, abandoned and forgotten. With a joint effort, we retrieved the TV and embarked on the arduous journey back home.

Upon closer inspection, I identified the main issue, the power lead inside the set had been severed. I skilfully reconnected the wires, and to my delight, the TV sprang to life. However, it was evident that the set required extensive adjustments. The primary colours were woefully misaligned, the image displayed black bars at the top and bottom due to misaligned scanning, and the sound quality was abysmal. Furthermore, the tuner proved to be unreliable.

Determined to restore the TV to its former glory, I subscribed to Practical Television magazine, which proved to be an invaluable resource. With the newfound knowledge at my disposal, I swiftly tackled the issues one by one. The poor sound was resolved by replacing a damaged speaker, while the misalignments simply required some careful adjustment. Yet, there remained one major challenge that eluded my expertise, the picture tube's impending end of life. It demanded regular tweaking every few weeks to maintain a stable image as the tube expired.

Despite its imperfections, it was a triumph to finally have a functioning colour TV. However, my parents, burdened with the costlier TV licence, held reservations about the new acquisition. Their concerns were assuaged when fate smiled upon me once again. Another old TV came my way, and I skilfully repaired it, providing my parents with their own dedicated set. As a result, my hard-won colour TV found its new home in the cosy confines of my loft bedroom.

With the newfound treasure of a functional colour TV in my possession, my loft bedroom became a sanctuary of entertainment and discovery. It was a haven where I could retreat from the outside world and immerse myself in the captivating programs and films that filled the airwaves.

It's only the dirty ones we don't want - Philip Wilkinson

The flickering glow of the television set became a constant companion, casting vibrant hues across the room as I delved into a myriad of shows and movies. From classic sitcoms to thrilling dramas, and even the occasional late-night horror film that would send shivers down my spine, the TV opened a vast world of storytelling and entertainment that captivated my imagination.

Beyond the realm of entertainment, the TV also became a gateway to knowledge and discovery. I would eagerly tune in to educational programs, fascinated by documentaries that explored the wonders of nature, history, and science. Each broadcast offered a window into a different realm of understanding, expanding my horizons and fuelling my curiosity.

In those moments of solitary bliss, I found solace and inspiration within the confines of my loft bedroom. The TV became more than just a piece of technology; it became a conduit for dreams and aspirations. It fuelled my imagination and ignited a passion for storytelling that would shape my future endeavours.

As time went on, I continued to refine my skills in television repair and maintenance. I honed my ability to fine-tune the picture tube and troubleshoot any issues that arose. With each repair, I gained a deeper understanding of the inner workings of television technology, cementing my love for electronics and engineering.

Beyond the technical aspects, the TV served as a catalyst for bonding moments with friends and family. It became a gathering point for shared experiences, whether it was watching a thrilling sporting event with friends or enjoying a movie night with loved ones. The magic of the television screen brought people together, fostering connections and creating lasting memories.

Looking back on those days, the abandoned TV discovered in the graveyard proved to be more than just a salvaged piece of technology. It became a symbol of resourcefulness, perseverance, and the power of curiosity. It ignited a passion for electronics, sparked a thirst for knowledge, and opened a world of entertainment and exploration.

In the end, my loft bedroom transformed into a personal haven, where the flickering glow of the colour TV illuminated not only the room but also my path in life. It was a reminder that great discoveries often lie hidden in unexpected places, waiting to be unearthed by those who dare to venture beyond the ordinary.

One thing the TV could not resolve was the lack of any insulation for my loft bedroom, it was tortuously hot in summer, and freezing cold in winter, to help out with the cold, I had an old free standing electric heater, this had a heating element in the base and a vent at the top of the front which I stood beside my bed and put my blankets over, this worked well to heat up my bed, however the heater also had a convection element in the front, on one occasion, this had been switched on without me being aware, after about half an hour, the mattress side caught fire, a bit of a rude awakening.

It's only the dirty ones we don't want - Philip Wilkinson

The long bus ride to school

The long bus ride provided us with a valuable opportunity to work on our homework. It was convenient for subjects like English and Maths, but when it came to technical drawing, things were a bit more challenging. The twins, with their A2 paper and limited supplies (using the back of my satchel as a makeshift drawing surface), struggled to produce high-quality work in this subject. Their attempts at technical drawing with a pencil and a broken ruler were less than ideal, to say the least.

It's only the dirty ones we don't want - Philip Wilkinson

Whenever we had to change buses at Bishopgate Street, our group would often make a stop at a small, intriguing shop nestled under the railway arches: M&B Radio. This unique establishment specialized in surplus government electronics, creating an enchanting atmosphere akin to an Aladdin's cave. Within its walls, one could find a treasure trove of captivating equipment, ranging from oscilloscopes and studio TV cameras to radio broadcast gear, reel-to-reel tape Dictaphone recorders, bench power supplies, radar equipment, flight masks, computer memory panels, and even landing lights for RAF jets. M&B Radio spares was in a railway arch close to Leeds railway station, it's now a fast-food cafe

It was in this remarkable store that Bilbo and another member of our group, a prodigious computer programming genius whose name eludes me now, stumbled upon a fascinating discovery. They purchased approximately fifty surplus memory PCBs, each adorned with around 40 integrated circuits. If my memory serves me correctly, each chip offered approximately 128 bytes of memory, resulting in roughly 5 kilobytes of memory per board. Armed with these components and an imposing power supply, they set out to construct a computer that would fulfil their hearts' desires.

A 1970's computer memory circuit bord like those used © Author

Their efforts culminated in the creation of a remarkable computer, boasting a series of two banks, each housing 16 lights. This ingenious contraption had the ability to play chess, indicating which piece to move and where it should be moved through the strategic illumination of these lights. For instance, if the computer deemed it appropriate to move a pawn to king 4, it would light up the corresponding lights for the pawn in one bank and illuminate its intended position on the second bank.

This achievement was quite extraordinary for its time. The brilliant individual behind this endeavour continued to soar to greater heights. In fact, he went on to secure a historic first in the UK. For three years, the examination board had offered a computer programming course at CSE level, starting in 1972. Yet, by 1975, no student had managed to pass at any level. Determined to change that, the course was elevated to the GCE level that year. And it was this very genius who emerged triumphant, becoming the sole student to pass the examination with an exceptional A* grade.

The tale of their adventure at M&B Radio and the subsequent accomplishments of this remarkable individual stand as testament to the awe-inspiring possibilities that lie within the realm of technology and human ingenuity.

It's only the dirty ones we don't want - Philip Wilkinson

Image of the old bridge at Sligachen with the Culin mountains   ©Author

Camping trip to Skye

The camping trip to the Isle of Skye was a truly unforgettable adventure, etched into my memory as one of the most remarkable experiences of my youth. The journey itself was an adventure, as we embarked on a long car ride to reach our destination. The lack of motorways in the early 1970s meant that the journey was slower, but it also allowed us to take in the scenic beauty of the countryside along the way.

Arriving at Skye by ferry was a moment filled with excitement and anticipation. As we set foot on the island, the air was filled with a sense of adventure and exploration. We wasted no time in setting up our campsite in the fields near the Sligachan Hotel, where we would spend the next few days immersed in the beauty of nature.

The campsite itself was nestled in the shadow of the magnificent Cuillin mountains, their rugged peaks standing tall and imposing. The views from our campsite were nothing short of breathtaking, with the river flowing nearby and the famous old stone bridge adding a touch of charm to the surroundings. It was a perfect spot to immerse ourselves in the tranquillity of nature and escape from the hustle and bustle of everyday life.

During our camping trip, there were certain rules in place, particularly regarding alcohol consumption. As teenagers, we were given some leeway, with beer being deemed acceptable if we were discreet and didn't get caught. In the evenings, our group would gather around the campfire, joining other outdoor enthusiasts who shared tales of their own adventures. It was during these moments that the three girls and I would venture out into the long grass, carefully hiding our beer bottles, and join the group, savouring the taste of freedom and the camaraderie of fellow campers.

Of course, no adventure is complete without a few misadventures along the way. It seemed that Nicky and I had a talent for finding trouble. The incident with the sewage settlement pond still brings a mix of amusement and embarrassment when recalled. Unbeknownst to us, we had been merrily throwing stones into the lake, unaware of its true nature. The resulting unpleasant odour that permeated the air caused quite a stir among the campsite, leading to some disapproving glances in our direction.

On another occasion, our youthful curiosity led us to swim across the river estuary, aiming to return to camp from the other side. We were strong swimmers and had carefully assessed the risks involved. However, when our feat was mentioned later, it sparked concerns and lectures from the adults about the potential dangers of swimming across an estuary. We quickly realized that sometimes it was best to keep our adventurous exploits to ourselves.

View from Elgin of the Culin Mountain range   ©Author

During the trip, we made sure to capture the essence of the experience through postcards, as we didn't have a camera with us. Those postcards serve as cherished mementos, preserving the beauty and memories of Skye, the towering Cuillin mountains, and the sense of freedom and exploration that defined the trip.

The majesty of the Cuillin mountains left an indelible mark on my soul. Sgurr nan Gillean, with its prominent peak and challenging climb, stood out among the rest, inspiring awe, and igniting a sense of adventure within me. The name itself, "peak of the young men," seemed fitting, as it symbolized the determination and resilience required to conquer such formidable heights.

It's only the dirty ones we don't want - Philip Wilkinson

The impact of this camping trip on my life was profound. It instilled in me a deep love for the outdoors, a fascination with nature's beauty, and a yearning for further exploration and adventure. Subsequent camping trips became a regular part of my life, providing a sense of freedom, tranquillity, and connection with the natural world. The Isle of Skye will forever hold a special place in my heart, as the place where my passion for camping and the great outdoors truly took root. three girls and I would discreetly collect bottles from the tent and sneak back to the group, hiding in the long grass common in the Highlands, where we would listen to age-inappropriate jokes and stories while enjoying our purloined beer

| Roger Youderian | Pete Fleming | Jim Elliot | Nate Saint | Ed McCully |

uncertain of copyright, please advise and I will add to the next revision
January 8, 1956, when all five—Jim Elliot, Nate Saint, Ed McCully, Peter Fleming, and Roger Youderian—were attacked and speared by a group of Huaorani warriors

The YL (young life)

The YL (Young Life) group, based in Headingley, held weekly prayer meetings every Friday, primarily attended by their supporters who were predominantly Evangelical Christians. You may have come across this group during a beach holiday, as they are often recognizable by their red and white attire. During the summer recess, they provide Sunday school-style teachings on various beaches across the UK.

On a particular occasion, I had the opportunity to attend one of their Friday meetings with my parents. That evening, the gathering featured special visitors who captivated our attention. They were the wives of the five missionaries who tragically lost their lives in Ecuador back in 1956. This mission, known as Operation Auca, aimed to establish contact with the previously unknown Waodani tribe residing in the rainforest. After months of dropping gifts to befriend them, the missionaries courageously ventured on foot to meet the Waodani people. Tragically, they were met with violence and lost their lives at Palm Beach, along the Curaray River. This extraordinary story later became the subject of the film "End of the Spear."

The meeting proved to be a deeply moving experience, leaving a lasting impression on me. It shed light on the profound sacrifices that some individuals are willing to make in the name of their religious beliefs. Witnessing the unwavering dedication and selflessness of these missionaries' wives, who carried the memory and legacy of their husbands, provided a powerful reminder of the profound impact that faith and devotion can have on people's lives. It served as a testament to the strength of the human spirit and the lengths individuals are willing to go to spread their message of love, compassion, and understanding.

© Pixababy

On another occasion, a planned walk brought together supporters of the YL and the local Evangelical Church. Coaches transported us to Pateley Bridge, where our journey was set to commence at the town's bridge over the river Nidd, proceeding along the southern bank into Nidderdale. The weather was delightful, and the atmosphere among the approximately 90 participants was cheerful as we embarked on our adventure. Our goal was to reach the Sportsman's Arms, where we could enjoy some refreshments before retracing our steps back to the waiting coaches.

During our walk, a peculiar incident unfolded. One of the fellow Christians in our group unexpectedly struck up a conversation with my father and me. Pointing to a nearby field, they remarked, "Not this one, but the next field over there is where I lost my cherry." Taken aback by the unexpected comment, my father responded with a hesitant, "Oh, okay." As we continued walking, the person continued, pointing towards a specific tree, and saying, "See that tree, second on the right? That's where it happened." My father grew increasingly embarrassed, yet the person persisted, pointing to another tree, and saying, "And over there, the third tree on that side, that's where her mother stood and watched." Unable to resist, my father fell into the trap and asked, "What on earth did she say?" To which the person replied with a sheepish "baaaaaaah." It was an inappropriate joke exchanged between two Christians, made more uncomfortable by the fact that it was shared in front of a 12-year-old. It highlighted the contrasting sides of human behaviour that exist within individuals, underscoring the complexity of human nature.

Chapter 6 – 1974

Life improves

Another camping trip in the Dales © Pixababy

The next camping trip to How Stean in the Dales was another thrilling adventure that left an indelible mark on my memory. This time, we were better prepared, having learned from our previous experiences. Our group had grown to fourteen, with familiar faces such as Erotic, Frodo, Bilbo (the twins), Ian, Teddy, and the addition of two girls, LTJ and her friend Jugsy. We were a spirited bunch, eager to explore the caves and embrace the beauty of the outdoors.

Prior to the trip, several of us had ordered wet suits from a catalogue, determined to delve into the world of cave exploration. Equipped with our wet suits and armed with two carbide lamps for better underground lighting, we were ready for the adventure that awaited us. Our Tilly lamps and stoves ensured that we could cook hearty meals and enjoy warm food even during nature's embrace.

One incident stands out in my memory, a mischievous escapade that involved us acquiring bottles of cider from a local shop. In our slightly inebriated state, we embarked on a noisy bike ride up the middle of a stream, revelling in our freedom and creating quite a ruckus along the way. Our rowdy antics did not go unnoticed, as they caught the attention of the local police. In a matter of moments, they arrived on the scene, kindly advising us to keep the noise down. It was a light-hearted encounter, reminding us to balance our enthusiasm with respect for others. Amidst the laughter and merriment, another memorable moment unfolded when one of the girls, LTJ, accidentally fell into the stream. She was wearing a cheesecloth top with nothing underneath, and the water caused her top to become transparent. The incident brought smiles and amusement to the faces of the lads in our group, a comical moment etched into the annals of our shared memories.

Riding a bicycle down a stream   © Pixababy

Little did we know that this camping trip would have far-reaching effects on the lives of some members of our group. Two individuals took their involvement with cave exploration to new heights. One of them went on to become a North Sea oil rig retrieval diver, leading a daring and adventurous life that included cave diving during his downtime. His love for exploration knew no bounds, pushing the boundaries of danger and excitement.

The other member, Bilbo, continued to contribute to the field of cave diving, expanding our knowledge of caves in Yorkshire and Lancashire. His affiliation with Leeds University and his role in building cutting-edge ULF radio transmitter/receivers allowed for innovative techniques in cave exploration. These devices were used to triangulate divers in caves, revolutionizing the safety and precision of underwater expeditions. The remarkable technology of that time is showcased in films made by Sid Perou, capturing the spirit of adventure and the state-of-the-art equipment employed in those thrilling explorations.

This camping trip in the Dales ignited a passion for the great outdoors and camping that would continue to fuel my sense of adventure for years to come. The camaraderie, the laughter, and the shared experiences created a bond among us that transcended the trip itself. The memories of that time spent exploring caves, riding bikes, and revelling in the joys of nature remain cherished and treasured, reminding me of the boundless beauty and excitement that can be found in the world around us.

Choosing Exam Subjects   © Pixababy

The process of choosing exam subjects in school was a significant milestone, shaping the academic path and prospects of each student. As the time arrived for us to make these important decisions, we were divided into two categories: CSE (Certificate of Secondary Education) and GCE (General Certificate of Education) candidates, based on our perceived abilities and interests.

With a keen interest in the sciences and a thirst for knowledge, I carefully selected my eight exam subjects. Mathematics, Physics, Chemistry, and Biology were the natural choices for me, as they provided a solid foundation in the scientific disciplines that fascinated me. These subjects promised to unlock the secrets of the universe and deepen my understanding of the world around me.

In addition to the sciences, I opted for English Language and English Literature. Language and literature had always captivated my imagination, allowing me to explore different perspectives, delve into the intricacies of storytelling, and express my thoughts with eloquence and precision. These subjects offered a creative outlet and fostered my love for literature and language.

Woodwork, an unconventional choice among the academic subjects, held a special allure for me. The prospect of working with my hands, shaping raw materials into functional and aesthetically pleasing objects, appealed to my sense of craftsmanship and practicality. Woodwork provided a welcome balance to the theoretical nature of the other subjects and allowed me to express my creativity in a different form.

Interestingly, our deputy headmaster was assigned as our Physics teacher, a role that initially evoked a sense of fear within me. He was a formidable figure, and I had observed his strict demeanour from a distance. However, my perceptions were quickly challenged as I experienced his teaching style firsthand. To my surprise, he turned out to be an exceptional educator, delivering complex concepts with clarity and instilling in us a deep passion for the

89

subject. He encouraged independent thinking, fostering an environment of intellectual freedom that allowed us to explore and question the principles of physics.

Under his guidance, my understanding of the subject flourished, and my confidence grew. I discovered that behind his stern exterior lay a genuine commitment to our education and a desire to see us succeed. He nurtured our curiosity, challenging us to push our limits and strive for excellence.

The process of choosing exam subjects was not just about selecting a set of subjects to study; it was a defining moment in our academic journey. It required careful consideration of our interests, abilities, and aspirations. The subjects we chose shaped our educational trajectory and set the stage for future opportunities and career paths.

Looking back, I am grateful for the subjects I chose and the dedicated teachers who guided me along the way. The sciences fuelled my passion for discovery and exploration, while the language and literature subjects refined my communication

skills and broadened my worldview. Woodwork provided a hands-on experience that complemented my academic pursuits, fostering creativity and practical problem-solving.

Ultimately, the process of choosing exam subjects was not just about the subjects themselves; it was about self-discovery, growth, and laying the foundation for a lifelong pursuit of knowledge. It set the stage for the academic challenges and triumphs that awaited me, instilling in me a love for learning that continues to shape my journey to this day.

© Pixababy

Teaching ourselves physics

In the unique setting of Mr. Haig's physics class, where three of us were deemed advanced compared to our peers, we were presented with an extraordinary opportunity: the chance to teach ourselves physics. Positioned at the back of the classroom, armed with A-level physics books as our reference materials, we embarked on a journey of independent learning and exploration.

This arrangement allowed us to delve into the intricacies of physics at our own pace, following our own interests within the boundaries of the subject. It was an empowering experience that fostered a deep sense of ownership and autonomy over our education. We had the freedom to select topics that captivated our curiosity, dive into them with fervour, and pursue a level of understanding beyond the confines of the regular curriculum.

It's only the dirty ones we don't want - Philip Wilkinson

The advantages of this self-teaching setup were manifold. We were able to explore complex concepts in detail, engaging in in-depth discussions and debates among ourselves. The small group dynamic fostered a collaborative environment, where we challenged and inspired one another to push the boundaries of our knowledge. We had the luxury of time to ponder, question, and experiment, allowing for a deeper grasp of the subject matter.

However, along with the advantages came a few downsides. Our experimental sessions, while fascinating, were not without risks. Accidents occasionally occurred, particularly during demonstrations involving reactive metals like potassium and sodium. These displays were both entertaining and educational, but on one ill-fated day, our experimentation with lithium took a dangerous turn. An oversized lump of lithium plunged into water, resulting in a massive explosion that sent debris flying, causing damage to the ceiling and lab lights. It was a moment of chaos and a stark reminder of the need for caution in our scientific pursuits.

Despite the occasional mishaps, our passion for physics remained undeterred. We were not content with solely theoretical knowledge; we wanted hands-on experience. During a rainy lunch break, when the school's oscilloscope was out of order, we took matters into our own hands. Venturing into the lab stores, we retrieved the oscilloscope from quarantine and embarked on a mission to repair it. Working together, we dismantled, examined, and meticulously fixed the device. By the time the next physics lesson arrived, our trio had successfully resurrected the oscilloscope. Our teacher was immensely grateful for our resourcefulness and swift resolution.

However, our unorthodox actions did not go unnoticed. Mr. Haig, fulfilling his duty, reported our unauthorized activities to the headmaster. Safety concerns were raised, prompting a thorough interview about our actions. As we reflected on the incident, we couldn't help but compare it to the open radios, televisions, and other electronic devices in our own homes, with exposed components and potential risks, especially considering the presence of younger siblings. It was a reminder that our pursuit of knowledge and exploration carried inherent responsibilities and required a balance between curiosity and safety.

In retrospect, our unconventional experiences in teaching ourselves physics were invaluable. They offered us a level of intellectual freedom and independence rarely found within the confines of a traditional classroom. We developed critical thinking skills, honed our problem-solving abilities, and forged a deep appreciation for the wonders of the physical world. The mishaps and challenges we encountered along the way served as valuable lessons, teaching us the importance of caution, responsibility, and the ethical considerations that accompany scientific exploration.

The experience of teaching ourselves physics left an indelible mark on our educational journey. It instilled in us a lifelong love for learning, a thirst for knowledge, and a resilience in the face of challenges. We emerged from that classroom with a profound understanding that education extends beyond the boundaries of formal instruction and that true mastery comes from embracing curiosity, taking risks, and embracing the joy of self-discovery.

Photo of an original advert and calculator   Author

The Sinclair Calculator

Practical Wireless magazine had recently celebrated the invention of the microprocessor, a ground-breaking development in technology. Sir Clive Sinclair, known for his innovative creations, utilised this new technology to introduce the world's first pocket calculator, the Sinclair Cambridge. Advertisements for this ground-breaking device could be found in every issue of the magazine that year.

The Sinclair Cambridge calculator was initially priced at £39.99 for a fully assembled and tested unit. Additionally, there was an option to purchase it as a self-assembly kit for just £29.99. Excited by the prospect of owning this cutting-edge technology, we eagerly followed the monthly updates as the prices gradually dropped. Eventually, the assembled calculator was available for £14.99, while the kit form could be purchased for a mere £9.99.

This significant reduction in price prompted several of us to order the kits and embark on the process of building our own calculators. The Sinclair Cambridge calculator was truly revolutionary for its time.

Shortly after acquiring our calculators, we had our mock exams. To our surprise, the math paper stated that logarithmic tables and calculating machines could be used if sufficient accuracy could be achieved. Intrigued by this statement, we approached our teacher's seeking clarification but received unsatisfactory answers. The discrepancy left us wondering about the true extent to which these advanced tools could be utilised during our exams.

By this stage in school, the first intake of the morons was absent most of the time, we were not sure if this was due to expulsion, police action or if they had left, but they really were not missed.

Fresh Blood   © Pixababy

A new intake of pupils this year had arrived, the 13-year-old middle school students, this brought fresh blood. Marsbar and Teddy were in their element, about 60 new and interesting girls were included in the intake, after a few months, they found two, we shall call them K and C, who were willing to sneak out of school and go to Marsbar's home on the local estate for sex. Neighbours reported to his parents that they were at home half the day three days a week, and running around naked, both in the house and the garden. At this point Marsbar's father, a barber, brought them a present, a box of 144 condoms, throwing them at him with the words, here son, be careful.

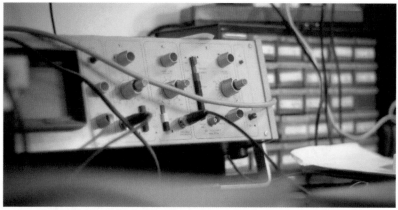

Building my own test equipment © Pixababy

I was engrossed in a project I had undertaken based on the instructions in the Practical Wireless magazine. It was a step-by-step guide to building your own oscilloscope, a fascinating endeavour. Gathering the necessary parts from work, I took on the challenge of constructing the case as a woodwork project.

Additionally, I enlisted the help of the twins to create an aluminium front plate with the required holes and engravings. However, as is often the case, I encountered a problem during this otherwise exciting project, finances were tight, and some parts were quite expensive. The costliest component was the 3-inch cathode ray tube needed for the instrument's display. I had managed to order it from work at an estimated cost of £8, but I needed to find a way to fund this expense.

Coincidentally, one of my parents' friends from church had recently purchased a new television. Their old set had been deemed irreparable by the engineer, and they kindly offered it to me for spare parts. We wasted no time in collecting it. Upon opening the set, I discovered that it had six pre-sets for the tuner. Keep in mind, at that time, there were only three channels: BBC1, BBC2, and ITV.

© Author

Six channel push button tuning capacitor from a vintage TV

Pressing one of the buttons caused an aluminium horizontal plate to rotate the fins in the tuning capacitor to a predetermined position. Turning the button allowed for fine-tuning. Once adjusted, each press of the button would move the capacitor to the same position, making channel selection a breeze. Previous sets had required a rotary knob for tuning, which was mechanically simpler but demanded more effort from the user.

Immediately, I noticed that the aluminium bar controlling the capacitor was detached from its seat at one end. This misalignment caused the set to be out of tune across all the buttons. I repositioned the bar and resoldered it into the correct location, effectively fixing the set. I then sold it for £20.

© Author

However, to my disappointment, I was instructed to give half of the money to the original owners, who were dismayed that the set could be repaired by a 15-year-old in his bedroom, when their engineer had failed, and now considered they had been conned, this left me feeling somewhat deflated.

To gather more funds, I made the decision to sell my old German rifle at an antiques shop. As I made my way up the road with the rifle in hand, a police car passed by, executed a U-turn, and approached me. T

They inquired about what I was doing and where I was headed. Proudly, I showed them the rifle and explained my intention to sell it. Concerned about the potential risks, they escorted me home, confiscated the firearm, and had a lengthy conversation with my parents. They emphasised that the IRA was employing makeshift firearms consisting of steel tubes and hammers, making a weapon like mine highly sought after.

Ultimately, the oscilloscope project proved to be more expensive than I could afford. Although I managed to assemble the entire unit, except for the cathode ray tube, its price had risen to £18 and, unfortunately, it never became available. Regrettably, the project had to be abandoned, remaining unfinished.

It's only the dirty ones we don't want - Philip Wilkinson

Unexpected noises   © Pixababy

Marsbar had a pair of trainers he wanted to sell, Erotic and I called round to his house to see these, whilst drinking water in the kitchen, he said the shoes were upstairs and he would go and get them when he could, suddenly there was a lot of loud banging and screaming ow! Ow! thinking someone was getting murdered.

Erotic asked innocently, what on earth is that. Marsbar replied, oh it's just mum and dad having sex. Half an hour later, his mum and dad appeared in the kitchen, oh hi, she said, I didn't know we had company, and then said they were just popping out, Marsbar could now go upstairs and collect the shoes.

Starting to lose interest in cycling   © Pixababy

I embarked on another cycle camping trip to How Stean, but by this time, I had managed to build an 18-speed road bicycle using mostly salvaged parts, thanks to the income from my part-time job. However, despite my efforts, I couldn't fully enjoy cycling due to my asthma which left me with limited lung capacity which made it difficult for me to exercise and breathe properly. This made cycling a tedious experience for both me and those accompanying me, as they often had to wait for me to catch up.

Other incidents while cycling proved to be discouraging. On one occasion, a group of around 20 of us embarked on a ride and reached the bottom of Otley Old Road in Otley. We decided to pause and wait for the stragglers to catch up. Unfortunately, this turned out to be a significant mistake. One of the stragglers, Erotic, was, after a cautious start, was now flying down the steep hill with failed brakes. Instead of walking down the hill, he attempted to ride down. However, as he couldn't stop, he chose to crash into the group, causing numerous cuts, bruises, sprains and a plethora of minor injuries and significant damage to our bikes.

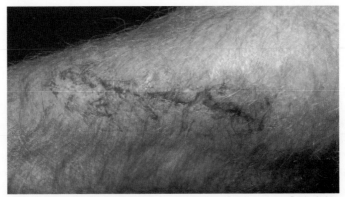

© Pixababy

The aftermath of the incident included scraped elbows, knees, and hands, sprained ankles, and one person suffering a head injury that bled profusely. Additionally, many of our bikes sustained bent or broken wheels, as well as damaged forks and frames. It was a rather unfortunate situation, and we were all left to walk home, carrying our bikes, and nursing our wounds. Erotic faced the consequences of his actions and became somewhat of an outcast within the group for several weeks.

Erotic was the type of friend who appeared mild-mannered and amiable in person, but whenever he hopped on any form of transportation, he seemed to grow horns and a tail, he was utterly fearless, never seemed to feel pain, and reckless to boot.

One Thursday, as we were riding through the park on our way to our regular meeting, I had no idea what was about to unfold. Unbeknownst to me, Erotic was speeding towards me from my left side, his sights set directly on my position. In an instant, he collided with me, causing both of us to tumble uncontrollably.

While Erotic found amusement in the situation and rolled on the floor laughing, I was left with cuts and bruises, unable to find any humour in the ordeal and called him several names I will not repeat here. To make matters worse, the impact had bent the frame of my bicycle, rendering it damaged beyond repair, and Erotic's front wheel was completely ruined, with the forks mounting on his bike broken as well. Two bikes written off in an instant, for fun!

It's only the dirty ones we don't want - Philip Wilkinson

Living with a squirrel   © Pixababy

Bilbo and Frodo (the twins), a group of friends and I would often gather at their house on Thursdays. Their mother, Cathy, a caring widow, had a deep love for animals of all kinds.

One day, she discovered a nearly lifeless creature by a stream, nursed it back to health, and hand-fed it for weeks. Curious about its identity, she took it to a veterinarian, who was startled when the box was opened, it turned out to be an escaped fur farm mink.

Known for their vicious and untameable nature, the mink, surprisingly, showed affection and gentleness in Cathy's hands.

The family had acquired a section of the old railway line in their backyard but struggled to tame the land. To address the issue, Cathy borrowed a goat, which successfully resolved the problem. However, when the goat escaped and caused havoc in the neighbouring gardens, it had to be rehomed.

On another occasion, Cathy hand-reared an orphaned grey squirrel. As it grew older, they encouraged it to venture outside, but the squirrel refused to leave. Recognizing the squirrel was a female capable of reproduction, and after consultation with a vet on sterilization which could not be done, they decided to keep it indoors as a pet.

The squirrel lived in the house for several years, providing both entertainment and moments of fright. It would perform acrobatics from the curtain poles, leap onto the ceiling lamp, and mysteriously appear on someone's shoulder only to vanish when they turned their head. Christmas was particularly eventful, as the squirrel would collect nuts and hide them in unexpected places. One might find their jacket pockets filled with nuts.

In addition, the squirrel would dig in plant pots and cause general mischief. Given an apple, it would nibble a coin-sized hole in the skin, remove the flesh, and consume only the pips. When presented with a tube of Smarties, it would open the bottom of the tube, discard the candies, and fling the tube across the room in disdain. The only nut it never cracked was a coconut won from a fair, which became a source of much frustration until Cathy finally removed it

It's only the dirty ones we don't want - Philip Wilkinson

© Pixababy   © Pixababy

The basement of their house served as a treasure trove, housing old World War II radios, dismantled motorcycles, a bicycle repair shop, and an assortment of tools. It was a true Aladdin's cave where items accumulated but seldom left. One notable addition was a wooden go-kart that I had built and taken for repairs. It ended up being fitted with a lawnmower petrol engine, providing us with immense fun in the park until the police confiscated it.

Another interest we had was air rifles, with most being break-action models where the barrel itself was in two parts, then bent to load a pellet, this style of rifles did not lend themselves to modification, although attempts were made to increase their power, they were largely unsuccessful due to their design. However, I owned an underlever rifle with a solid barrel, offering greater strength and efficiency. Pellets were loaded using a turn buckle that rotated 90 degrees to expose a recess for insertion. By cocking the spring with the lever, the weapon was armed. This rifle lent itself to modifications, and I was able to dismantle and install a more powerful spring. With this upgrade, the lead pellets could penetrate half-inch plywood.

© Pixababy

Owning such a modified gun required a license, but we managed to use it on the old railway line and farmland without detection, until one day when my brother took it for a spin in the park, he never got away with anything, so it was not a surprise when he got arrested. The weapon was subsequently destroyed.

99

It's only the dirty ones we don't want - Philip Wilkinson

Photo of an original advent from the era   © Author

The Sinclair Scientific

Sir Clive Sinclair had unveiled an upgraded version of his pocket calculator, this time in a sleek white plastic design. It retained the same size and number of keys as the previous Cambridge model but introduced triple functions for each key. A select key allowed users to choose specific functions for the calculator to perform. Among our group, Bilbo, who had not yet purchased the Cambridge, decided to acquire this new scientific calculator.

The scientific calculator, in essence, was like the Cambridge model. It could perform scientific calculations by utilizing algorithms based on the basic operations of addition, subtraction, multiplication, and division. Whilst the Cambridge could perform the same calculations by manually entering the algorithms, this was tedious and time consuming, requiring hundreds of calculations to be performed for even a simple output. The Scientific however could automate these algorithms, the display featured rotating lines to indicate that the calculator was in the process of calculating the answer.

However, despite its advancements, the calculator had its limitations. When asked to calculate the tangent of an angle greater than about 87 degrees, it would consume a fresh set of batteries, compute for days, and eventually display an incorrect answer of "EEEEEEEE." It seemed that our expectations may have been too high for the device's capabilities.

100

It's only the dirty ones we don't want - Philip Wilkinson

Sinking of the HMS Ark Royal © Shutterstock

In the chaotic classroom of Mr Sherwood's Maths class, disorder and mischief seemed to be the norm. Students were unruly, and the teacher, seeking refuge behind his desk, tried to shield himself from the commotion by hiding behind a large book. This only fuelled the chaos further, as one of the troublemakers who wasn't even part of our top set seized an opportunity for mischief.

His eyes landed on the impressive plastic model of the HMS Ark Royal that Mr Sherwood had proudly displayed on top of the blackboard. A mischievous plan formed in his mind, and he reached for his catapult and a marble. Pulling the catapult to its maximum tension, he took aim at the ship and released the marble, which hit its target with precision, causing the model to crumble and crash to the floor in pieces.

The room fell silent as everyone witnessed the destruction of Mr Sherwood's prized possession. Realizing the magnitude of what had just happened, the teacher sank to the floor, overcome with sadness as he tried to collect the shattered fragments of his beloved model. The empathy of some students welled up, recognising the devastation that Mr Sherwood must be feeling in that moment.

While many of us felt sympathy for our distraught teacher, it was evident that his emotional response to the incident didn't magically transform him into a better educator. The chaos and lack of discipline persisted in the classroom, and Mr

Sherwood's teaching methods remained ineffective. The broken model served as a poignant reminder of the need for a conducive learning environment and a teacher who could effectively engage and inspire his students.

It's only the dirty ones we don't want - Philip Wilkinson

Copyright unsure, please advise and I will add on next revision
Model of the HMS Ark Royal

Mr Sherwood had the model in its prominent location since HMS Ark Royal, once a symbol of the Royal Navy's power, held a special place in the hearts of the people of Leeds. When the ship was torpedoed in World War II, the city raised £9 million to rebuild it. In 1973, the Queen Mother awarded the ship Freedom of the City, resulting in a grand celebration with thousands of people cheering and waving flags.

Now, ten years after its decommissioning, former crew members remember their time on the "Mighty Ark" and its enduring legacy. Leeds's connection with the ship dates to the war when the city adopted it as part of a fundraising campaign. The ship sank shortly after but was replaced by Ark Royal IV, which served for 25 years and received the Freedom of the City. The crew members marched through Leeds during ceremonial occasions, creating lasting memories for both the sailors and the city's residents. The ship's decommissioning in 2011 was a cost-saving measure by the Ministry of Defence. The Ark Royal holds a significant place in Leeds's history, and many hope that another ship bearing the name will emerge in the future.

Chapter 7 – 1975

Leaving school

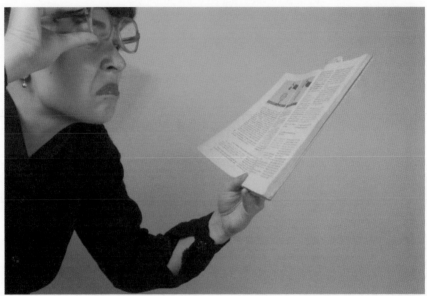

An unusual request from our RE teacher   © Pixababy

Sex education in the 1970s was a period of significant change and evolving attitudes towards sexuality and reproductive health. While discussions about sex were often seen as taboo, there was a growing recognition of the importance of providing young people with accurate information. In schools, sex education was gradually introduced, although it varied greatly depending on the region and school. The content typically focused on basic biological aspects, such as puberty and reproductive systems and emphasized the importance of abstinence and traditional gender roles.

Discussions about contraception and sexually transmitted infections were often limited or omitted altogether. Controversies and debates surrounding sex education reflected societal norms and cultural values of the time, highlighting the ongoing struggle to strike a balance between providing comprehensive information and addressing moral concerns.

It's only the dirty ones we don't want - Philip Wilkinson

© Author

Overall, sex education in the 1970s marked a crucial step towards acknowledging the importance of educating young people about sexuality, even though the approach and depth of instruction varied significantly.

A few days before summer recess, Miss Brent, the 40+ year old RE and French teacher mentioned previously showed her true colours, advising us that the next lesson would be an open and frank discussion on sex.

She asked all five classes in my year to bring in pornographic literature for the next class, there was no time to organise anything other than a few lads' mags such as Mayfair and Fiesta. Sure enough in her next class, the magazines were handed around for open discussion, the girls were embarrassed, the boys loved it and at the end of the class, Miss Brent took the magazines home with her.

Miss brent, during the lesson, had asked everyone to provide a rude word, as the class called these out, getting braver as the list grew, Miss Brent wrote each word on the blackboard to remind us of them for part of the open discussion, as we left, she was distracted with some of the girls wanting to ask personal questions, and of course rounding up the lads mags, so I rolled the blackboard over to it's clean side, leaving the list of words not erased and ready for the next classroom teacher to discover, hopefully in the middle of a maths class, or similar.

A former female student commented on the Abbey Grange Facebook page that Miss Brent was in her opinion a lesbian, she based this upon the fact she insisted on showering with the students and would insist that the girls all cleaned carefully between their legs whilst she watched, sometimes insisting they repeat the procedure more than once.

It's only the dirty ones we don't want - Philip Wilkinson

Maths exam tribulations   © Pixababy

The question of whether we could use our Sinclair Cambridge calculators in the maths exam had been a point of contention. To address this, five of us who had built these calculators decided to display them on our desks in full view of the exam adjudicator before the papers were handed out. Surprisingly, no one raised any objections, and upon checking the exam paper, it once again stated that log tables and calculating machines could be used if sufficient accuracy could be achieved, the exact same wording as on the mock exam paper.

As the exam began, I took the first 15 minutes to read through all the questions and promptly answered the ones that were simple and straightforward.

I then proceeded to tackle the more challenging questions in order of their value, starting with the highest. However, throughout the entire exam I found that I couldn't use the calculator to answer a single question listed in the paper, every question required much higher maths than could be computed, trig, geometry, algebra, simultaneous equations, identifying geometric shapes, correctly recording logs from the log tables for numbers etc. were the order of the day. Approximately 10 minutes before the end of the exam, another adjudicator entered the room and upon seeing the calculators, considered ending the exam. However, they ultimately decided to collect the calculators and report the incident.

Later that afternoon, we received an unwelcome invitation to the headmaster's office, Mr. Slack. Unfortunately, he was not interested in hearing our explanations regarding the exam paper's guidelines or our consultations with teachers. He resorted to his usual approach, shouting at us, administering canings, and downgrading our exam grades by two levels because of the breach of exam rules we had committed in his opinion.

It's only the dirty ones we don't want - Philip Wilkinson

© Pixababy

It was only to be expected we would receive such unfair treatment from our renowned headmaster. Despite the downgraded grade of 3, I have always maintained my belief in the grade I felt entitled to, which is grade 1, and have declared this result on all job applications, CVs, and resumes ever since.

Abbey Grange c1974 – The hated light grey and pale blue blazers © Pixababy

As the school year ended and the exams were behind us, anticipation for the summer season was palpable. However, tensions were rising as some unruly individuals, the morons, had returned after failing to attend their exams, causing trouble once again.

It's only the dirty ones we don't want - Philip Wilkinson

© Pixababy

One unfortunate incident involved a new student being shot with a bow and arrow in the playground, leading to the involvement of both the hospital and the police.

Suddenly, just two days before the official last day of school, we were informed that today would be our final day. We were instructed to report to our respective form rooms and that we would be called to the hall to queue for our exam grades. While waiting in line for mine,

I overheard the headmaster, Mr. Slack, remarking to several of my friends that he believed they didn't deserve the grades they had received. According to him, they hadn't put in enough effort to earn such high-level grades. When it was my turn, Mr. Slack continued his streak of sour grapes and declared that I, too, didn't deserve the results I had obtained, six grade 1 certificates. He repeated his belief in a previously expressed opinion that I would never amount to anything, how wrong can one be!

I chose to remain silent, aware that my past actions were not in my favour. The pile of documents in my file, including my deliberately provocative punishment essay from about 18 months earlier where I had written "blah blah blah" for four sides to test if anyone read the essays, along with incidents involving fireworks, repairs to the oscilloscope, and laboratory mishaps, seemed to reinforce Mr. Slack's negative perception of me.

© Pixababy

It's only the dirty ones we don't want - Philip Wilkinson

Meanwhile, some of the more unruly students, including a few of my friends, expressed their frustration by hanging their bags and books from the school gate by their ties and setting them on fire. It was an unsettling and chaotic end to an era.

Despite the challenges and unjust judgments, the conclusion of that school year marked the beginning of a new chapter in our lives.

A leather school satchel – similar to the one I left burning on the gates ©
Author

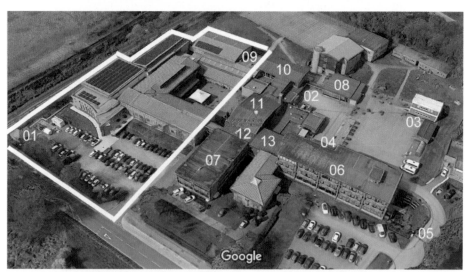

Abbey Grange CofE High School

For reference, the image shows many of the parts of the building I refer to in the book, prominently in the foreground marked No. 6 we see the three-story classroom block, the cause of much confusion due to the way the school numbered the classrooms, also the location for the toilets through the windows incident No. 04 and the firework incident No. 03.

No. 12 is the administration block which was originally designed to link all three sections, until bureaucracy deemed the constant passing of pupils every 40 minutes was unbearable, and pupils were no longer allowed to cross the hallway except for using the bridge (in silence for fear of penalties), effectively cutting the school into three with the hall (the curved roof section) No. 11 changing rooms between No. 10 and No. 11 and gym No. 10, now only accessible by going outside and walking round, there was at least a partial covered way seen in the photograph No. 02 which was the location for the dinner queue mentioned in my book.

The classroom block No. 06 and science block No. 07 were connected by the bridge at first floor level only, the stairwell that produced the stampede at dinner and home time is located at No. 13.

The car park where the teachers cars had their windows broken in year 1, can be seen in the foreground in front of No. 06 the location of the main gates, the place where the school leavers set fire to their bags is No. 05

The incident with the pupil shot using a catapult took place near to the dinner queue covered way, the pupil on the receiving end was on the top right-hand corner of the hard surfaced area in the right of the image No. 03.

The image shows the metalwork/woodwork block, the single storey flat roofed building centre right No. 08, with the sixth form block on the small hill behind. (The new building between the workshops and the sixth form block encircled was not bult in my time.

All the buildings and car park encircled between 01 and 09 were not present in my tenure they have been built on what used to be a playing area behind the gym/changing rooms, these locations are where students were targeted with the sniper rifle from No. 01 location on the railway line footpath, the deputy head witnessed the marbles exiting the changing room windows and the burnt out car ended up against the wall at No. 09

It's only the dirty ones we don't want - Philip Wilkinson

Working at a glassblowers   © Pixababy

When school finally came to an end, like many of my peers, I found myself uncertain about what to do next. It was then that Chinner, a school friend of mine, informed me about a job opportunity for the summer at Hailwood and Ackroyds, a glass blowing factory in Morley. Intrigued, I applied for a position and was fortunate enough to be offered a spot. The factory's plan was to take on several school leavers, providing them with a comprehensive experience of the various tasks involved in glass blowing. The hope was that some of us would decide to pursue an apprenticeship with them.

On the first day of work, Chinner and I found ourselves seated on wooden stools, positioned on the factory floor. In front of us stood an empty glass mould made of wood, hinged at the back and with a latch on the front, while above us loomed a mesh stage where the skilled glassblowing team operated. Adjacent to the stage were five blazing glass furnaces.

The glassblowers would start by dipping a glass blowing tube into the furnace, gathering a blob of molten glass. With skilled precision, they would blow and swing the tube, shaping the glass into a hollow sphere. Once ready, they would hang the tube by the mould, and it was our task to promptly close and lock the mould upon their foot tap. After a few seconds, the foot would tap again, signalling for us to unlock and open the mould, once clear, we would hose the inside down to cool it. It was hot, demanding work for novices like us.

True to their word, the factory exposed us to every aspect of their production process over the course of approximately ten weeks. We experienced tasks ranging from loading the Lear cooling oven to cutting, grinding, and even acid etching the finished glass products. We even had a stint working night shifts. By the end of our time there, a college placement awaited me, and I decided not to pursue the apprenticeship program any further.

During lunch breaks, the glass blowers often used their time to create useful objects they could sell for additional income, yards of ale glasses were popular along with multi coloured paperweights, I manged to persuade one of the teams to make me a paperweight which I still have to this day.

© Author

© Author

Although I never mentioned it to my father, during those few weeks, I was earning double his income as a decorator and signwriter. This experience provided me with a significant boost, as I entered college where the grant offered was a mere £6 per week. With my newfound earnings, I treated myself to a high-quality audio system, including a Garrard SP25 MKII turntable, Teleton amplifier, and Sony SS70 bookshelf speakers.

© Author

This marked the beginning of a lifelong love affair with hi-fi and music, one that continues to bring me immense joy to this day.

I vividly remember the precise moments when I first listened to numerous seminal LPs from the likes of Supertramp, Genesis, Pink Floyd, and many others that defined the music of that decade. Each album became a gateway to a new sonic experience, transporting me to different realms of creativity and emotion. The melodies, the lyrics, and the intricate production captivated my senses and left an indelible impression on my musical journey.

Chapter 8

Discovering motorcycles

One morning, Erotic awoke to find his father sitting at the kitchen table, wearing only his vest. It was a peculiar sight because his father had never skipped work before. As Erotic joined him at the table, his father casually tossed a set of keys in his direction. "I've retired, lad," his father announced, "and I don't need the motorbike anymore. It's yours now."

© Author & Pixababy

In an instant, Erotic found himself transformed into a motorcyclist, albeit on a Honda 50 cub. This model was legal to ride at the age of 16, and it was a thrilling prospect for Erotic.

He could hardly contain his excitement as he imagined the adventures and freedom that awaited him on the open road. With a sense of gratitude and anticipation, Erotic accepted the keys, ready to embark on his new journey as a motorbike owner.

© Author & Pixababy

At the Thursday club, Richie from Woodhouse collected Marsbar from Meanwood on his Yamaha FS1E moped swelling the numbers at the meeting, also adding to the interest growing swiftly in motorcycles in our group.

Soon after, Bilbo and Frodo (the twins) bought motorcycles meaning that most of us now had moved on from cycling.

During my time at Kitson College of Technology, I had the pleasure of befriending a fellow student who owned a sleek and impressive moped, a new Honda SS50. We would often hang out at his parents' house, which happened to be located close to

wasteland frequently used by trial bikes. He also possessed an old 50cc Yamaha, which, although not road legal, served us well for riding around the area and exploring the trails. It didn't take long for me to realise that owning a motorbike was the perfect solution to my commuting needs, replacing the laborious task of cycling.

I wasted no time and made my first motorbike purchase, acquiring a Honda CD50 50cc bike for a mere £25. Its chrome tank sides, sporty appearance, and handy indicators made it an ideal choice. Suddenly, my daily college commutes became significantly easier and faster, transforming my experience entirely.

My first bike, a Honda CD50   Author & Pixababy

Unfortunately, the joyous occasion of purchasing my Honda was marred by an unfortunate incident. On that very same day, my friend decided to follow me home to ensure my safe arrival. Tragically, as he set off back home, he was involved in a collision with a car just a few hundred yards from my house.

The impact sent him flying over a nearby wall and into a church graveyard, resulting in a severe leg fracture that required months of traction and hospitalisation. I made sure to visit him regularly in the ward designated for such injuries at St. James's Hospital, often stopping by the Florence Nightingale pub to pick up a few pints along the way.

Chapter 9

Discovering alcohol

© Pixababy

During this time, our youthful curiosity led us to experiment with alcohol. We discovered that with just a pound in our pockets, we could catch a bus into Leeds, enjoy four pints, and still have some change left. Walking home afterwards became our strategy to sober up and avoid parental scrutiny.

However, one eventful evening, our usual route was obstructed by the newly constructed M621 motorway. In our tipsy and confused state, we unwittingly ended up walking up the slip road and onto the motorway's hard shoulder. It didn't take long for a police car to spot us and offer us a ride off the motorway, along with a £15 fine each. Teddy, who was seriously underage, had given his older brother's name, Bilbo, which didn't sit well with him when the summons and fine arrived.

On another occasion, during a Thursday gathering at the twins' house, our beer and cider-fuelled hunger prompted us to send Erotic and Teddy on a mission to the local Chinese takeaway. Equipped with Erotic's Honda 50 Cub, complete with a large white fiberglass top box, we believed it would be perfect for carrying our order.

What we expected, a delicious Chinese takeaway © iStock

However, their return took an unexpectedly long time. When they finally arrived, the food was ice-cold, and the aluminium takeout boxes had disintegrated, leaving a congealed mess about two inches thick at the bottom of the box. The food had melded with the oil and dirt in the box, rendering it unappetizing. Despite our hunger, we had no choice but to go without as the takeaway had closed for the night.

When questioned about the delay, Erotic confessed that after collecting the order, he and Teddy had ventured to Hugh Gaitskell school. The school had two grass playing fields with a public footpath running through the middle, and grass ramps on either side to protect pedestrians during games. Their misguided attempt was to ride across the field, up the ramp, and attempt a jump over the gap, repeatedly and unsuccessfully. Erotic, oblivious to our annoyance, genuinely failed to understand what he had done wrong. To this day, he remains steadfast in his perspective.

During lunch breaks at Kitson College, a now-demolished 12-story concrete and glass building that Pink Floyd famously used to record their single "See Emily Play," my classmates and I had a peculiar routine.

German barmaid with stein and pretzel © Pixababy

116

We would drop our bags off in the top-floor classroom and then make our way to the Hofbrau house. This establishment aimed to recreate a German-style experience akin to the Oktoberfest in Munich, complete with steins of lager, bratwurst, pretzels lederhosen and live strippers on stage. Despite most of us being underage, it was an adventure not to be missed. The atmosphere could be quite seedy, attracting its fair share of unsavoury characters.

A pint between funerals　　　　　　　　　　　　　© Pixababy

The twins, Bilbo and Frodo, their brother Teddy, and several of my friends had been part of the choir at St. Mary's Parish Church on Town Street in Beeston for many years. One day, during our lunch break, we decided to enjoy a pint at the Old White Heart pub.

It was Colin's turn to buy the round, so he walked up to the bar. However, as he made his way, he bumped into Mr. Smithies, the vicar of the church, who was dressed in his full cassock and robes, also enjoying a pint.

Teddy, noticing the vicar, couldn't help but be intrigued and asked him what he was doing there. The vicar's response was unexpected and caused half of the people at the bar to spit out their beer in surprise. He simply said, "Just popped in for a quick pint between funerals." It was a humorous and memorable moment, showcasing .he vicar's down-to-earth nature and providing a light-hearted anecdote for our group to share.

117

© https://www.leeds-live.co.uk/news/leeds-news/leeds-college-technology-could-demolished-15847089

Hung out to dry on the eleventh floor

On one occasion, as we returned to the top floor classroom at Kitson after alcohol for lunch, we noticed that one of our classmates was running late. This individual had been particularly annoying in recent weeks, so a lesson was in order. The previous day, he had taken several of our bags and playfully hung them out of the windows by their straps. We managed to retrieve them by holding onto the visible part of the straps and opening the windows. As a form of retaliation, we decided to teach him a similar lesson.

Taking his bag, we opened the pivoting window and trapped the strap in the frame by closing the window, then severing the portion of the strap remaining indoors.

When he finally arrived, he could see that opening the window would cause his bag to plummet 11 stories onto the roof below. With not many options, in a panic, he searched for a solution. His only option, opening another window, climbing out onto the ledge, shuffling along to reach his bag, and attempting to free it. Sensing his desperation, we decided to intervene. We slightly opened the window to release the trapped strap, and at the same time, closed the other window he had climbed out of. This left him with no choice but to shuffle along to the adjacent classroom's windows and draw the attention of the lecturer inside.

Thankfully, the lecturer let him back in, and after his high-rise escapade, he became significantly less annoying. It was a memorable lesson for everyone involved.

118

It's only the dirty ones we don't want - Philip Wilkinson

Alcohol, Motorcycles and Malham Image capture: Apr 2022 © 2023 Google

During another memorable escapade, Frodo, Erotic, and I embarked on an exhilarating motorcycle journey to the Buck Inn in Malham. Our primary mission was to relish the renowned Theakston's Old Peculiar, a beer celebrated for its potent alcoholic content. While it currently stands at 5.6%, back in the late 1970s, it packed an even mightier punch at 6.4%. Just a few pints of this brew had the potential to
unleash chaos. After bidding farewell to the pub, we impulsively decided to push our motorcycles to their limits as we headed towards Malham Tarn.

© Pixababy

Fuelled by excitement, our high-speed adventure came to an abrupt halt when we encountered a road closure. A telegraph pole, mounted on sturdy posts, served as a barrier to restrict motor vehicle access. Thankfully, Frodo was the first to spot this obstruction and urgently tried to grab Erotic's attention through a series of kicks and hits. Eventually, Erotic's gaze fell upon the pole, and in a spontaneous act, he threw his bike to the ground. Sliding along the road, they skilfully maneuverer beneath the pole and landed in an adjacent ditch.

Although slightly battered and scraped, they regrouped and hoisted the bike back onto the road. The only significant casualty was a broken clutch lever, presenting a formidable challenge for the journey home with minimal stops. Naturally, faced with such a predicament, our immediate response was to return to the pub for another pint.

Sometime later, as we reached City Square in Leeds, Erotic found himself compelled to halt at a red traffic light. While stopping and shifting gears while riding posed no significant issues, commencing the ride required a forceful kick and full throttle to engage the gears. This often resulted in either a wheelie, a stall, or an unsteady start. On this occasion, our less-than-graceful departure caught the attention of two passing WPCs. Their intervention caused the bike to topple over onto its side, effectively blocking the road. Both Erotic and Frodo found themselves lying on their backs, gazing up at the police officers. Reacting swiftly, Erotic jumped to his feet and promptly righted the fallen motorcycle, attempting to lighten the situation in the hopes of evading a Breathalyser test, arrest, or any charges.

Meanwhile, Frodo, still lying on his back in the middle of the road, clutching half a bottle of beer, cheekily remarked to the WPC leaning over him, "Eyup love, you're f****ng gorgeous. Fancy a cheeky kiss?", and the WPC helped him back onto Erotic's bike, then gave him his requested kiss.

Erotic the brave   © Pixababy

On a different occasion, Teddy joined Erotic as a passenger on the CB125 motorcycle. They embarked on a journey down a narrow road with only one lane. As they approached an articulated flatbed truck, they decided to overtake it. However, a van approached from the opposite direction and began flashing its lights frantically, signalling that it wouldn't clear the truck in time.

It's only the dirty ones we don't want - Philip Wilkinson

The Honda motorcycle was already traveling at its maximum speed of 60 miles per hour, leaving no room for acceleration. Thinking quickly, Erotic swiftly manoeuvred the bike by ducking underneath the flatbed, skilfully navigating the tight space between the truck's cabin and rear wheels. The van, blaring its horn in urgency, passed by just as Erotic completed the manoeuvre, allowing them to continue their overtaking safely.

© https://compassliveart.org.uk/lost-pub-competition/
The Market Tavern – a rough pub in 1975

On January 16, 1995, when The Market Tavern, served its last pint there was a mixture of relief and sadness. The pub had long been known as the "Mad House" and according to some, the "Bucket of Blood" such was the kind of evening, or afternoon, you could expect in there. The Market Tavern stood on the corner of George Street and Harewood Street.

Across the road from Kirkgate Market, it was popular with market traders, but it was also a haunt of less savoury characters and misfits. David Oluwale, a Nigerian immigrant "hounded to his death" by racist Leeds police, drank at the Market Tavern although according to regulars, he did it alone. Read more: The lovely Leeds pub once home to Yorkshire's only female serial killer

The Market Tavern was originally a dwelling but was converted into a pub in 1850. By 1914, when four of five of the photos below were taken, the pub, then run by landlord Job Dixon, was looking worse for wear.

When plans were unveiled to demolish the pub, Leeds Civic Trust led a campaign to save it. The plan went ahead, and the Tavern was pulled down to make way for an open car park. On its last night, landlords John and Margaret Jackson sold the pub's remaining drinks at cost price. It is now the site of the upmarket Victoria Gate shopping centre. The irony probably isn't lost on some of the Mad House's old customers. Text reproduced from

It's only the dirty ones we don't want - Philip Wilkinson

During one of our outings in Leeds, we found ourselves at the Market Tavern. Excitedly, we entered the tap room and ordered a round of a dozen pints. As we collected our drinks and made our way towards the games room, the landlord called out, "Oy! You can't take those beers in there!" We exchanged puzzled glances, unsure of what he meant. "The price is for the tap room only, not the games room," he clarified. Reluctantly, we paid an extra penny per pint and proceeded to the games room.

However, our anticipation quickly turned to disappointment when we discovered a revolting scene. Someone had regrettably vomited all over the pool table we had hoped to use. The mess was substantial, with large piles of vomit in three different spots on the table. To make matters worse, it had even made its way into the corner pocket, dripping onto the floor and ball storage area. Disheartened, we abandoned our plans and moved to the "lounge" area.

© Author

The lounge had windows that overlooked the pub's back yard. The yard was covered in worn-out corrugated plastic sheeting, which had taken on a yellow hue and was covered in moss. Peering through the windows, we could see the far wall of the yard, which had been whitewashed years ago but was now mostly just exposed red brick. It came to our attention that the yard served as the toilets—a rather unusual setup.

These unisex facilities lacked any handwashing amenities and were simply rinsed down periodically with a hosepipe. It was disconcerting to think that this pub, which held a special license allowing alcohol sales from 5am for market stall holders, likely had patrons who had used these makeshift toilets earlier in the day.

It dampened our enthusiasm for purchasing fruits and vegetables from Leeds Market, knowing that they might have been associated with these less-than-sanitary facilities.

Many years later, a close friend, who used to run a major branch of a pensions administrator here in Leeds, recalled that he had organised a pub adventure for a number of his staff, they would visit a nice pub, followed by one not so nice, when it came to the Market Tavern, one of his staff asked if my friend would accompany him to the toilet, and he replied, it's OK I can watch you from here, pointing to the window overlooking the yard containing the facilities'.

It's only the dirty ones we don't want - Philip Wilkinson

Incidents in the workshop   © iStock

During our college days, we had a memorable study session held in a dedicated workshop for electrical equipment assembly. The lecturer in charge possessed an astonishingly high body resistance, allowing him to grasp 415VAC bus bars with his bare hands and boldly declare, "Yes, they are live." It was truly an impressive feat.

On a particular day, while experimenting with an oscilloscope to create Lissajous loops, I faced a component shortage. The only power supply I could find was rated at 600V, and the large paper electrolytic capacitor I had was designed for 3KV. The oscilloscope didn't mind the high voltages; it solely focused on the frequency of the wave generated on the x and y axes. However, we soon discovered that the capacitor was polarity sensitive.

Despite the limitations, I managed to achieve a visually pleasing triple loop display on the scope and called the lecturer over to witness my success. He leaned over the workbench to get a closer look just as the capacitor, improperly connected, exploded with a deafening bang. Smoke, bits of paper, and tar were scattered all around. The lecturer turned back to face the class, resembling a toffee apple wrapped in silver paper and covered in sticky brown tar. Smoke even rose from his hair. It was a comical sight. From then on, whenever I claimed to have a working experiment, the lecturer would quip, "I'll just give it a few minutes first."

In another incident involving the same lecturer, we were in the process of removing the armature, the heavy metal core with copper wire wound around it, from a motor. It was a sizable and weighty object, and there were three of us, including a West African student, struggling to slide it out of its casing. Suddenly, the lecturer made an inappropriate remark, saying, "Come on lads, imagine you're pulling a n****r off your granny."

123

It's only the dirty ones we don't want - Philip Wilkinson

We all stared at him in disbelief, then turned to the West Indian student in the class. The lecturer quickly became aware of what he had said and deeply apologized. Unfortunately, such language had been common for the lecturer in his youth, and it had unintentionally slipped out without him being fully conscious of it. Even then, it was not politically correct, and today such remarks would not be tolerated.

The college course in electrical and electronic engineering was demanding. Originally designed to be completed over four years on a part-time basis, we chose to undertake it as full-time students, completing it within one year.

The course encompassed three A-level equivalent subjects: Mathematics, Engineering Drawing, and Electronics, with a specific focus on electrical engineering and distribution. Some days, we wrote so much that our hands felt as though they might fall off, but at least the college allowed us to use ballpoint pens instead of the old-fashioned and despised fountain pens from my school days.

©iStock

One day, our late class was scheduled to take place in a portacabin on the college site. We arrived to find the door unlocked and entered to escape the cold. Just as the lecturer walked in, one of the guys let out an incredibly loud and unmistakable fart.

The stench that followed was indescribable, we as one evacuated the classroom back into the cold. Amidst the embarrassment, the guy quickly apologised, attributing his dinner of Greek food as the cause.

In response, the lecturer casually remarked, "Of course, you do know why they smell, don't you?" Our minds immediately started to contemplate the chemical composition of the gas, thinking about methane and such. However, before we could respond, the lecturer added with a mischievous smile, "It's for the benefit of the deaf!".

After completing the course at Kitson College, I was lucky enough to receive an offer as an apprentice intruder alarm engineer with Chubb Alarms, a prestigious security company, I also continued to attend Kitson College for the duration of the training, the story of this era is told in my book, Alarming Stories, tales of an apprentice intruder alarm engineer.

It's only the dirty ones we don't want - Philip Wilkinson

Another unusual request in RE © Pixababy

Meanwhile, back at Abbey Grange school, Miss Brent did once again request the boys bring pornographic material into her class for open discussion, as we had predicted she might. This must have been an annual event going on for years.

This time however we had been gifted a year's notice to find the most disgusting material we could get our hands on, Teddy, the twin's younger brother had asked a long-distance lorry driver neighbour to obtain some whilst travelling in Europe, and boy had he had come up with the goods. These two magazines included sex with animals and highly successful experiments with enemas and were very explicit.

On the day, the elderly gentlemen employed by the school to watch over us during dinner, (the diner gimmers), frisked Teddy and took the magazines from him, however, an hour later they gave them back as the content was beyond what most could cope with and way beyond their comfort zone.

So, the class went ahead, Miss Brent, eagerly awaiting the arrival of Teddy's class with the literature was I for a shock, the magazines were opened for all to view and discuss in her RE class, all the girls and half the boys, expecting a titillating light adventure into soft porn and sex education, were in floods of tears.

The headmaster now got involved and serious questions were asked of Miss Brent. It was not known if Miss Brent took these magazines home with her, but I suspect this was the last time she ever requested any such material be brought in for open class discussion Unless you know different!

History does not record if Miss Brent took these books home.

125

It's only the dirty ones we don't want - Philip Wilkinson

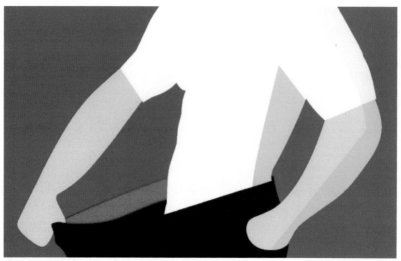

A change of trousers   © Pixababy

A week later, as the school year ended, Teddy encountered an unfortunate incident. He realized that he had unintentionally sat on a piece of chewing gum with his only remaining pair of school trousers the day before, rendering them unwearable. Left with no other option, Teddy decided to wear his vibrant blue Oxford bags instead.

However, it didn't take long for a teacher to notice that his trousers did not adhere to the school's uniform code. In response, the teacher sternly instructed Teddy, "Go home immediately, change your trousers, and report back to me." Curiously, the teacher didn't inquire about Teddy's address.

Following the teacher's directive, Teddy left the school premises, walked to the nearest bus stop, and boarded a bus headed for the city centre. After transferring to another bus, he embarked on a journey that lasted around 90 minutes, considering the less frequent midday bus schedule.

Upon reaching home, Teddy spent an hour having lunch and then proceeded to change his trousers. He then embarked on a return journey, taking two buses to reach the opposite side of the city.

Approximately four and a half hours had passed since the teacher had dispatched him.
Teddy dutifully sought out the teacher, who was now sporting bright green Oxford bags. With a hint of amusement in his voice, Teddy recounted the entire tale, remarking, "Well, he didn't specify the colour of trousers I should change into."

Chapter 10 – 1977

Work and play

Another family holiday in Staithes   © Pixababy

During that summer, my family embarked on another delightful two-week retreat in the cozy cottage nestled in Staithes. This time around, I made the decision to ride my motorcycle to the coastal village, while the rest of my family opted to travel in my parents' Mini Clubman car. Staithes, being an ancient fishing village, wasn't designed to accommodate cars, so all vehicles were expected to park at a designated car park situated at the cliff's top. From there, the occupants had to make their way down to the town on foot. However, due to the compact size of my motorcycle, I found a clever solution. I managed to discreetly conceal it within the narrow passageway flanked by our cottage and Captain Cook's cottage. This afforded me the luxury of riding down to the town and effortlessly returning up to the cottage, while the rest of the family had to make the journey on foot.

On a specific day, our collective decision led us to Saltburn, a town that had initially been developed as a seaside destination for affluent individuals seeking rejuvenating sea bathing experiences. However, due to the resort's incomplete construction, there were very few visitors and limited entertainment options available. The beach, extending across a vast expanse, appeared extensive, level, and devoid of tide boards. The scarcity of people presented an ideal opportunity for me to indulge in some exhilarating motorcycle riding. To my delight, several members of my family also had the chance to partake in the excitement of riding along the beach.

© Pixababy

The cliffs encircling the town of Staithes boast the distinction of being the highest in England. Among these majestic cliffs, one prominent feature that looms over the town is Cowbar. Over time, the relentless forces of erosion have gradually reshaped it, and will eventually transform it into a stack. In the spirit of the adventurous nature that was common among children back then, a group of three of us decided to embark on an exploration of the cliff top. To gain access, we scaled a gate, only to find that the scrubby land at the top served as nesting grounds for gulls.

As we made our way through the nests, the gulls became increasingly agitated, squawking loudly and swooping around us to impede our progress. Undeterred, we pressed on, eventually reaching the cliff top to take in the breath-taking view. In a regrettable turn of events, we unwittingly collected around a dozen gull eggs and brought them back to the cottage as mementos of our adventure.

It was only later that we came to realize the gravity of our actions. Cowbar was designated as a nature reserve, carefully protected to ensure the undisturbed nesting of the gulls. Our unintended disturbance of their nests and removal of their eggs violated the sanctity of the reserve. We learned a valuable lesson about the importance of respecting and preserving wildlife habitats, realizing the need to treat such areas with the utmost care and reverence.

It's only the dirty ones we don't want - Philip Wilkinson

Temping

© Pixababy

During the period when Teddy and I were actively seeking employment following my college recess and his completion of school, we realized that temporary work offered a swift opportunity to earn a decent income. Our routine involved arriving at a modest agency office tucked away in a backyard off Park Square in Leeds promptly at 7 a.m. on Monday mornings, where we would be assigned various jobs for the week.

On our very first day, we parked our motorcycles in the narrow alley adjacent to the entrance of the temp agency. To our dismay, upon returning a few minutes later, we discovered that a builder's van had reversed into the alley, leaving only a slim gap that seemed impossible for us to squeeze our bikes through. Aware that time was ticking, and we risked being late for our initial assignment, we decided to improvise a solution.

Resourcefully, we unloaded some scaffolding planks from the back of the van and cleverly assembled them to create a makeshift ramp. With determination and a touch of ingenuity, we crafted a pathway, first leading up onto the flatbed, then continuing from the flatbed to the cab, and finally descending from the cab to the ground. Through this makeshift ramp system, we successfully rode our motorcycles over the van, ensuring our timely departure to the day's job.

In that moment, we relied on our resourcefulness and teamwork to overcome an unexpected obstacle. Our impromptu ramp not only saved us from potential tardiness but also demonstrated our willingness to find creative solutions in the face of challenges. This experience marked the beginning of our temporary work adventures, where we would encounter a diverse range of tasks and continue to adapt and overcome obstacles along the way.

It's only the dirty ones we don't want - Philip Wilkinson

Throughout our temporary work assignments, we found ourselves in various settings, including bottling plants for companies like Schweppes, Britvic, and Mathers Black Beer. As is often the case, we were typically assigned the less glamorous tasks that others preferred to avoid. For instance, we often found ourselves stationed in the yard, diligently washing crates filled with musty bottles to ensure they were not filled with contaminants, they were then machine washed before the refilling process.

However, amidst the monotonous routines, Teddy's resourcefulness shone through at one bottling factory where sherry production was underway. Recognising an opportunity, he devised a clever plan to take advantage of the situation. During our allotted cigarette breaks, Teddy would discreetly lift the crate counter, allowing one crate to pass through without being counted. Seizing the moment, he swiftly slid the unaccounted crate off the production line and out the back door, carefully concealing it from prying eyes.

On his way home, Teddy would make a detour, guiding the liberated crate down a grassy slope until it came to a gentle rest against the railings. It was during these moments that he discreetly collected the "acquired" crate. Little did we know at the time that this would result in an unexpected outcome. When Christmas arrived, we were pleasantly surprised to find that everyone received a delightful gift of sherry, courtesy of Teddy's ingenuity and the fruits of his covert operation.

The sherry became a memorable part of our Christmas celebrations that year, serving as a testament to Teddy's knack for making the most out of any situation. Although our temporary work assignments often involved less glamorous tasks, we found ways to inject a bit of adventure and create fond memories along the way.

During Teddy's temporary assignment at the newly constructed Lloyd's bank building in Park Row, he found himself tackling a rather unenviable task. Despite the building being brand new, an unforeseen issue had arisen with its drainage system. The main sewage pipe had become clogged, resulting in a rather unpleasant predicament. Whenever a toilet was flushed on the upper floors, an unexpected eruption would occur in the basement toilets, propelling a geyser of sewage into the air, sometimes reaching astonishing heights that even touched the ceiling.

It's only the dirty ones we don't want - Philip Wilkinson

© Pixababy

On that eventful day, Teddy's responsibility was to assist in cleaning up the aftermath caused by these unpredictable eruptions. As you can imagine, the task proved to be quite challenging and far from glamorous. The experience was, without a doubt, unforgettable. Teddy's work attire bore the marks of his valiant efforts, and his distinctive odour served as an unintended deterrent, leading even the most eccentric individuals on the bus ride home to keep a safe distance.

It was a day filled with unexpected surprises and a job that demanded Teddy's resilience and resourcefulness. Although the circumstances were far from ideal, Teddy approached the task with a can-do attitude and did his best to mitigate the unpleasant situation. While the day may have been filled with less-than-desirable encounters, it undoubtedly left Teddy with a unique story to tell and a heightened appreciation for more agreeable working environments.

© Pixababy

One day was sent to help at a wine and spirits distribution warehouse in Garforth for the week, all went well on the Monday, my job entailed taking a shopping style trolley around the facility and picking orders to be dispatched to pubs, clubs etc. Waking the next day, the weather had taken a severe turn, overnight heavy rain had fallen washing all the grit from the roads throughout the whole city, the temperature had then plummeted, and the fallen rain had frozen solid, the whole cist was now an ice skating rink, setting off, after pouring warm water all over the bike to clear the ice, I found progress very slow, sliding around I could not exceed 5mph, even with both feet on the ground, unfortunately, cars, busses etc. were out in force, and had no control.

© Pixababy

I witnessed dozens of collisions, vehicles sideways, or even facing backwards having spun out, busses on their sides, Jac knifed articulated lorries and even a snow plough/gritter on its side. At one point, the traffic had stopped, and I slid to a graceful rest behind the queue, I realised that the next vehicle may not be capable of stopping, so drove onto the pavement to circumvent the queue and avoid being crushed, as I did so, a bus careened into the back of the car I had just been behind. It took hours to get to work, and I was not paid travelling time, however it as an adventure.

A birthday in the bridewell   © Pixababy

On the twins' birthday, we decided to have a night out in town. Around 10pm, we collected a generous amount of money from strangers in the pub, filling two-pint glasses with notes and coins. It was surprising to see how much people contributed to our drinking fund. The landlord poured two pints of mixed shorts from the bar optics, but just as he did, Bilbo disappeared, leaving Frodo to drink both pints himself. Frodo downed the first pint in one go. Later, we noticed that Frodo, having consumed the second pint glass of mixed shorts, had himself gone missing.

During our next Thursday gathering, Frodo recounted what had happened after he finished both pints. He woke up at 6am to the sound of his digital watch alarm, only to find himself in a cell at Leeds Bridewell. Confused, he started banging on the door to get someone's attention. Eventually, a police officer came by and looked through the cell hatch, Frodo, convinced it was all part of a prank (as one of our friends at the event was a police officer), demanded to be let out, claiming he needed to go to work. The officer looked bewildered but denied his request.

© Pixababy

A few days later, Bilbo appeared in front of a magistrate. The arresting officer testified, explaining that while driving along Water Lane in Leeds, he had noticed what appeared to be rubbish or sacks partially blocking the pavement and road. As he approached, he realised it was a person.

When questioned, the person responded with a groan. Believing him to be drunk and causing a disturbance in a public place, the officer arrested him for his own safety and held him overnight in Leeds Bridewell. The magistrate turned to Frodo and asked how much he earned, to which Frodo replied £26 per week. The magistrate quipped, "I presume you see your wages as beer tokens." He then fined Frodo £25 and released him.

The twins' birthday celebration took an unexpected turn, resulting in an eventful night for Frodo and an interesting encounter with the legal system

It's only the dirty ones we don't want - Philip Wilkinson

The continuing story of Marsbar and K   © Pixababy

It appears that Marsbar's relationship with K took a tumultuous turn. Marsbar related to the Thursday club meeting that he had fallen out with K, and she had reconnected with her old friends while she was going through a difficult time. However, despite the rift, K managed to convince Marsbar to have sex with her again, leading to speculation about a possible pregnancy. Initially, K denied the rumours, but when she returned to school after a few months for her final exams, she was heavily pregnant, and it became clear that Marsbar would have to take responsibility.

Marsbar had to leave school and find employment to support his impending marriage with K. He began working at a garage, utilising his skills in car repair, which allowed him to earn a decent income, (some hundreds of pounds a week paid in cash, against our typical apprentice pay iro £25 a week). Marsbar and K were able to buy a terraced house in Meanwood and started a new life together with their baby. However, their neighbourhood in Meanwood was rough, as demonstrated by an incident Marsbar encountered while walking home one day.

A car abruptly stopped, and the driver quickly got out, attacking Marsbar by punching him in the gut. Marsbar was left gasping for breath on the ground, astonished that the driver was demanding money from him. Dressed in his painting
overalls and lacking any money, Marsbar attempted to stand up when the driver threatened him again. In an act of self-defence, Marsbar extended his hand to calm the driver but swiftly retaliated by delivering a forceful kick to the driver's groin using his steel-toed boots. The impact was significant, the driver was subsequently taken to the hospital by ambulance in extreme discomfort, the incident led to the police intervening and arresting the driver. and his car was impounded as it was not taxed, tested, or insured and he had no licence to drive, not what you would describe as a successful mugging.

It's only the dirty ones we don't want - Philip Wilkinson

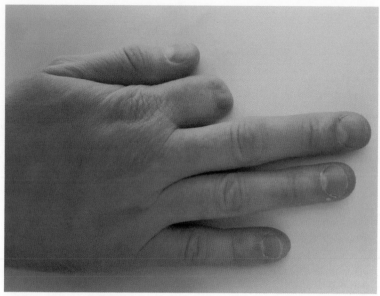

We believe these are your fingers

The situation Marsbar encountered while driving through the estate late at night turned into a dangerous and confrontational encounter. His way was blocked by a large group of men staggering around the road, when he sounded the horn, it angered the group of intoxicated individuals who then surrounded his car banging on the roof and bonnet. Suddenly the car door opened, sensing the imminent threat of being pulled out of the vehicle, Marsbar quickly shut the driver's door and proceeded to drive forward, knocking several of the individuals to the ground in the

process. Amid the chaos of shouting, swearing, and objects being thrown, Marsbar managed to escape from the scene.Feeling shocked and shaken by the incident, Marsbar decided to report it to the nearest police station, as well as the damage to his car. However, when he opened the driver's door at the station, he discovered that two fingers had fallen onto the floor. Realizing their significance, he collected the severed fingers and handed them over to the police. Through fingerprinting, the police were able to identify the owner of the fingers and found a match in their system. The individual who had lost two fingers on his right hand was subsequently arrested and could hardly deny his presence at the scene, you could say he was banged to rights. Can you imagine being arrested, and in the interview the statement of fact, we believe these are your fingers, coming up. As a result of his actions, the individual and his companions faced legal consequences. He received a substantial fine and a six-month prison sentence in addition to the physical injury he sustained, serving as a costly lesson for his behaviour that night.

It's only the dirty ones we don't want - Philip Wilkinson

Aire Valley MCC run to Malham approx. 1979   © AVMCC

The formation of the Aire Valley MCC

Through a chance encounter outside my local shop with a lad called Spawny, who so happened to work with Frodo and Bilbo in engineering, he advised me that he was starting up a motorcycle club in the area and that I should consider going, all motorcyclists would be welcome.

This marked the beginning of a new era of freedom and adventure for me and my friends. With most of us now owning motorcycles, we started planning camping trips once a month, forming the Aire Valley Motorcycle Club. These camping excursions became an extreme form of adventure, especially during the winter trips that tested our survival skills.

As a club, we preferred attending winter rallies to avoid rally spoilers, such as car-driving ex-motorcyclists, scooter drivers looking to recreate the mod and rocker conflicts, and troublemaking Hell's Angels.

In the main, the Aire Valley MCC were a group of hard working, reliable and successful likeminded people with good jobs and careers, I was an apprentice intruder alarm engineer working for Chubb Alarms, Spawny, Bilbo and Frodo were apprenticed to one of the premier engineering companies in Leeds and we had multiple members from the police, telecoms, mining, and North Sea oil organisations. Our mantra was to have fun, drink a lot, ride motorcycles, and try wherever possible to prevent conflicts and to teach the public that not all motorcyclists are hells angels. To that end, we would often stop on the way back from camping for Sunday lunch at a nice pub or restaurant to demonstrate we knew how to behave.

It's only the dirty ones we don't want - Philip Wilkinson

The Spring Close Pub   © Stephen Craven

One of the first meeting venues for the club was the Spring Close Pub in Cross Green, a Tetley's house serving hand draw ale and within the catchment area of the brewery, so drey deliveries were still by cart and horse, a magnificent sight in the city in this era.

An early photo of the Aire Valley MCC location and date not known © Bilbo

It's only the dirty ones we don't want - Philip Wilkinson

The Fishermans Hut pub, Cross Green   © Yorkshire Post Newspapers

Regular pub crawls around the Tetley's houses in Cross Green always resulted in a lot of laughs, some drunkenness, hangovers and occasional fights with some of the less agreeable locals. Two regular haunts were The Fishermans and The Black Dog

The Black Dog pub, Cross Green   © Yorkshire Post Newspapers

Chapter 11

Leaving home

Leaving home for better food

I had reached a point of desperation to leave my family home, where I had endured my mother's cooking for over 17 years. The opportunity finally arose when Richie, who worked for the family business, a vehicle repair shop and MOT station in Woodhouse, mentioned that the living accommodation attached to the garage was available for rent. His parents had recently renovated the top-floor flat, which had its own separate entrance. Without hesitation, we decided to move in together and share the responsibilities of chores, including food shopping and cooking.

This newfound independence brought a sense of liberation. Suddenly, I was free from financial constraints and could indulge myself at the grocery store. I no longer had to scrutinise the prices or hold back; I could simply select the foods I desired and relish in the pleasure of buying them without hesitation. It was a delightful and empowering experience to finally have the freedom to enjoy the food I craved without any reservations.

It's only the dirty ones we don't want - Philip Wilkinson

When Richie and I moved into our new place, we were both equipped with stereo systems and TV sets. We quickly realised that combining our audio equipment would create the ultimate music setup. My turntable seamlessly merged with Richie's excellent amplifier and speakers, providing us with a fantastic audio experience.

However, our TV situation posed a bit of a challenge. My TV had suffered a tube failure, leaving it with sound but no picture. On the other hand, Richie's TV had encountered an audio malfunction, leaving us with a mute screen. Determined to make the most of our resources, we decided to stack the TVs on top of each other, running both simultaneously to achieve both picture and sound. Unfortunately, it was the black and white TV that still displayed a clear picture.

It's only the dirty ones we don't want - Philip Wilkinson

Despite the comical mismatch and the absence of colour, we embraced our unique TV setup. We found ourselves huddling around the stack of TVs, eagerly watching our favourite shows and movies. The monochromatic display added a touch of nostalgia, transporting us back to a simpler time when black and white screens were the norm.

In our living room, music filled the air from our combined stereo system, while the mismatched TVs provided entertainment and served as a testament to our resourcefulness. We laughed at the absurdity of the situation but appreciated the joy it brought us. It became a quirky symbol of our shared journey and the willingness to make the best of any circumstance.

As I settled into my new living arrangement, I began to explore other skills and alternative ways of managing certain chores. One such example was ironing my jeans after washing, which I found tedious and time-consuming. Instead of ironing, Richie showed me a shortcut, by folding them flat and placing them under the mattress of my bed for a few days. Surprisingly, this method worked well enough to keep my jeans relatively wrinkle-free.

© Pixababy

Another newfound hobby that brought me satisfaction was home brewing. After accumulating around 60-pint bottles, Richie and I decided to purchase a plastic brew bin and a brewing kit. We meticulously sterilised the bin and bottles, then began the brewing process.

After several days, when the specific gravity was at the correct level, we transferred the brew into the bottles, added a small amount of sugar to each bottle for carbonation, and sealed them with crown corks. With a few more days of patience, the beer cleared and was ready to be enjoyed. Brewing beer at home cost us only around 4p per pint, compared to the rising price of 38p per pint in pubs at that time. It was a significant cost-saving endeavour.

However, we did encounter a minor issue with our homebrew when we hosted a party. Our friends, unaccustomed to drinking live bottled beer with sediment, struggled to pour it properly into a glass in a single action. As a result, some of them experienced epic headaches the following day, a consequence of consuming the sediment-laden beer.

Austin Gipsy MK4   © Author & Pixababy

Richie's father was a really odd bugger, often when I arrived he would just ignore me, so I got to the point of not conversing with him much, one hobby he enjoyed was pretending to cycle, he had an Austin Gipsy long wheelbase 4X4 (looks a lot like a Land Rover), this was set up to burn pink diesel, he had a tank on site and a tractor with a forklift attachment to legitimise the supply and use on site.

The Gipsy had been modified with a tube into the tank, removing the filler cap exposed regular diesel within the tube, but a secret catch released the tube allowing pink diesel to be pumped to fill.

He would put the bike in the back, set off to say Malham for the day, parking two miles up the road, he would cycle the last bit to the pub, locals would ask where he was from, and he just replied Leeds, they always assumed he had cycled the whole way and he loved it.

It's only the dirty ones we don't want - Philip Wilkinson

The Fenton pub & Chakwal Curry house © Author

By this stage our Thursday meet had moved to the Fenton pub near Leeds Uni, a number of additional friends had joined in and we had started to pick up nicknames, there was now a Mutt, one with short curly hair was renamed Pube, Pat (the postman), Erotic, Julie Belstaff, Boz, The Animal (known for his annoying habit of putting his member into your pint, and it reaching the bottom of the glass), Student Ron (still called this today), Pop Frog, Terrifying, Pansy, Flaps, Spawny and I had become The Prof to name but a few. Despite having very rude nicknames for each other, most had responsible jobs as engineers, coal miners, North Sea oil rig recovery divers, plumbers, mechanics, electronics engineers, telecoms experts, we just shared a love of beer, curry, motorcycles, and camping.

© Pixababy

After a night of imbibing, we would bravely venture across the road to The Chakwal, a curry house not known for its quality but rather for catering to Leeds Uni students. With its

143

bench seating and bowls straight out of a school cafeteria, the food was anything but gourmet. Each dish resembled a bowl of thin brown gravy with meat, often still clinging to the bone, floating within. Served alongside chapatis and tap water, these curries were renowned for their "put the toilet paper in the fridge" level of spiciness.

Despite the inevitable regret that would follow on Friday and the swearing we would never do that again; it was a tradition we couldn't resist repeating when Thursday rolled around again.

Years later, one friend recalled an interesting incident at the Chakwal. His wife's friend had discovered a 12-inch bone in their chicken curry, which led them to question its authenticity. Concerned about what they had been served, they took the bone to the biology department at the university for analysis. After several days, the results came back, confirming that it was indeed chicken. It seems that the Chakwal's culinary surprises extended beyond its spicy curries.

My brother, a dropout   © Pixababy

During this time, my younger brother seemed to have an uncanny knack for finding himself in amusing predicaments involving alcohol, motorcycles, the authorities, and oily clothes. Unfortunately, he was also the one who always got caught red-handed whenever he stepped out of line. At the tender age of thirteen, he and a friend stumbled upon a motorcycle in Middleton woods around 1 AM. Engrossed in their attempt to start it, they unknowingly attracted the attention of the police, who promptly arrested them. My brother, dressed in tattered jeans and a sleeveless denim jacket layered over a leather jacket, refused to cooperate, which led to a case of mistaken age and a few rough encounters with the police.

It's only the dirty ones we don't want - Philip Wilkinson

Suddenly, he found himself facing charges for offenses like TWOCing (taking without owner's consent), riding without a license or insurance, no helmet, lacking L plates, and neglecting road tax, just to name a few. And that was only the beginning of his escapades.

Rountrees chocolates were renowned for placing damaged stock on the windowsills to deter potential burglars. My brother, arriving a tad too late one evening, resorted to using a spade to pry open the fire door, only to activate the silent alarm, and be apprehended by the arriving police officers.

As he repaired a motorcycle he had recently acquired, he decided to take it for a test drive. Careening down the cobblestone street where we lived, he reached the end only to find himself in yet another arrest situation, riding underage without licence, insurance, helmet, tax disk, or L plates.

Our local corner shop had a makeshift repair job on its front window using cardboard and tape. Cunning kids knew that by moving the cardboard aside, they could reach in and grab a bottle or can of pop. On his first attempt, my brother 's hand was caught by the vigilant shopkeeper, resulting in another call to the police.

I vividly recall my mother describing my brother to a neighbour during one of those typical conversations about her children's progress. "How's your son? He must be all grown up by now," our neighbour inquired. With a sly smile, my mother replied, "He thinks he's a dropout, but really he needs dropping out of the bathroom window."

© Pixababy

The list of my brother 's offenses grew longer and longer, but the most absurd incident that I'm aware of involved him stumbling home one night inebriated. Realizing he was a bit lost, he resorted to trying car door handles with the intention of stealing a vehicle as a means of finding his way. To his surprise, he discovered an unlocked car, hopped in, and drove around the estate to navigate his way home. However, his joyride was short-lived as he was pulled over by a police car. The conversation with the officer began with a question we all know too well, "Is this your vehicle?" The observant officer quickly realised that my brother was in no condition to drive and decided to give him a chance. He said, "I'm off duty in an hour, and I really don't want to stay late dealing with all the paperwork your arrest will cause.

Consider yourself lucky. Park the car here, walk home, and never let me catch you driving in this state again."

My brother, grateful for the leniency, complied with the officer's request. However, in his state of disorientation, he soon found himself still lost. In an act of desperation, he resorted to trying car doors once more, this time finding an unlocked van. Determined to find his way home, he took the van and drove out of the estate, only to be stopped by the police yet again. And yes, it was the same officer.

You bend fork © Author & Pixababy

During an evening out in town, my brother, my girlfriend, Erotic, his girlfriend, and I decided to have dinner at a Chinese restaurant. As we sat at the table, waiting to be served, my brother surprisingly ate the daffodils from the vase placed in the centre. Soon after, the waitress approached us to take our orders but spoke with a broken accent. She seemed to say, "you bend fork." Initially, we misheard her and asked her to repeat herself. It was then that my girlfriend noticed her fork was severely bent. She handed it to the waitress, claiming innocence in the matter. The waitress took note and proceeded to take our orders.

Later, when the waitress returned with another fork, she immediately noticed a problem with our table. Pointing out two more damaged items of cutlery, one in front of Erotic and another in front of my embarrassed girlfriend, she exclaimed, "See, I tell you, you bend fork!" Erotic kindly offered to pay for the damaged forks, while my brother pretended that the situation had nothing to do with him. To add to the unusual circumstances, my brother even reached over to the neighbouring table and began eating the daffodils from their vase.

As time went on, and My brother reached the age to apply for a driving license, he needed extra pages to accommodate the long list of offenses he had accumulated. However, things eventually took a turn for the better.

Following his release from Armley Prison, he embarked on a journey to Matlock Bath and stayed with my parents who were training with an Evangelical group in a grand house called Bulstrode for several months. It was there that he met a Brazilian woman who was training for the mission field, asked to listen to her English so she could practice they grew close. Eventually, they got married in Sau Paulo, and my brother became a missionary, dedicating his life to living with a tribe of indigenous people three weeks away by small boat up the Amazon. Funny how life works out in the end.

16 cans of wee on the mantle   © Pixababy

As an interesting side-line to the story, my parents trusted my little brother to stay in the house during their trip, I called several times, just to check the house was OK and everything was fine, no issues and the house was clean enough, that was until the Thursday before my parents were due to return Saturday, his mates persuaded him that a party was now or never, they promised they would help to clean up before the imminent return of authority, and he agreed to go ahead. Far more people arrived than had been invited, some were strangers who must have noticed the lights and music, and simply invited themselves, beer, spirits and other substances flowed freely most of the evening and until the early hours.

The party wound down when the neighbours called the police to stop the noise about 4AM on Friday. Around 10AM however, my parent arrived home, a full day early, they walked into a scene of utter devastation, there was a layer of crisps, biscuits, sandwiches, cigarette ends and bottle tops about an inch thick throughout the whole ground floor, (ironically the most food ever in the house at one time), they found sixteen cans of pee on the mantlepiece in the lounge, cigarette burns on the table in the dining room and next doors teenage son in their bed with three girls.

The notorious student house © Author

Five of us from the group happened to be students at Leeds Uni, and we shared a delightful abode on Marlborough Grove in Blenheim, Leeds. Now, this house was something straight out of "The Young Ones" TV series, with comings and goings that rivalled their chaotic adventures. Its reputation was legendary, and we shamelessly used it as a bargaining chip with our parents. All it took was the threat of moving into the student house for them to surrender in defeat.

Let me paint a vivid picture of this remarkable establishment. The front door had gracefully collapsed into the hallway, becoming an impromptu obstacle course for everyone walking or riding motorcycles over it. Speaking of motorcycles, we had not one, not two, but three of them parked right in the hallway. The lounge, decorated with an assortment of beer towels pilfered from pubs, presented a unique sight. Alas, these towels were not washed, and over time, they had developed a charming layer of mould.

© Pixababy

But wait, there's more! We had our very own resident band, complete with a drummer who seemed to practice nonstop in the cellar. The rhythmic cacophony was the soundtrack to our daily lives. In the kitchen, you'd find not one, not two, but three refrigerators. However, none of them worked, so they had cleverly repurposed them as smelly, mouldy cupboards.

© iStock

One of the lads, whilst I was round at the house asked, do you want to see my pet mould, intrigued I said I would like to, at this moment, he went to the kitchen, lifted down a large clear glass bottle with a metal screw down lid, the bottle was full of a clear liquid, and a large white free floating blob the size of a tennis ball, here you go, he said, my pet mould.

The surrounding landscape was a sight to behold. Thistles and nettles grew in abundance, and they put them to good use by incorporating them into culinary experiments. Thistle curry and nettle tea became unexpected delicacies of the house. Broken windows added a touch of rustic charm, while the absence of curtains meant privacy was a foreign concept. And let's not forget about the lack of heating. They all relied on layers of sweaters and endless cups of tea to stay warm.

Now, let's talk about the toilet experience. You were greeted with torn-up newspaper for wiping, a true testament to student resourcefulness. And just to add a touch of sophistication, they had proudly displayed a newspaper heading on the wall that proclaimed, "The Leeds Weekly News, the only free weekly to Reach the whole of Leeds." Truly, it was a house filled with character, quirks, and an unwavering sense of adventure.

Breaking the rules   © Pixababy

One evening, after having already imbibed a skinful including the ubiquitous last minute double pint rush at last orders, myself, Frodo, and several of the students from the rented dump in Blenheim, were walking back to said accommodation, as we walked, we started to sober up slightly, next we came across a small drunk man, obviously the worse for wear and drunk as a skunk. As we approached, he backed away a bit and stumbled onto the floor in the middle of the road, helping him to his feet and off the road the small, inebriated chap simply asked, do you know where we can get another drink.

We knew there was no alcohol at the student let, there never was, after all this is a student let, we are talking about. So, challenge accepted we considered a plan, one of the students some months before had visited a large house nearby and been able to get drinks after time, he thought he could remember the address, so we set off and followed his lead.

Suddenly the small man pulled away from us and burst into sobs of tears, we tried to reassure him, but he pulled away further, I know what you are going to do, he proclaimed, you're going to beat me up and rob me. When pressed as to why he thought we would attack him, he sobbed and said, because I'm gay, we assured him that we were not the least concerned and he finally calmed down.

Arriving at the house, a regular, if large, detached property, the lights were on, music was playing and it looked to the world like there was a party in full swing, which of course is how they circumvented the licensing laws, at the door raffle tickets were being sold, each ticket won a prize, an alcoholic drink, buying a few each, we ventured inside.

It's only the dirty ones we don't want - Philip Wilkinson

Almost immediately, the small, inebriated man was surrounded, several of the party goers had recognised him as Marc Almond from Soft Cell. We enjoyed our additional illicit alcohol at the house, however, try as we might, Marc was the only one of the motley crew that evening to pull.

It's only the dirty ones we don't want - Philip Wilkinson

Three Christmas dinners   © Pixababy

Erotic was now the man with two girlfriends and a monumental appetite! Christmas day turned out to be quite the feast for him, but also a logistical nightmare. With girlfriend one scheduled for 3 PM and girlfriend two at 7 PM, he had to plan his meals with military precision.

The day started innocently enough, with Erotic sitting down to a lavish Christmas dinner at home with his family. Little did he know what awaited him. After polishing off platefuls of turkey, stuffing, and all the trimmings, he found himself in a precarious situation. It was time to make his excuses, escape the clutches of his family's lovingly prepared spread, and embark on a journey through the land of awkward excuses.

With his belly already stretched to the limits, Erotic dashed over to girlfriend one's house, hoping to blend in with her family's festive gathering. As he pulled up a chair, he couldn't help but notice the tantalizing aromas wafting from the kitchen. The sight of a second Christmas dinner, with its succulent roast, mountains of mashed potatoes, and rivers of gravy, made Erotic's heart race... or was that just indigestion?

But the show must go on! With a sense of duty (and a growling stomach), Erotic soldiered through the second feast, attempting to find room for that extra serving of Christmas pudding. As the dishes piled up and the belt around his waist tightened, he bid a hasty farewell, leaving girlfriend one's house with a full belly and a guilty conscience.

Yet, there was still one more stop on Erotic's culinary adventure. Girlfriend two's family awaited him with open arms and a table groaning under the weight of yet another gastronomic masterpiece. It was as if the universe conspired against his waistline. With each bite, the joy of the holiday feast slowly turned into a test of sheer endurance.

Finally, the day ended, the dishes were conquered, and Erotic had tales of Christmas dinner conquests to share. Reflecting on his epic food odyssey, he confessed that while he managed to devour all three feasts, the second and third plates required Herculean effort to tackle with the same enthusiasm as the occasion commanded. One can only imagine the state of his poor waistband by the end of the night.

Chapter 12

Bigger and better motorcycles

I now owned a Suzuki S100   © Author & Pixababy

I had recently upgraded to a 100CC Suzuki, which I considered my pride and joy. However, it didn't take long for my friend Erotic to approach me with a desperate plea. He begged for a chance to ride my prised possession. Against my better judgment, I reluctantly handed him the keys.

Off he went, zooming up the street with a mix of excitement and trepidation. However, his joyride was short-lived. Just ten minutes later, Erotic returned, but the sight that greeted my eyes was nothing short of a disaster. My once gleaming Yamaha had suffered a scrape on the engine and tank from the unfortunate meeting with the ground. Both mirrors were shattered, and one indicator hung limply, barely clinging to its thread.

Stunned and dismayed, I couldn't help but express my shock at the pitiful state of my "new to me" bike. Erotic, however, nonchalantly shrugged off the mishap with a simple statement, "It doesn't handle very well," as if it were the most obvious explanation in the world. With that, he casually walked away.

Erotic had moved on from the Honda cub and now had a Honda CB125, his driving skills were legendary, he really did not need a bike any larger to keep up with the rest of the group, and he never bought another bike.

Erotic now had a Honda CB125   © Author &Pixababy

Bilbo had also moved on, now the proud owner of a Honda CB175, this bike was so utterly reliable, with no maintenance, that it became his winter bike, despite owning much larger and faster machines in the future, he kept the little Honda.

Bilbo had a Honda CB175   © Author & Pixababy

Teddy's motorcycle escapades were nothing short of disastrous. In his brief motorcycle-riding career, which lasted a mere half an hour for each of the two bikes he owned, he managed to have two serious crashes.

One unfortunate incident left him with both legs severely broken, requiring extensive pots that stretched from foot to groin. I remember walking into the pub toilets only to find Teddy resembling a caution wet floor sign, tangled in a comical struggle. After slipping, he was attempting to get up using both clutches, but they kept slipping, leaving him in a crumpled heap on the floor with his crutches forming a peculiar wigwam shape around him.

It's only the dirty ones we don't want - Philip Wilkinson

Teddy had a red BSA   © Author & Pixababy

Several days later, desperate to reclaim his passion for riding, Teddy came up with a rather unconventional solution. With sheer determination, he drilled holes in the bottom of both pots, removed the rubbers from the foot pegs, and miraculously found a way to ride again with both legs encased in plaster. And so, a group of about six of us set off towards Otley, brimming with excitement. Our plan was to swing by Tinshill to pick up another friend, but fate had a different plan in store for us.

Teddy, in his relentless pursuit of adventure, decided to cut a bend in the road. However, his daring manoeuvre ended in disaster as he was side swiped by an oncoming car, resulting in a severely broken right ankle. It was off to the hospital once again, where the bewildered nurses couldn't believe they had to remove a pot from a leg broken in a recent motorcycle crash, only to treat and repair a broken ankle from a second motorcycle crash. Teddy ended up in St James's hospital, joining a ward full of fellow motorcyclists all sporting various forms of traction and plaster.

In an act of light-heartedness, a few of us decided to pay Teddy a visit a day or so later. Before heading to the hospital, we made a pit stop at the now-demolished Florence Nightingale pub, conveniently located opposite the medical facility. With a mischievous twinkle in our eyes, we purchased two pints each for ourselves and a generous three pints for Teddy. As we entered the ward, the nurses couldn't help but chuckle at our arrival. In good spirits, they decided to fine us by playfully taking a sip from our spare pints, adding a touch of laughter to the healing atmosphere.

During one of our group rides, Frodo found himself being pursued by a car flashing its lights. Curious about the situation, he decided to stop and investigate. As the driver approached, he informed Frodo that something had fallen off his bike. It didn't take long for Frodo to realise that his gear lever was missing, leaving only the splined shaft behind.

Undeterred by the setback, Frodo improvised a solution by grabbing a pair of trusty mole grips. With a firm grip on the splined shaft, the mole grips became the makeshift gear lever, serving Frodo well for the rest of the ride and beyond. From that day forward, Frodo's Honda CD175 earned the endearing nickname "the tractor," as it never failed to deliver him to his intended destination, even in the face of unexpected gear lever mishaps.

It's only the dirty ones we don't want - Philip Wilkinson

Camping on a low budget   © Author

On a memorable camping trip near Kirby Lonsdale, our ragtag group of motorcycle enthusiasts woke up to the enticing aroma of a luxurious breakfast being prepared by the posh caravaners nearby. They had all the bells and whistles, fancy tables, chairs, tablecloths, and those snazzy multi-ring gas stoves for their culinary endeavours. Meanwhile, we scrounged through our meagre supplies, Mutt managed to find half a loaf of bread, Frodo proudly revealed his prised possession, a large tin of beans, and Bilbo... well, he had a blowlamp (don't even ask).

There was just one tiny problem, we didn't have a tin opener. As we clumsily brainstormed a solution, the caravaners couldn't help but watch, clearly amused by our predicament. Determination in our eyes, we grabbed a rock and a trusty screwdriver, poking holes in the lid of the bean can. And then, behold, the ingenious use of Frodo's beloved mole grips came into play, removing them from their semi-permanent use as a gear lever on "the tractor" we haphazardly tore off the can lid, making a mental note to reattach them to his trusty Honda CD175 later.

With Bilbo's blowlamp finally lit, we set the can on a rock, giving it a fiery blast. The label instantly went up in flames, and soon enough, one side of the can was glowing red hot. Convinced that the contents were adequately heated, we took the screwdriver and expertly stirred the can's contents, mixing the charred bits with the cold beans from the other side. It resulted in a peculiar concoction that we poured from the can onto a slice of bread, forming a rather challenging sandwich to eat.

And so, with beans cascading onto the grass as we leaned forward in a valiant attempt to devour our creation, we munched away, fully aware of the scrutinising gazes of the other, more sophisticated campers. We may not have had the trappings of a lavish breakfast setup, but our resourcefulness and culinary innovation certainly left an impression, one that the caravaners who witnessed the event won't soon forget.

Chapter 13 – 1977

Anything goes

Three men and a Datsun Cherry   © Author & Pixababy

During the summer, Richie, Erotic and I went camping in the Lake District, a week in Wasdale followed by a week at Buttermere was planned, Richie had bought a Datsun Cherry very cheaply, it's paint was in poor condition and the engine was in

bits in the boot, the car had been heavily modified by the previous owner and was sporting extra wide wheels with flared wheel arches, fortunately Richie was able to use his families garage to repair the car making it fit for a road trip.

As our journey unfolded in the captivating Lake District, we found ourselves at the shores of Windermere, ready to embark on a scenic drive. With excitement fuelling our spirits, we circled the crown of the lake, passing the charming town of Ambleside, and venturing onward towards Skelwith Bridge. Here, our path took an

adventurous turn as we veered onto a narrow single-track road that wound its way through the enchanting landscapes of Little Langdale, eventually leading us to the famed Wrynose and Hardknott Pass.

Known far and wide as one of the steepest roads in all of England, this rugged stretch of asphalt carried the moniker of "Britain's wildest road" for good reason. The pass tested the limits of our courage and driving skills as we navigated its treacherous bends and vertiginous gradients. The road, often no wider than a few feet, made passing another vehicle a near-impossible feat for most of its length.

Image capture: Sept 2011 © 2023 Google

Covering a mere 10 miles, our journey across both passes was a captivating, albeit time-consuming, endeavour. On a fair day, it would take us a full hour to traverse the twisting and turning roads, always mindful of the awe-inspiring sights that unfolded before us. As we pressed on, the remnants of Hardknott Roman fort came

into view, a testament to the historical tapestry woven within these rugged lands. Our path led us further, through the picturesque valley of Eskdale, until finally, we arrived at our destination, Wastwater, cradled within the breath-taking embrace of Wasdale Valley

Wastwater lake   © Author

This dramatic body of water, stretching for three miles in length and half a mile in width, possessed a mysterious allure that captured our hearts. And as if to deepen its mystique, Wastwater plunged to astonishing depths, reaching an impressive 260

158

feet, the deepest among all the lakes in England. It was here, at the edge of this untamed beauty, that we pitched our camp, ready to immerse ourselves in the wonders of the Lake District. At the base of Scafell Pike, proudly standing at 3,123 feet, the highest mountain in all of Britain, rested the serene lake of Wastwater. After an arduous trek through rugged terrain, our weary legs brought us to the doorstep of the welcoming Wasdale Head Inn, a true haven for tired adventurers. The aroma of hearty stew filled the air, drawing us in with its irresistible allure. With pints of refreshing beer in hand, we sank into cosy chairs, indulging in the warmth and shared experiences of fellow explorers. A generous bowl of steaming hot soup, accompanied by a substantial hunk of bread, proved to be a modest indulgence that revived our spirits. And to our pleasant surprise, these humble delights came at a price that was as light on the wallet as they were filling

The Wasdale Head Inn   image capture: Oct 2021 © 2023 Google

During that summer, the water level of the lake was lower than usual. Embarking on a circular walk around the lake, our steps guided us to the grand scree section at its western end. There, amidst nature's splendour, we paused and assembled a simple yet satisfying lunch, generously filled tinned salmon sandwiches, crisp apples, and a medley of tinned fruit luxuriating in sweet syrup, a feast fit for intrepid souls like us.

© Pixababy

As we continued our journey, following the meandering path along the stream that cascaded from the lake's western edge, a delightful sight caught our eye. Brown trout, ensnared by the receding waters, had found themselves temporarily trapped.

Seizing the opportunity, we put our resourcefulness to the test, fashioning impromptu fishing gear from whatever we could find at hand. With a stroke of luck, we managed to secure three plump specimens.

© Pixababy

With the sun dipping below the horizon, casting a warm glow upon our campsite, we kindled a crackling campfire and prepared our freshly caught bounty. The sizzle of the fish, kissed by the dancing flames, wafted through the air, intensifying our anticipation. Succulent and flavoursome, those trout were a testament to the rewards of venturing into the great outdoors and embracing the simplicity of life under the open sky. With every mouthful, my love for the wonders of camping was reignited, reminding me of the joys found in the simple things in life.

Image capture: Jul 2022 © 2023 Google

The Bridge Inn Buttermere where we camped behind for the second week

It's only the dirty ones we don't want - Philip Wilkinson

Finally, we bid farewell to Wasdale and embarked on a picturesque drive to Buttermere. Our chosen abode for the duration of our stay was the Syke Farm campsite, nestled serenely behind the Bridge Hotel. From this idyllic base, we set out to explore the enchanting northern lakes that adorned the region. Looking for something a bit different, Richie suggested we walk over the farm early that morning where we delighted in the purchase of farm-fresh green top milk straight out of the chiller and milked as we watched. The creamy goodness provided a delightful accompaniment to our morning walk, adding a touch of authenticity to our camping experience, and, no longer legal for sale, hence this part of the trip cannot now be experienced, what a shame.

Eager to immerse ourselves in the natural wonders that surrounded us, we embarked on leisurely walks around the captivating landscapes of both Buttermere Lake and Crummock Water. These shimmering bodies of water, basking under the summer sun, showcased the epitome of tranquillity and beauty. Each step revealed new vistas that evoked a sense of awe. Now, let's talk about Richie's car, a true character. The previous owner, in a fit of whimsy, had equipped it with a whoopy whistle. Oh, the mischievous joy we derived from giving passing girls a playful whistle! Alas, the unsuspecting sheep grazing peacefully in the meadows and blocking our passing on many roads, remained thoroughly unimpressed by our antics.

Buttermere lake   © Author

As we cruised along the winding roads, an 8-track cassette player serenaded us with an eclectic mix of tunes. Unfortunately, the assortment left behind by the previous owner featured many recordings of chart-topping hits, including the likes of Lionel Ritchie, Boney M, Captain & Tennille, and Rose Royce.

It's only the dirty ones we don't want - Philip Wilkinson

While they may not have aligned with our musical tastes, we discovered a saving grace in the form of Genesis' "Selling England By The Pound", a true prog rock album featuring characters and concepts far beyond the Top of the Pops fare, where have you encountered undinal songs, father Tiresias, a lawn mower who you can tell by the way he walks and concepts such as "there is in fact more earth than sea", the final track lyrics start with a lady called Tess who thankful for here fine fare discount, Tess co-operates, then the lyrics drift into the discounts available in the supermarkets that week, the lyrics over sung to sound like several singers are ethereal an example being, Peak Freans beans slashed from twenty p to seventeen and a half, which goes to show you can sing anything, so long as you do it right . To this day, whenever those familiar melodies fill the air, my mind drifts back to the enchanting landscapes of the Lake District, forever intertwined with those enduring songs.

© Pixababy

Engineering apprentices

The twins, Bilbo, and Frodo along with Spawny worked as engineering apprentices for one of the major engineering companies In Leeds, their tales of fun at work were some of the best I have heard.

Being sent to the stores for a long stand, rubber hammer, left-handed screwdriver etc. did not catch them out, they would simply take a break for an hour in the canteen, when reporting back to work, they would say that the stores were all out of long stands, or similar.

One day, someone came up with an idea following a chance remark over lunch, the remark revealed that the individual stood up to wipe after using the toilet, as most sit, an idea came to the fore, a survey to get a measure on who stood, and who remained seated, over the next few weeks, there were some choice words shouted at them in the gents whilst the survey

162

took place, looking over the toilet cubicle was not deemed acceptable by most of the workforce singled out for the survey, it turned out that the result was split almost 50:50, in the main, the larger individuals sat, whilst the slender ones tended to stand.

One day, one of the lads arrived with his mother's catalogue, as she had become an agent, she was looking for customers that would earn her points, the catalogue was scrutinised carefully and five of the lads in the bike club decided to make a significant purchase, a Wendy house for the princely sum of £6 or 15p a week for 40 weeks. The Wendy house, when it arrived, was used as a joke tent for camping several times and caused quite a stir at several bike rallies.

Spawny on one of his hand-built Kawasaki drag racing motorcycles © AVMCC

Spawny, building a street legal drag bike, was finding it increasingly tough to work on the parts during his lunch break, the box section swinging arm was not too difficult as the sections were similar to work he would have been conducting for the company, however, stealing the milling machine, re programming it and skimming the cylinder head was a bit more tricky, and as for the custom exhaust pipe and turbocharger service, well it was obvious that these were not authorised jobs.

A cylinder head from an engine © Author

Imagine sneaking this into work, hiding it until lunch break, commandeering a machine and setting it up to skim the surface, running the machine, then hiding the head again until it was time to go home

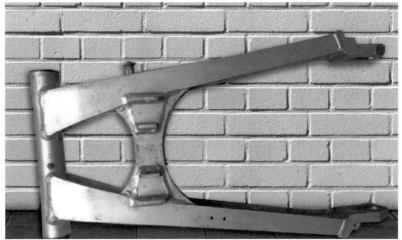

© Author & Pixababy
Box section rear swinging arm, designed to not twist under extreme torque

Chapter 14

Discovering girls

© Pixababy

On a wintery Thursday evening, amidst the cosy ambiance of the Chemic Tavern, Frodo and I found ourselves engaged in light-hearted banter over drinks. Amidst the jovial atmosphere, Frodo whispered to me, his eyes darting toward a group of girls at the adjacent table. "Those girls keep stealing glances at us," he confided mischievously. "When their dad heads to the loo, I'm going to make a move. It might work better if you join in too."

Returning from the toilet myself, I noticed Frodo had made his move and intrigued by his audacious plan, I played along, joining him at the table with the girls we struck up a conversation. The father, clearly miffed at being momentarily side-lined, couldn't dampen our spirits and we plied them with drinks, which seemed to appease him (we leaned later he was an alcoholic).

Against all odds, the girls agreed to meet us in town on Saturday, an outcome that surprised even us.

It's only the dirty ones we don't want - Philip Wilkinson

The Chemic Tavern, Woodhouse, Leeds   © Mtaylor848

As the appointed day arrived, I must admit, I harboured doubts that they would show up. Yet, to my astonishment, they did, and among them was T, the more attractive of the duo we had met the night before and, in my eyes, the epitome of beauty. Unbeknownst to me, she had taken an interest in me, rather than Frodo, who had always been the "babe magnet" of our duo, Frodo only stayed for about 20 minutes and having been disappointed by T's interest in me, made up some excuse and left, at this the other girl, rather than play piggy in the middle, also left.

Seeking a casual setting for our outing, we indulged in some delectable fish 'n chips from Graveley's, a renowned take-away by the bustling city market and sat on the low wall opposite to tuck in. With a touch of excitement, I arranged to pick T up on my motorcycle the following day, eager to embark on a new chapter of adventure and romance.

We drove out to Settle and walked up the top of the limestone escarpment where I showed her the caves where fossilised fish had been found giving an insight into the geological age of the earth in the 19th century, she must have been impressed.

By now, T had admitted that she was only 15, she assured me here birthday was in a few weeks and as I was seeking a long-term relationship, I was not too concerned, we had already arranged to meet for a midweek drink, an appointment I intended to keep.

It's only the dirty ones we don't want - Philip Wilkinson

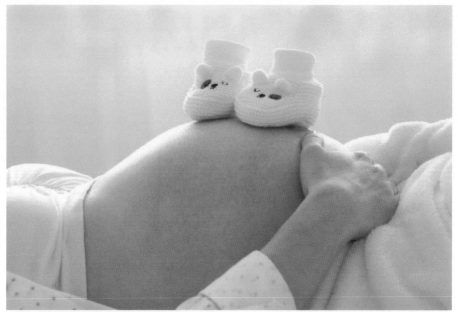

Richie's encounter © Pixababy

I received a phone call from T an hour before the agreed time for collecting her on my motorbike, pleading for someone to collect her sister, C, who had an inexplicable desire to join the evening's festivities. I enrolled Erotic and his motorcycle. Intrigued and fuelled by a desire for adventure, we set off to the Little London estate.

To Erotic's surprise, as we arrived to gather the duo, a wild sight greets his eyes. C, braving the winter weather like a fashion rebel, appears before us in a Japanese-style silk mini dress with a daring thigh-high split and high heels. The sheer audacity of her attire in such inclement conditions leaves everyone flabbergasted.

Undeterred by the biting cold and the inevitable consequences of poor outfit choices, C hops onto Erotic's motorbike, who had kindly offered her a lift. However, little did C know that Erotic had recently wax-oiled his bike for the winter, turning it into a slippery, greasy uninviting place for a girl made up to the nines.

As their journey unfolds, disaster strikes. C, desperately clutching onto the bike for dear life, unwittingly smears her hands with oily residue. The moment of truth arrives as she triumphantly removes her helmet, only to wipe her now oily hands across her face and hair, unwittingly transforming herself into a bedraggled, slicked-back mess.

In a twist of fate, Erotic's romantic prospects with C come crashing down, His greasy bike proved to be an insurmountable obstacle to any budding love connections. But alas, it was Richie who would become the unwitting target of C's affections. With his family business, own flat, own car and an aura of easy prey surrounding him, he inadvertently fell into her tangled web of charm.

It's only the dirty ones we don't want - Philip Wilkinson

And so, as if following a script penned by the cruellest of comedic writers, C swiftly moved into the shared apartment, leaving me in a state of perpetual couch surfing. The one-bedroom abode, equipped with two singles in the bedroom, became a battleground of space, comfort, and sleepless nights.

Oh, the hilarity of it all! From the ill-fated choice of clothing to the slippery embrace of a motorbike, this tale of misadventures and romantic entanglements serves as a reminder that life's comedic timing knows no bounds. As I resigned myself to the couch, they can only laugh at the absurdity of it all.

C managed to convince Richie that they didn't need to worry about family planning due to an accident she had as a child, which supposedly rendered her infertile. Erotic, when Richie related this said oh year, and you believe her? And he was right, against all odds, she miraculously became pregnant. Their wedding was a rather sombre affair, with C being 8 months pregnant and wearing a worn-out wedding dress to the registry office. To add to the melancholy, the bride's father, who struggled with alcoholism, failed to show up, worse, Richie's father, who he had to work with every day, cut him off.

It was revealed that C, along with her sister T and younger brother, had spent their entire lives in a high-rise block without access to electricity. Their father's alcoholism led to the power being disconnected, leaving them without the necessities of washing, lighting, heating, cooking, and even entertainment through television. It was difficult to fathom the challenges they faced, growing up in such circumstances without the essential resources that many take for granted.

C barely married and with a 4-month-old son, took to having sex regularly, not always with Richie, in an unexplained twist, a guy known simply as Shoes had moved in with the newlyweds, Erotic once tried to ask Richie who Shoes was and why had he moved in, he is a lodger came a reluctant and unsure reply.

After a few years and the arrival of another unexpected baby, C and Richie's relationship came to an end. C embarked on a new journey with a conman, traveling across Europe and engaging in fraudulent schemes. As their activities drew the attention of the police, including Interpol, C found herself in a desperate situation. She made a distressed call to her mother, claiming that her partner had passed away, she had no funds, and needed assistance to repatriate his body back to the UK.

Her mother, despite having raised three children with an alcoholic husband and no electricity, had managed to save several thousand pounds throughout her life, which she promptly wired to her daughter. However, this heart-breaking plea turned out to be a scam. It's difficult to imagine the depth of betrayal felt by a mother who had struggled to provide for her daughter during their challenging upbringing, only to be deceived and robbed of her life savings in such a callous manner.

Shortly after, while watching the television program Crimewatch, C's face appeared as one of Interpol's most wanted criminals. Witnessing a close acquaintance's wife on such a notorious platform is an extraordinary and unsettling experience.

It's only the dirty ones we don't want - Philip Wilkinson

The Milk Bar, Sherburn in Elmet   © AVMCC
famous "Banana Boat" Tuned Honda CB 750 K2

Frodo's close call

I encountered T once more, we decided to drive to Sherbourne in Elmet, a popular gathering spot for motorcyclists on Sunday afternoons. We headed to the milk bar, a renowned hangout where bikers from all over Yorkshire would converge. However, to my surprise, T quickly abandoned me and joined a group of motorcyclists, effectively disappearing from my sight and my life.

Months later, T reached out to Frodo after learning through her sister, via Richie, about a planned weekend camping trip to the Hill Inn in Chapel le Dale, Ingleton. Frodo agreed to pick her up and drove out to the inn with her as his pillion with the intention of spending the weekend camping with her. His brother Bilbo also needed a lift, so Frodo set off back to Leeds to collect him, However, upon his arrival back at the Hill Inn, T was nowhere to be found. Instead, he noticed a large van belonging to a group of cavers parked in the car park. It became evident that T had joined forces with the cavers, spending the entire weekend in the van engaging in sexual encounters with each of them. Disturbingly, they seemed unconcerned about her age, despite her being only 15 and potentially even younger.

It's only the dirty ones we don't want - Philip Wilkinson

By Sunday afternoon, T was standing in the car park, waiting for Frodo to provide her with a ride back home. Though reluctantly, Frodo, being a gentleman, drove her to a bus stop and bid her farewell, expressing a simple wish for her to have a good life. He then had to return to the inn to collect his brother Bilbo. From that moment on, T earned herself the unfortunate nickname "mattress back," reflecting the promiscuous behaviour she had displayed.

Mattress back went on to marry, never had children and then divorce about ten years later, however around ten years after her divorce, somehow, she hooked up with Frodo, after a few weekends, she got pregnant with his child, this just went to demonstrate that the wise, after dodging a bullet in a game of Russian roulette, should not try firing the pistol again.

© Author

Erotic's near misses

Erotic paid a visit to Richie's apartment with a specific purpose in mind, he was keen on purchasing the amplifier that Richie had put up for sale. After listening to the amplifier and negotiating a price, Erotic secured the deal and strapped the newly acquired item to the back of his motorcycle. As he made his way home, an unexpected encounter occurred. Jugsy, whom Erotic happened to run into on the street, engaged him in conversation. However, her interest in the amplifier was minimal, as she abruptly propositioned Erotic to come over to her house for a sexual encounter, making her intentions explicitly clear due to Erotic's reputation for missing subtle hints.

Suddenly faced with two enticing opportunities, Erotic found himself torn between indulging in sex and eagerly listening to his new amplifier. With a hint of regret, Erotic explained that he had just purchased the amplifier and was eager to go home and enjoy it, and that if she still wanted to, they could have sex next week. Disappointed, Jugsy withdrew her offer. Three years later, Erotic ran into Jugsy again, she now had a child, aged two and a half, leading him to wonder what his life could have been like had he accepted her proposition that day. Even after many years, Erotic still ponders the path not taken and the alternate life that could have unfolded had he made a different choice.

It's only the dirty ones we don't want - Philip Wilkinson

© Pixababy

Erotic's Second Chance

On one occasion, Erotic, C, and mattress back along with their mother were at the apartment watching pornography on the video recorder, Erotic had never seen women who enjoyed porn before and found the situation both fascinating and dangerous in equal measures, especially when the mother opened her bag and a 10inch vibrator rolled out. He made up some excuse and left them to it, but he did borrow their favourite VHS recording as he left.

© iStock

Erotic did eventually get engaged and married, I took the wedding photographs for him, and Richy borrowed the 1939 Rolls Royce Silver Ghost from his parents to use as the wedding car, we drove to the front of Temple Newsom House for some of the photographs, he went on to have a long and happy marriage which is what really counts.

© Pixababy

Teddy's experience

Teddy never had a close call, he was probably the most experienced of the whole group with girls, he never had a time when he had less than half a dozen female acquaintances on the go at once, occasionally the number would reach double figures, of course in those days the only way to communicate was by a land line telephone in the home, or to call around and knock on the door. Cath, his mother had a whiteboard on the wall by the phone, listed upon this were the girls names, and in another column, the answer she was to give, should the telephone or visit, she would remind him that he must keep it current as whatever was written on the board would be the answer she would give, issues arose with the system when Teddy started to date two girls with the same name.

He went on to marry a daughter of one of the Satan's Slaves in Leeds, had a son and then it all went very wrong, his wife signed legal documents for a loan for another member of her family in Teddys name, when the fraud was discovered, it was the end of the marriage.

Teddy and his mother sold up in Leeds and went to live on the Isle of Skye where he re married, has several successful children who own businesses on the island, has recently built himself a new house on the family 44acre island on the northern tip of Skye and is very happy with his life achievements to date.

He has recently purchased a large, custom Harley Davidson motorcycle, and confesses to setting out on a day off to ride 70 miles round trip, for a bacon sandwich.

It's only the dirty ones we don't want - Philip Wilkinson

My life changer   © Bilbo

Life has a funny way of surprising us when we least expect it. Amidst the chaos and challenges of living with Richie and his amorous escapades, a glimmer of hope emerged. Little did I know that my upcoming birthday party would become the catalyst for a life-changing encounter. As the day of celebration approached, we extended invitations to Marsbar, his wife, and her friends. The prospect of their presence infused the air with anticipation and excitement. Our modest flat, once a haven for hilarious mishaps and shared laughter, was soon transformed into a vibrant gathering place.

As the guests arrived, I couldn't help but notice the presence of a group of attractive girls, adding an extra touch of enchantment to the evening. Encouraged by the lively atmosphere, I summoned my courage and, in a moment of spontaneity, leaned in to share a kiss with one of them. The connection was instantaneous, and the spark between us was undeniable.

In the days that followed, my thoughts were consumed by the memory of that fleeting but meaningful encounter. Fate seemed to be at work, intertwining our lives in unexpected ways. Through Marsbar, I discreetly inquired about her identity, and to my delight, I discovered her name was C.

Curiosity piqued, C sought the opinion of her friend, Marsbar's wife K, to discern if our connection was worth pursuing. The affirmation she received emboldened her to take a chance, and we eagerly made plans to meet once again. That subsequent meeting was nothing short of magical. Conversation flowed effortlessly as we discovered shared interests, dreams, and aspirations. Having been at the same high school, both born in adjacent suburbs of Leeds, either side of Headingley cricket club (which incidentally was built by one of my relatives Lord Airey) and having both grown up in terraced housing, we had a lot in common. Our connection deepened with each passing moment, and before we knew it, we had embarked on a journey of love and companionship.

In the years that followed, our relationship blossomed, enduring the tests of time and the challenges that life inevitably brings. Two years after our initial encounter, we took a momentous step forward together, purchasing a house that would become the foundation of our shared future. As the years rolled by, our love grew stronger, we celebrated our union in a joyous wedding ceremony, surrounded by friends and family who had witnessed our love story unfold. Our commitment to each other was solidified, and we embarked on the journey of marriage with hope and determination.

Four beautiful children blessed our lives, filling our home with laughter, chaos, and unconditional love. They became the embodiment of our love, a testament to the life we had built together.

Recently, we marked a milestone in our journey, celebrating our Ruby wedding anniversary, a testament to the enduring strength of our love over more than four decades. The years have been filled with ups and downs, joys, and challenges, but through it all, we have remained steadfast and supportive of one another.

An incident with the tractor © Author & Pixababy

Frodo, while riding his Honda CD175 tractor back home from work one evening, was unexpectedly stopped by the police just 500 yards away from his destination. They informed him that his indicators were not functioning properly. Frodo calmly explained that he was aware of the issue and had been using hand signals instead. Despite his explanation, the police issued him a ticket, stating that if indicators were installed on a motorbike, they must be in working order. Resignedly, Frodo accepted the ticket and prepared to ride his bike home. However, as he started the engine, the police officers promptly instructed him to turn it off, claiming that he couldn't ride the bike with faulty indicators. Frustrated, Frodo reached into his tool bag, retrieved a hacksaw, and promptly cut off the non-functional indicators. With a cheeky glance at the perplexed police officers, he asked, "Can I go now?" To their bewilderment, they waved him on, and Frodo continued his journey.

The Sportsman Pub   © Chemical Engineer

A new venue for the Aire Valley MCC

The Aire Valley MCC initially started with a small group of members who would gather at The Spring Close pub in Cross Green, enjoying beer and music. However, as the club grew, they quickly outgrew this location. They decided to move their weekly meetings to the Sportsman Inn on Stony Rock Lane in Leeds. This pub was selected for various reasons: it was conveniently situated for most members, located in an area where there was little opposition to motorcycles, drinking, and lively behaviour, and the landlord kindly provided them us a room once a week.

These meetings primarily revolved around social drinking and light-hearted fun. However, they also used this time to plan events for the upcoming weekends. Upon arrival, members would learn about the next rally or camping trip scheduled. These meetings took on the atmosphere of a mini rally, with everyone arriving on their motorcycles and engaging in heavy drinking, fun, and pranks. It was during this period that many members earned their nicknames used in my book to conceal their identities.

One member, known as "The Animal," gained notoriety for a peculiar act. On more than one occasion, he would take another member's glass of beer and perform a surprising feat by inserting his manhood into the glass, astonishing the witnesses as it touched the bottom.

175

Meanwhile, another member named Erotic had a new girlfriend who earned the nickname "Terrifying." Her behaviour at these meetings took the bawdiness to a whole new level, and her intimidating antics made everyone present genuinely afraid of her. Tampons would appear in your drink, occasionally used, she could arm wrestle anyone to defeat, when she grabbed hold of your genitals and squeezed hard it was not an erotic experience, and she could drink most under the table.

Erotic shared an intriguing incident involving his girlfriend, Terrifying. While visiting her at her home on one occasion, he was pleasantly surprised to discover that she had a younger sister. As Erotic sat in the lounge, the door swung open, revealing a very attractive young blonde girl dressed in a leotard. She was on her way to ballet class. Erotic found himself unable to avert his gaze, admiring every inch of her and even experiencing a bit of drooling.

Once the aspiring ballet dancer had left the room, Terrifying leaned over and whispered a chilling message in Erotic's ear. She sternly warned him, saying, "If you ever lay a finger on her, I will use a blunt knife to castrate you." She then leaned back, grinning at Erotic. This sudden threat caught him off guard. Firstly, the fact that Terrifying chose to whisper the threat heightened its seriousness, intensifying the level of danger. Secondly, Erotic believed that Terrifying was fully capable of following through on her words if the need ever arose. This incident served as a stark reminder to Erotic that Terrifying was fiercely protective of her younger sister. It made him realise the potential consequences he would face should he ever cross that line.

Postman Pat © Author

One of the Thursday club friends, and a former resident of the student house, despite having a degree in civil engineering, saw himself as staunch working class, to this end he worked as a postman hence his nickname, lived in a back-to-back terraced house in Leeds 4 off the A65 Kirkstall Road, his choice of employment was

deliberate, it ticked all the boxes, a working-class role, a 4AM start and more significantly a 11AM finish, this gave him time to study, and study he did, using the

Open University he enrolled for a different degree course approx. every three years, building up multiple degrees over a long period.

One day at the Thursday meet, we were discussing the torrential monsoon type rainfall overnight in the area, to which Pat chirped in with a tale. That morning, as he went back to the depot to collect a second bag for delivery despite the torrential rain, he happened to overhear his supervisor on the telephone, he could only hear one side of the conversation, but that was enough, he was asking a complaining member of the public, ringing to say their mail was wet, if they could see their postman out of the window, because he wondered if she could tell if he was doing the breaststroke, or the crawl.

Encounters with the police   © Pixababy

In the past, there was a more lenient attitude towards drinking and driving, and the members of the bike club would often consume alcohol beyond the legal limit before riding their motorcycles home. They had several encounters with the police, but the law enforcement officers did not vigorously pursue them for a few reasons. Firstly, it was unlikely that the police could catch up with the speeding motorcycles. Secondly, engaging in a chase could potentially cause accidents, putting both the motorcyclists and the public at risk. Lastly, the police had more pressing concerns than individuals who had consumed a few pints over the limit.

I personally experienced being targeted for a stop on multiple occasions. The first encounter occurred while driving down Cemetery Road in Beeston, heading towards the newly completed M621 slip road. I noticed a marked police car following me. Although I had initially planned to take the motorway into the city centre, I decided to confirm if I was being singled out for a stop. I slowed down and turned into Brown Lane East, revealing the police car's intention as they continued to follow me. I then made a left turn into Crosby

Road, and another left into Recreation Mount, which had road bollards closing off its east end. Without hesitation, I drove through the bollards and onto Top Moor Side, reaching the motorway slip road, leaving the police car stranded behind. Another encounter with the police occurred on the Leeds Inner Ring Road. After being followed off the motorway, I travelled along Wellington Street towards the Armley Gyratory roundabout. Remaining vigilant for any manoeuvres the police driver might attempt, I adhered to the speed limits. Upon reaching the roundabout, I took a left turn onto a footpath. At this point, the A643 was elevated above the railway lines, with a series of arches supporting it. The footpath utilised one of these narrow arches, which my bike easily passed through. Once again, the police car was unable to continue pursuit and was left behind.

Most of the club members had similar experiences, and we delighted in sharing our stories of daring escapades and how we managed to outsmart the police.

© Pixababy

Frodo, who, after a jolly session in the town centre, found himself moseying along, heading home. As fate would have it, he stumbled upon some road works and noticed a mighty handy tool left unattended, an abandoned pickaxe. Without a second thought, Frodo lifted the pickaxe onto his shoulder, feeling like the king of the construction site, and continued his way.

He then encounters a police car slowly chugging along Beeston Town Street, completely oblivious to the fact that its lights were absent. And there, in his slightly inebriated state, Frodo had an epiphany. He was struck by the brilliant idea that it was his moral duty to inform these unsuspecting officers about their lack of luminosity.

So, with the pickaxe resting comfortably on his shoulder, Frodo approached the car, determined to grab their attention. He began banging on the passenger side window, walking alongside the car like a persistent troubadour. Eventually, the officer, no doubt perplexed by the commotion, rolled down the window to investigate.

It's only the dirty ones we don't want - Philip Wilkinson

Without missing a beat, Frodo pointed out their lightless situation, emphasizing the potential danger of driving without proper illumination. However, instead of receiving a grateful nod of appreciation, the officer responded with a curt command for Frodo to go away. But our resilient hero was having none of it!

Undeterred, Frodo raised his voice and continued his passionate plea, exclaiming that driving without lights was a recipe for disaster. The officer, undoubtedly growing more exasperated by the second, tried frantically to shoo Frodo away, desperately signalling for him to retreat. But Frodo, fuelled by his sense of

righteousness, wasn't about to back down. He persisted, shouting at the top of his lungs, "You could cause an accident!"

And just when you thought things couldn't get any stranger, the police car suddenly decided to make its grand escape. With the officer likely preferring to avoid any further confrontation, they swiftly drove off, leaving Frodo behind, contemplating the bizarre events of that fateful evening.

When Frodo later recounted his journey to his bewildered friends, he couldn't help but remark on two astonishing aspects of that peculiar night. First, not a single soul uttered a word to him throughout his eventful walk. It was as if he were a mysterious figure, moving through the world in his own peculiar bubble. And second, to his utmost surprise, the police officers showed absolutely no interest in the fact that he was carrying a pickaxe on his shoulder, despite his rather obvious state of inebriation. It was as if the pickaxe was just another fashionable accessory to them.

And so, the tale of Frodo, the pickaxe-wielding advocate for road safety, and his encounter with nonchalant law enforcement officers, became a legendary anecdote that left many scratching their heads in disbelief.

© Pixababy

Across from the twins' humble abode lay a patch of wasteland, easily accessible from the road. Right next door to this seemingly desolate place, there was a house infamous for providing certain adult services in exchange for some monetary compensation. And what a sight it was on many an evening! Two or more police

cars could often be spotted discreetly parked on that waste ground, well out of sight, undoubtedly taking advantage of the services offered by the adjacent house.

It's only the dirty ones we don't want - Philip Wilkinson

Now, Teddy, being the observant brother, couldn't help but notice this peculiar pattern after witnessing a dozen such incidents over the course of several months. Late one evening, upon returning home, he came across an astonishing sight, four marked police cars discreetly tucked away, hidden from prying eyes. It was a moment of revelation for Teddy, realizing that living across from a "lady of the night" was one thing, but discovering that the very police officers who were meant to enforce the law were blatantly partaking in the services, well, that was an entirely different story.

With a fire in his heart and mischief in his mind, Teddy quietly sneaked into the basement of his home, where he stumbled upon two tins of trusty spray paint and a lathe cutting tool. In a matter of minutes, he embarked on a mission.

© Pixababy

Teddy meticulously spray painted the address onto the bonnet and roof of each police car, leaving an indelible mark for all to see. And just to ensure that the officers couldn't simply clean off the paint and brush it aside as a mere prank, Teddy took it a step further. He employed the tungsten carbide lathe tool to scratch the address, time, and date onto several of the car's glass windows. That ought to make a lasting impression!

As one can imagine, it must have been quite the surprise for the serving officers returning to their vehicles, only to find them marked with full details revealing at a minimum that they had all been left together unattended. Picture their baffled expressions and the inevitable scramble to come up with some tricky explanations when they got back to the station. I can't help but chuckle at the mental image of those officers, trying to justify their mysterious connection to the infamous house of indulgence.

After Teddy's bold act, a remarkable thing happened. No further marked police cars were seen hidden off the road. It seems his cheeky act had a lasting effect, dissuading the officers from indulging in their extracurricular activities at the expense of their duty.

My little brother Stephen   © Author

One last tale, by now I had left home but I took my new girlfriend round for tea and meet at my parents' house, brave I know, but there was no change from the routine, the food was served in stages, with bread, butter and a bowl of meat spread to start with, a large pot of tea was on the table and I poured my girlfriend a cup, as I reached for the potted meat, my middle brother grabbed it and the meat leapt out of the pot and landed in her tea with a splash. The main course, fish fingers, peas, carrots, and chips came next, then when we had finished, gravy arrived.

I noticed that my little brother was not there and when I asked, I was told that he had been missing all day, as he was eleven, I was concerned.

© Author

Watching TV later, we had asked my mother to make some supper, she had managed pilchards (from a tin) on toast and this was actually fairly tasty, an experience I was not altogether familiar with, baying for more and having been told that it was the last tin, suddenly she re appeared with another round of 'fish' on toast, my mother warned us that it was from a different tin and may taste different, and she was correct, it was soggy and unpleasant, to this day we believe she served us fish flavoured tinned cat food on toast, a tale my wife regales to this day.

It's only the dirty ones we don't want - Philip Wilkinson

Later that evening, just as we intended to leave, my little brother fell into the house through the front door unconscious, he was vomiting profusely, his pallor was grey and he needed urgent medical attention, an ambulance was called, and he received urgent resuscitation from the crew who saved his life. It transpired that he had taken magic mushrooms, solvents and brandy in quantities that were lethal and had in fact attempted suicide.

No explanation was given by my brother when he recovered, other than it was a deliberate attempt. It became obvious that he had serious mental issues, and he went on to take almost every type of drug he could obtain, he persisted in managing his mental health himself by taking uppers and downers with alcohol for many years and got into all sorts of scrapes along the way.

By the time he was fifteen, he was starting to receive professional mental care and medication, but he was so paranoid that he could never take the care advice of medication for long before distrusting it, and the carers.

At this point to fund his habits he took up professional signwriting having learned much about this trade from my father, he earned good money cutting vinyl for vehicles and illuminated signs, but it was never enough, so he resorted to tricks like selling raffle tickets in the centre of town to unsuspecting passers by.

When he first met people, he trusted them implicitly and they often fell for his charm and politeness, offering him places to live with them and even money, he would accept these offers but they were always doomed as he would after a few weeks become distrustful of his new house mate/s on one occasion, believing they were plotting to kill him, he grabbed what he could and jumped out of the bedroom window to escape them.

By this stage, he had been diagnosed as bipolar, he was hearing voices and behaving very strangely, sitting in a pub with him and my girlfriend, he suddenly stood up and shouted at a group on another table to fuck off and mind their own business, sitting down again he explained that they had been watching him all evening and, in his mind, plotting to stab us.

He was always involved in fights; he could not even wait in a queue for a bus without getting beaten up for his bad attitude. Eventually he was sectioned in Roundhay wing at St James's hospital. Visiting him on the first occasion, I and my girlfriend were horrified to discover he was on fifteen-minute suicide checks, and he demanded that I obtain a horses head for him to use for a warning to protect the family from our enemies. On the second visit he had calmed down a bit, but he insisted that the previous evening he had played a tough game of chess with the SAS marksmen on the roof of the hospital, when questioned he said they were there to prevent him from leaving.

However, he did leave the ward, but rather than simply walk out which he was permitted to do, he helped himself to the beat box owned by one of the nurses and climbed out of a third floor window and down a drainpipe to escape, having sold the beat box he was next seen by the same nurse as they drove home, he was thumbing a lift at the side of the M621 in Leeds and a car had stopped to offer him a lift. The nurse provided the registration mark, and the owner lived in London, my mother provided an address of a friend he had stayed with, and the police turned up to wait for him to arrive, and sure enough the car pulled up and my brother was taken into custody, the owner of the car was advised that he had given a lift to an escaped mental patient, I dare say that was the last time he ever picked up a hitch hiker.

Once more, within a few weeks he was refusing to take his medication and could not trust the doctors, so the hospital took him off the medication in the expectation that he would get worse and come back to them for help, my parents, listed as his carers were not informed of this decision putting them and the rest of the family at risk.

Now living rough, he was reduced to catching brown trout out of the decorative ponds at the Canal Gardens, Roundhay Park, Leeds and barbequing them. He arrived out of the blue and caused trouble at my parents home threatening my father and mother, and my sisters baby with a carving knife, and when the police arrived, he jumped out of the bedroom window and disappeared into Gipton Wood, the police failed to catch him, but I am not so sure I would want to search for a nutter, in the woods, at night, so we forgave them. However, he came back a few days later for his possessions, once again the carving knife was brandished, and police called to no avail.

The next morning the police arrived at the chemist where he received his daily methadone only, they missed him by a few minutes, he turned up the following day, threatened the chemist with the knife to try to obtain a larger dose, and when this failed he ran out into the middle of Roundhay Road, laying down in front t of a bus he screamed for it to run over him and end it.

© https://www.yorkshireeveningpost.co.uk/news/crime/joiner-found-dead-in-armley-cell-received-satisfactory-care-from-leeds-prison-service-inquest-hears-3733253

The police arrived and he was placed in Armley prison, (now renamed Leeds prison) for his safety, on arrival, he told the prison doctor that he was receiving 250ml of methadone a day (he was actually prescribed 100ml but they did not check), he spent a month in the prison before an incident occurred, he refused to go on exercise, and when the cell was opened for his watch inmate, he was hanging from the bars having used a boot lace ligature and was unconscious, the guards cut him down and performed CPR and the prison doctor was called,

It's only the dirty ones we don't want - Philip Wilkinson

when he arrived he collapsed into a corner of the cell in tears whist the guards shouted at him to help, eventually he crawled over to my brother and picked up his hand, after a second or two he said he is dead and at that they stopped CPR, minutes later the ambulance crew were on the scene, hooking my brother to a machine, they found his heart was still beating, and resumed CPR, but even after an hour in the ambulance and at the hospital, he was proclaimed dead. At the inquest, the coroner discovered that the doctor employed by the prison was not qualified to carry out his duties on his own, and needed a second doctor present at all times, however the prison claimed that they could not easily recruit doctors and had to take what they could find, the coroner then turned to the hospital and the withdrawal of the medication, blasting them for this failure. H found both the prison and the hospital were guilty of neglect, a very serious breach of care.

It was also evident that the lethal dose of methadone being prescribed to him every day, at his request, was not being taken, he had no drugs in his system at time of death and showed clear of drugs for several weeks, so we presume he was using this as currency in the prison. When I heard he had died, it was an unusual mixture of grief for a wasted life, and relief that he had hurt himself, rather than others. Not long before in 1995 a Steven Wilkinson had broken into Hall Garth school in Middlesborough with a gun and a knife and killed one child and stabbed two more whilst claiming it was not him, but his dark alter ego. My parents received many phone calls fishing about my brother, so friends obviously wondered if he was the same person.

My bother (left) in happier times RIP   © Author

Chapter 15

An apprenticeship in beer drinking

An apprenticeship in beer drinking   © Pixababy

Upon returning to the student dump late one evening, we couldn't help but notice a delivery of new black plastic dustbins from the council, intended to replace the old, galvanised bins in the neighbourhood. Seizing the opportunity, we swiftly gathered five of them and stashed them in the hallway. A few days later, these bins were filled with fermenting mash for some homemade beer. Impatience got the better of us, and instead of waiting for the brew to be properly bottled, we resorted to dipping glasses directly into the mash and consuming it in its unfinished state. Unfortunately, this impulsive decision led to a series of severe hangovers for the next two weeks, until the beer was finally depleted.

This was the heyday of pub crawls, a time when the quest for a perfect pint of hand-pulled Tetley's bitter took centre stage in the bustling city centre and Cross Green pubs. This delightful trend gained momentum shortly after CAMRA (Campaign for Real Ale) successfully put a stop to the insidious invasion of keg beer from the breweries. With that victory under their belt, beer enthusiasts flocked to the vibrant streets, eager to explore the myriad of pubs that awaited them.

185

It's only the dirty ones we don't want - Philip Wilkinson

Oh, the city was a treasure trove of establishments, each boasting a unique and intriguing name that beckoned patrons inside. Let me regale you with a few of these

legendary watering holes. First, we had the Plasterers Arms, where locals and visitors alike sought solace in the comforting embrace of a well-pulled pint. Then there was The Black Horse, a mysterious haunt that whispered tales of dark secrets and hidden delights to those who dared venture through its doors.

Ah, the Fish Hut, a whimsical name that conjured visions of maritime adventures and salty tales. The White Swan, affectionately known as the Mucky Duck, where raucous laughter, ugly barfly transvestites and good cheer flowed as freely as the ale. Now, the Hampton, a word of caution to the unsuspecting traveller, for asking strangers for directions to this establishment could lead you astray into a labyrinth of confusion.

But the city didn't stop there in its pub-proud glory. We had the City of Mabgate, a place that embraced the spirit of community. The Bridgefield, where friendships were forged amidst clinking glasses and lively conversations. The Florence Nightingale, a tribute to the lady of the lamp, where the weary found solace in the company of kindred spirits. The Granville, a faded but still grand establishment where elegance and libations merged seamlessly. The Victoria, a regal name that hinted at a warm embrace and a royal welcome. And let us not forget the enigmatic

Headless Horse and Trumpet, named after the carving above its entrance, an ode to a horse with a mysteriously missing head and a trumpet held aloft.

Now to the joys of camping and pub hopping! There's something magical about planning your outdoor adventures to align perfectly with fantastic country pubs. It's like a match made in heaven, where the great outdoors and delightful libations intertwine to create unforgettable memories.

You see, our camping escapades weren't just about pitching tents and roasting marshmallows. No, no, they were epic journeys filled with laughter and, of course, the indulgence of good ol' liquid courage. Weekends away meant we could fully embrace the joys of the pub scene without worrying about having to drive back home the same evening. That meant one thing: the freedom to imbibe to our hearts' content.

As the ale flowed freely, we embraced the spirit of merriment, each of us quenching our thirst with approximately a gallon of ale on Friday alone. And that was just the warm-up! Come Saturday, we'd kickstart the day with a midday session, sipping our way through yet another gallon of liquid happiness. But wait, the day was far from over. As the evening sun painted the sky with its vibrant hues, we'd gather around for another round of laughter and libations, ensuring that our Saturday night was nothing short of legendary.

Now, as you can probably imagine, such indulgence often resulted in waking up the next morning with a reminder of the revelry that had transpired. Ah, the infamous hangover! But fear not, for we had a secret weapon to combat those pounding headaches and unsettled stomachs, a refreshing strip wash in a bone-chilling, freezing cold stream. Yes, the shock of icy water against our skin was like a miraculous cure for our ailing bodies, rejuvenating us with a jolt of invigoration

And to complete our morning ritual, we'd venture to the nearest greasy spoon café, where the sizzle of bacon, the aroma of fried goodness, and the comforting embrace of a full

It's only the dirty ones we don't want - Philip Wilkinson

English breakfast awaited us. With each bite, we felt the hangover slowly receding, replaced by contentment and a renewed sense of vitality.

.

© iStock

So, there you have it, our camping adventures were a delightful blend of outdoor escapades, pub discoveries, and the perfect excuse to indulge in ale-filled revelry. It was a recipe for unforgettable moments, shared laughter, and courage forged through shared experiences. Cheers to camping, pub hopping, and the joyous pursuit of the full English breakfast cure!

© Author

It's only the dirty ones we don't want - Philip Wilkinson

Then we have Eppy, the guy who bought a scooter rather than a motorcycle, we met him in the Whistlestop pub, Beeston Town Street one evening, he had some papers for Bilbo, when we arrived he was already waiting for us with a pint, after a while he stood saying I'll just go get those papers, they are under the seat of my scooter, he arrived back a few minutes later saying he would get them later, then he said, when I got to my scooter, half a dozen motorcyclists were peeing on it, so what did you do, we asked in amazement, I peed on it too, he replied.

One of the favourite pubs among pub crawlers was surprisingly not a Tetley's establishment but a Samuel Smith's house called the Eagle Tavern on North Street. While it still sells Sam Smith's beer, there was a brief period when the landlord was granted a ten-year license to operate as a free house. This immediately attracted a massive crowd, and the pub was bustling from opening to closing time every day. The beers on offer included Timothy Taylor's renowned brews such as Best Bitter, Dark Mild, Black Bees Stout, and Ramtam, which were not easily available in Leeds.

© Author

The adventures at the Eagle Tavern were legendary. Dart games were played down the middle of the tap room with benches on either side filled with people. Wearing a leather jacket was advisable to protect against wayward darts. I once had a dart fly into the air and land in the back of my hand. Student Ron and Postman Pat were enlisted (in exchange for free beer) to clear out the bottle and barrel store yard, which they then adorned with painted grass, sky, clouds, trees, and more. The landlord proudly erected a sign that read "Visit our beer garden."

The gents' toilets were a haven for high-quality graffiti, but the presence of a blackboard above the urinals kept most of it confined to one manageable location. Nevertheless, other areas were not spared. I remember one witty inscription on the blackboard that read "Also available in paperback," which sparked an idea.

Many of the wall writings were later compiled into books like "The Scrawl of the Wild (and other tales from the wall)." Here's just a sampling of the humorous and thought-provoking graffiti: "On the condom machine: Insert baby for refund." "On the chalk wall: Captain Kirk had three ears, left, right, and final front." "I'm into bestiality, flagellation, and necrophilia. Do you think I'm flogging a dead horse?" In one cubicle, a poetic line from John Cooper Clarke, a local punk poet, was scrawled.

> Sing a song of syphilis
> A fanny full of scabs
> Some of them were blackheads
> Some of them are crabs
> And when the blackheads opened
> The crabs begin to sing
> Oh, wasn't it a stupid sod who flopped his chopper in

And in the next cubicle, on the back of the door the following unattributed ditty; -

> It's no use standing on the seat
> The crabs in here can jump six feet
> If you think that's flipping high
> Go next door where the beggars fly

After several years, we found ourselves banned from the Eagle Tavern when one drunken evening, we decided it would be a good idea to steal the dartboard. We did return it the following day, but the damage was already done. We were no longer welcome.

Years had passed since my last visit to the pub, but on a scorching afternoon, a spontaneous impulse led me to pull over and step inside for a refreshing pint. As I entered the establishment, I couldn't help but notice the sparse gathering of loyal patrons huddled near the bar. Most of the hand pumps remained concealed, leaving only Tim Taylor's Ram Tam as the sole remaining option. To my dismay, the familiar and beloved chalkboard that once adorned the gents' toilets was absent, a sign of the ongoing renovations taking place in the lounge bar.

Curiosity piqued, I ordered a pint of Ram Tam and was taken aback by its price. The landlord, sensing my surprise, proceeded to enlighten me about the recent developments. It turned out that the esteemed Sam Smith's brewery had rescinded the pub's license to sell other brands, limiting their selection to their own offerings. Today marked the landlord's final day, and in a bittersweet gesture, he had decided to sell off the remaining beer and merchandise at half price.

As we engaged in conversation, the landlord expressed his melancholy over the impending changes that awaited the pub. He foresaw a future where its cherished character would be eroded, ultimately leading to a decline in sales. The very essence that had drawn patrons like me in the past was in jeopardy of being lost.

Sipping my pint of Ram Tam, I couldn't help but reflect on the passage of time and the inevitable transformations that come with it. The pub, once a bastion of tradition and camaraderie, stood on the precipice of change. The loyal drinkers, like stalwart sentinels, gathered, savouring their last moments within the familiar walls that had housed countless memories.

It was a bittersweet moment, sipping on that last pint of Ram Tam realizing the end of an era for the Eagle Tavern and the fond memories we had shared within its walls.

An unfortunate habit   © Author

The basement of the twins' home served as a versatile workshop, accommodating a wide array of projects ranging from bicycle repairs and motorbike maintenance to go-kart tinkering, DIY endeavours, and electronics experimentation. Frodo, having honed his skills as an apprentice engineer over several years, had developed a rather unfortunate habit during his work. Whenever he accidentally dropped an item he was working on, his instinct was to swiftly extend his foot to catch it, mitigating potential damage and preserving the progress invested in the object. This practice, sensible and effective when executed in a work environment, was primarily facilitated by his trusty steel-toed boots, offering protection and support.

However, one fateful day in the basement workshop, an unforeseen mishap occurred. The vice, a substantial and weighty casting, unexpectedly came loose from the workbench, hurtling toward the ground. Instantly and instinctively, Frodo extended his foot, relying on his ingrained reflex to soften the impending impact. Unfortunately, on that day, he had opted for lighter trainers instead of his customary steel-toed boots. The vice, devoid of mercy, unleashed a crushing blow upon his foot, leaving him in excruciating pain and grappling with the consequences of his reflexive action.

It's only the dirty ones we don't want - Philip Wilkinson

Watermill Rally badge 1977 © Author

Watermill Rally The Watermill Inn, near Pateley Bridge, October 1977, Pudsey MCC

In October 1977, I travelled to my very first motorcycle rally, my motorcycle was kitted out with tent and sleeping bag, pocket full of cash from my wages, ready for anything, or so I thought....

My first bike rally was a truly eye-opening experience. The Pudsey Motorcycle Club had spent years convincing the Watermill Inn in Pateley Bridge to host a rally. They had put in a tremendous effort to prepare the venue, including repairing the impressive 34-foot diameter water wheel, clearing the storage ponds, and getting the wheel to turn under water pressure once again. Although the wheel was no longer connected to any machinery, its revival was a captivating sight.

The watermill, formerly the watermill inn near Pateley Bridge © Author

It's only the dirty ones we don't want - Philip Wilkinson

Upon arriving at the rally on a Friday evening, I was immediately struck by the sight before me. The vast car park was filled with rows of motorcycles, and I estimated there were already over 1000 bikes present. Motorcycles continuously rode up and down the road between the inn and Pateley Bridge, creating a lively atmosphere. The snack van, Melvin's, was stationed near the base of the impressive water wheel, which turned in the background. People moved up and down the steps, carrying camping gear, as they accessed the field behind the pub.

Along the walkway running alongside the water race, connecting the storage ponds to the top of the wheel, about twenty motorcyclists waved their tankards of beer at arriving bikers.

Pudsey MCC had set up a tent and table to welcome and register attendees. I joined my friends and provided my name, the name of my club, my bike's registration number, and the distance I had travelled. Although there were awards for the furthest travelled individual and the most miles travelled by a group, my hopes were dashed when my friend pointed out that a club from Denmark was leading the list.

The registration fee charged by Pudsey MCC was (to the best of my recollection) £1.50, which included a lovely enamel badge featuring the mill and the rally's name and date, a bacon sandwich from Melvin's snack van, permission to park and camp until Sunday afternoon, access to a late bar on both Friday and Saturday nights, and live music. It was a great deal.

In total, around 2600 participants registered for the rally. The locals seemed to retreat, and the shops, cafes, and pubs in Pateley Bridge closed their doors. An overreaction in my opinion, however this led to the presence of a single police officer in the village to maintain law and order having a busy weekend, even though the main event was limited to the inn and its surroundings.

The landlord had prepared for the rally by stocking extra beer, including Theakston's bitter and Old Peculiar on tap. Many seasoned rally enthusiasts had brought their own pewter tankards, as glasses were often in short supply.

However, the demand for pints quickly overwhelmed the bar service, prompting the landlord to bring out several hundred pre-filled 6-pint metal jugs, which worked like a charm. During that time, beer was priced at around 28p a pint. As an apprentice earning £18 per week, I could afford about 30 pints after covering my expenses. This should have been sufficient for the weekend, but many surpassed that quantity between Friday evening and Sunday afternoon.

The finale event on Saturday night was a live band who rocked the evening, the last number, accompanied by a screening of an old sepia-toned film from the 1930s, "The Dance of the Seven Veils," set to the resounding anthem of Queen's "Fat Bottomed Girls" as the track ended, the girl in the film turned around, dropped the last veil, and had the words 'the end' written upon her voluptuous bottom. Well, let's just say it caused quite a ruckus. Fireworks were set off inside the pub, joining the cacophony of airhorns and football rattles. The place was absolute mayhem!

Now, picture this. There we were, queuing for the gents, and to our dismay, there were only three urinals. Desperate times call for desperate measures, right? So, we had a stroke of genius and started using the sinks to speed up the queue. Picture four motorcyclists at a time, relieving themselves in each of the sinks like it was a perfectly normal thing to do. Well, when the landlord himself walked in, peeing into one of the sinks, he took one look and quipped, "I guess I need to install more sinks in here.", as he spoke a banger exploded in one of the cubicles and a drunk motorcyclist fell foreword out of the cubicle unconscious on the floor, smoke rose from the cubicle and his hair, he had lit the firework with the intention of dropping it into the wate in the toilet, likely to result in the destruction of the porcelain, but had been so drunk he had not managed to let go, fortunately he was not injured, but it had been a close-run thing.

© Pixababy

Camping during these motorcycle rallies presented a range of experiences. Some campers opted to sleep out in the open, while others had tents of varying quality.

Unfortunately, not all the tents were well-maintained, which led to some problems. Fire hazards were a significant concern, with fires being lit outside many tents. Unfortunately, there were instances where these fires got out of control, resulting in some tents catching fire. Additionally, the use of Tilly-style lamps and cookers posed inherent dangers. These devices occasionally sprayed a stream of burning paraffin over a significant distance, leading to fires. It's important to note that such lamps and cookers were not recommended for use inside tents, however, when you have consumed large quantities of alcohol, and get the munchies, these rules were not followed. That weekend we only say two tents lost to cooking blazes, and fortunately no one was injured.

As it was close to bonfire night, the campers got together and built, then lit a massive bonfire on the field above the inn (now built upon with houses), the flames seemed to my mind to reach the stars, and sparks were many times higher. Fireworks were set off randomly around the campsite and you needed to be wary, as the users were mainly inebriated the firework could go in any direction.

It's only the dirty ones we don't want - Philip Wilkinson

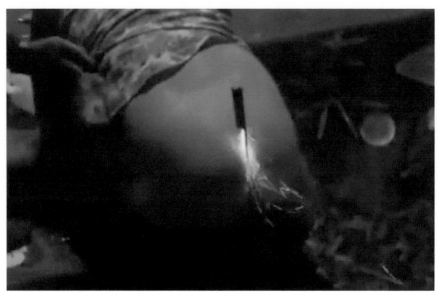

Image © https://www.joe.ie/uncategorized/video-using-your-arse-to-launch-a-bottle-rocket-is-a-contender-for-worst-idea-ever-43331

I spotted one idiot with his trousers round his ankles, bent over and a small rocket clenched between his butt cheeks, his mate lit the rocket, the rocket motor flames burning has bare bottom for a second as it was launching, as he cried out and jumped about on the spot, then the rocket took off, flew sideways across the whole camp, and landed in the mill pond. Others were running around the camp site holding air bombs or Roman candles and firing them at each other, then you got the real idiot, demonstrating how to hold a firework whilst lit, he clenched his fist around a banger and lit it, fortunately his mate grabbed his arm and twisted, the banger fell to the floor and exploded, just a second longer and he would not have been able to pick his nose with his right hand for the rest of his life.

A Standard Fireworks Air Bomb © Author

The Old Hill Inn, Chapel Le Dale   Image capture: Jun 2022 © 2023 Google

Beer, caving, and a goat barn

The XS250 had its fair share of adventures, but one trip that stands out is when a bunch of us decided to combine our love for caving and motorcycles for a beer-fuelled weekend at the Hill Inn in Chapel le Dale Ingleton. We set up our tents and the fun began. Frodo, tired of his makeshift cooking equipment, stumbled upon a Tilley-style stove. Now, these stoves usually ran on paraffin, with a pump to pressurise the fuel tank and turn it into a high-pressure gas for burning. However, Frodo's genius find ran on petrol drained from his bike. So, with cautious anticipation, we watched as Frodo lit the stove, half-expecting a fiery explosion. Surprisingly, it worked like a charm this time, much to our relief.

In the pub, amidst the merry crowd of cavers and walkers, a familiar sight caught our attention. They were using ice axes to hammer coins into the support poles for the bar. And if that wasn't enough, some of them were climbing through the cartwheels, roped to the alcoves, renowned as a rite of passage. Clearly, this was a bunch of cavers we had joined for the weekend!

The next day, we drove to Gaping Gill, where the Craven Pot Holing club had set up their annual winch to lower people 630 feet deep into the cave. The club insisted that the descent was free but charged for the ascent. Naturally, we tried to argue that we only needed the descent since we planned to find our own way out. Alas, our clever reasoning didn't earn us a free pass.

Gaping Ghyll Pot, Yorkshire   © BBC

As night fell, the inn was bursting at the seams with rowdy patrons. That's when the landlord made an announcement, suggesting we relocate to the barn a few hundred yards behind the inn. Like a group of eager rodents following the Pied Piper, we followed him to the barn, which had been transformed into a makeshift party venue. Straw bales served as seating, a basic bar was set up, and there was even a DJ spinning tunes. But the barn had a quirky feature—a ground floor and a first floor.

Just below the ceiling, a row of timber poles had been strategically placed at four-foot intervals and about nine inches below the ceiling, presumably for structural support.

Among the revellers, one loud and obnoxious guy stood out. He had a knack for knocking over drinks, annoying the DJ with his terrible song requests, and generally causing trouble.

As the night progressed and the drinks flowed, some brave lads began to climb and traverse the telegraph poles, showing off their acrobatic skills.

Of course, Mr. Loudmouth couldn't resist the chance to impress everyone. He decided to swim across the poles, Olympic style. However, his little stunt backfired, quite literally. As he pulled himself forward, his trousers and pants came tumbling down, leaving his manhood on full display, swinging from the barn's roof. The crowd couldn't help but notice his less-than-impressive appendage and erupted in a football supporter-style chant. He quickly pulled himself up, embarrassed and significantly quieter for the rest of the night.

Finally, after some persuasive negotiation (and probably a few pints), we managed to convince the inn landlord to let us sleep in the old goat barn opposite the inn's entrance.

The old goat barn opposite the Old Hill Inn   © Roger Templeman

This small stone building had a pitched roof, a single door leading to the central section, and stone shelves on either side for food storage. The shelves could accommodate about eight people in their sleeping bags, but the top bunk was always a risky proposition. With no edge to keep you from toppling out, falling onto the floor was a constant concern. A perilous sleep indeed!

Photo inside the Hill Inn barn, the bars just below the ceiling are visible   © Bilbo

© Leodis

The Gaiety

The Gaiety pub was a lunch time strip club venue at this time, it had gained a reputation as "Britain's most notorious". I cover more from this era in my book Alarming Stories, Tales of an apprentice intruder alarm engineer.

The Leeds Teddy Boys in the Gaiety © https://www.edwardianteddyboy.com/page39.html

According to Leeds Live website The Gaiety, on Roundhay Road, Harehills, straddled Gipton Beck and so was designed with a central archway under which the beck ran through a culvert. A bridge connected the two sides of the pub.

It's only the dirty ones we don't want - Philip Wilkinson

Inside were five bars. On the ground floor was Roundhay Public Bar, which could fit up to 400 people, another bar, and a restaurant. Upstairs was The Variety Room where live entertainment and private functions took place. On the bridge itself, was another bar, The Vaudeville. The decor, meanwhile, harked back to the Edwardian period.

By the 1970s, the pub was in one of Leeds's principal red light areas. Yorkshire Ripper Peter Sutcliffe picked up two of his victims, Emily Jackson, and Irene Richardson, from outside the Gaiety where they were soliciting.

Extract from https://www.leeds-live.co.uk/news/history/gallery/leeds-lost-super-pub-became-24039916

Monday nights at the Gaiety, a pub located near Chapeltown's red light district in Leeds, were known for their rock 'n' roll-themed events. These rock n roll nights attracted a crowd of people dressed in 1950s-style teddy boy outfits. The music played during those nights was carefully selected from that era, creating a fantastic atmosphere for all attendees.

After one of these lively dance evenings, we decided to continue the festivities by heading across the street to the Rendezvous café, another notorious spot in Leeds. It was there that Teddy, perhaps caught up in the moment, engaged in negotiations with an aging prostitute present at the café. He jokingly tried to arrange a deal involving all of us, including the girls present. However, when the prostitute realised, he wasn't being serious, she became infuriated. In a fit of rage, she started throwing cups of tea and coffee at us while unleashing a barrage of profanity.

© Pixababy

It was an unexpected and chaotic turn of events, but it added to the wild and unforgettable experiences associated with those Monday nights at the Gaiety and the surrounding area.

The Gaiety whist itself achieving the accolade of the most notorious pub in the UK, it was not the only pub in Leeds that was renowned for it's notoriety, the Viaduct in Lower Briggate, the Fforde Green Roundhay Road, The Whip pub in Duncan Street, alongside the Mucky Duck (White Swan), Brannigans Bar in the Calls, The Brougham Arms (The Duck and Drake since 1985) Kirgate all vied for the top title and were not considered safe for lone drinkers or the wrong groups.

It's only the dirty ones we don't want - Philip Wilkinson

The Travellers Rest, Halton   © Betty Longbottom

One of our regular haunts was the Travellers Rest in Halton, many a session and much driving home whilst seriously under the influence occurred from here

The Florence Nightingale   © Betty Longbottom

The Florence Nightingale, opposite St James's Hospital, many pints were bought to take up onto the ward visiting mates with broken limbs following motorcycle mishaps

Chapter 16 – 1978

The bike rally era

Me with the XS250 setting off to then Monkey Hanger rally   © Bilbo

An unlucky bike

Around this time, I made a significant purchase, an exciting new red Suzuki XS250. It was the first-ever four-stroke twin from Suzuki, and it came with a sleek white fiberglass cockpit mini fairing designed to reduce wind drag. I was thrilled with my new bike and having recently discovered bike rallies I couldn't wait to ride it.

However, just a few days later, as I was on my way to meet with the Thursday club at the twins' house, my joyride took an unfortunate turn. A car, failing to notice me approaching, pulled out of a side street, turning right across my path. I had no choice but to lay my bike on the ground and skid along the road until my wheels collided with the car, near the driver's door position. The bike was in terrible shape, and I had injured my left hand, breaking a finger, and my legs were badly grazed.

An ambulance arrived to take me to the hospital while the police took care of recovering the bike. It was disheartening to realise that I would be making monthly payments for a bike that would spend the next ten months in the garage, awaiting insurance coverage for repairs. Finally, after what felt like an eternity, I got my bike back. However, just three weeks later, as Eric and I were driving to Woodhouse to meet another friend, a car crashed into the back of my bike at a speed of around 30 mph. Once again, the bike was rendered unrideable and left in a mangled mess.

A close up image of the Yamaha XS250 c1977   © Classic Super Bikes

It seemed that my purchase had been plagued by misfortune, I then made a significant discovery, the petrol tank, despite having a locking cap, contained handfuls of metal filings, these had collected in the carburettors pitting the ports and airways and no doubt had caused damage within the cylinders and valves comprising the top end of the engine. I made the difficult decision to sell the bike shortly after it had been repaired. It was an unfortunate series of events that led me to part ways with my beloved Suzuki XS250 after only about 18 months.

It's only the dirty ones we don't want - Philip Wilkinson

Hartlepool rally badge © Author

Hartlepool Rally

Hartlepool Rally, Trimdon, March 1978, Monkey Hanger MCC

The rally, normally held by the Hartlepool and District MCC would this year be hosted by the Monkey Hangers MCC, set in a field opposite a pub in Trimdon, Hartlepool. The area was steeped in history, and the club had pulled out all the stops to make it a memorable event. They secured a fantastic pub as the main venue, a field across the road for camping, and even arranged coaches to take us to the legendary "End of the World Disco and Laser Show." The stage was set for a wild time.

Back at the pub, the atmosphere was buzzing, and the beer was flowing freely. However, the landlord, in his wisdom, had acquired a stash of substandard glasses with sharp edges. It was like drinking from a weapon rather than a vessel of joy. But that didn't dampen our spirits. The evening progressed with the customary round of bawdy songs, with folks jumping on tables, fully immersing themselves in the spirit of the rally. And then, out of the blue, the group next to us decided to moon us. Well, we couldn't let that slide, so we returned the favour, leading to a hilarious back-and-forth of mooning antics. One lad, unfortunately, hadn't paid much attention to personal hygiene, and his skid marks became the talk of the night, inspiring football-like chants about our superior wiping skills.

As the pub began to run dry, the coaches arrived to transport us to the club. But before we left, we had a glass-throwing competition in the car park to bid farewell
to those shoddy glasses. It was a cathartic moment, watching them shatter and disappear into oblivion.

Arriving at the club, we found a lively scene. The bar was conveniently positioned at one end, a spacious dance floor occupied the centre, and tables and chairs were scattered around. The "End of the World Disco and Laser Show" had commenced, although, to our dismay, the laser wasn't quite cooperating. Thankfully, the DJ had selected a playlist that perfectly matched the vibe of the rally. From the timeless tunes of "House of the Rising Sun" to the infectious beats of "Black Betty" and the soulful melodies of Judie Tzuke, Queen, Deep Purple, Rainbow, and even a sprinkle of Led Zeppelin, the dance floor was a haven for merriment.

It's only the dirty ones we don't want - Philip Wilkinson

As the night ended, and the club's beer supply dwindled, Bilbo, never one to back down from a challenge, made sure to squeeze in a couple of pints before last orders. Meanwhile, some of the first timers, who had indulged a bit too much in the festivities, were being unceremoniously dragged back and forth through the beer-soaked dance floor. It was a chaotic yet strangely amusing sight, perfectly encapsulating the spirit of the rally.

Photo of me (right) from the rally

It's only the dirty ones we don't want - Philip Wilkinson

The next day, our thirst for beer was unquenchable as we prepared for the lunchtime session. The pub had received a fresh delivery, but the staff were ill-prepared for the onslaught of motorcyclists pouring in through the doors. The bar was packed, nine deep, with tankard-waving bikers, all clamouring for service and ordering rounds of 10 pints or more.

Being in the front row, pressed against the bar amidst the chaos, I suddenly found myself unable to contain a bout of flatulence brought on by the whirlwind of the past 24 hours. With a discreet release, I unleashed an SBD (silent but deadly) and feigned innocence, hoping that perhaps it would help disperse the crowd at the bar. Little did I know, the odour that filled the air was beyond description, and instead of thinning out the crowd, it seemed to exacerbate the situation as even the bar staff left in search of fresher air.

Returning triumphantly to our group of club members with a tray of full tankards, Spawny couldn't help but notice the effect my silent emission had on the hardened motorcyclists at the bar. Pointing out their visibly green complexions, he jokingly asked, "Was that you responsible for that potent aroma?" With a nod and a grin, I confirmed that I was indeed the culprit, eliciting laughter and a mix of admiration and disbelief from our fellow riders.

As the day progressed and the pub regained its equilibrium, we continued to revel in each other's company, swapping stories, toasting to new adventures, and savouring the communal spirit that only a group of motorcyclists on an adventure could understand.

Photo of me (right) from the rally © Bilbo

It's only the dirty ones we don't want - Philip Wilkinson

My badge from the rally © Author

The Dark Wet Cold and Gloomy Rally

Wincham, Cheshire 1978, WMCC

I do not have much recollection of this rally and cannot find any details from the internet to fill in the blanks, what I do recall is it was very cold, by late Saturday night a gale had blown in, this lasted most of the night, we spent a lot of time clinging onto our tents and suffered damage to several. In the morning when the wind subsided the rally campsite field was best described as chaos.

This was the era pre sewn in groundsheets and we noticed that many tents were missing, simply blown away, the motorcyclists losing their tents had been so inebriated that they simply had not noticed they were missing, torn to shreds on nearby barbed wire. They must have suffered some hangovers that morning, waking with no tent, soaked to the skin and no respite until the pub opened.

It's only the dirty ones we don't want - Philip Wilkinson

Picking fights with the wrong guy   © Pixababy

Teddy, with his distinct 1950s Ted appearance complete with a blue suede jacket, matching trousers with silk trim, DA, and blue suede shoes, certainly stood out from the crowd. People often made fun of him in pubs and other places, unaware of his true strength. During the day, Teddy worked lifting hydraulic arms for JCBs onto grinding machines, building up impressive muscles in the process.

There were instances when individuals mistakenly thought Teddy was an easy target for trouble. Little did they know, they had picked on the wrong person. On multiple occasions, Teddy would leave the pub only to return alone a few seconds later. It became a regular sight. Teddy took to wearing large rings on all his fingers, these acted as a knuckle duster but did not attract attention from the boys in blue investigating several of the fights he had been involved in. One night, as Teddy, I, and Erotic were walking through the Merrion Centre in Leeds, we found ourselves surrounded by a group of tough individuals from West Africa who had singled out Teddy for trouble. In complete silence, the group circled us and confronted Teddy, leaving Erotic and I frightened for what might happen next. In a matter of moments, without uttering a word, Teddy swiftly incapacitated four of them, leaving them lying unconscious on the ground. Two others were nursing injuries to their testicles, teeth, and noses. The remaining individuals scattered, fleeing from the scene.

It was a clear demonstration that Teddy was not someone to be trifled with. Despite his unique appearance and friendly demeanour, he possessed a formidable strength that demanded respect.

It's only the dirty ones we don't want - Philip Wilkinson

Notted Bear rally badge © Author

Notted Bear Rally

Litchfield, 1978, North Midland Motorcycle Club

This is a rally I really cannot recall, sorry, I have the badge in my hand, the spelling is correct, notted, the badge has heraldry on a shield motif, the heraldry has a rope in a knot over a crown on the left side, and the motto, in English "The Knot Unites", on the right half, a depiction of a bear, chained to a tree along with the motto, this time I believe French, "Mon Sanz Droict", which translates to English as exactly the same?

A fan calling himself Jasper has posted the following on the LPMCC website https://www.lpmcc.net/rallies/rally_nottedbear.htm

It was held at Alrewas just up the road from Lichfield. My old club the North Midland Motorcycle Club ran it. It did move for a while to Market Bosworth Rugby Club. Everyone should remember the goat fenced off at the side of the field and the scooter throwing. As an aside what happened to the two rally fanzines Rally Review and Big Bollards? Dave Richmond's column and dedicated rally pages in MCN and Motorcycle Weekly? The memories just come flooding back. I could write all night about the rallies but probably end up homeless though. Only do a couple or three a year now.

REMEMBER-THERE'S ONLY ONE WAY OF LIFE.

Regards to all.

It's only the dirty ones we don't want - Philip Wilkinson

Brontosaurus rally badge ©Author

Brontosaurus Rally

Northamptonshire Grand Canal, 1978, Leicester Phoenix MCC

Just arriving at the Brontosaurus Rally   © Bilbo

Once again, a cold weekend, as I recall it was minus 4 degrees and the tents along with £5 nylon summer sleeping bags were not up to these sub-zero rallies at the time, made it more fun though as you felt like you had survived an expedition.

It's only the dirty ones we don't want - Philip Wilkinson

The pub was about 2 miles from the field we camped in which was inconvenient, as I recall, Mutt, one of the Aire Valley MCC remained sober-ish and ferried us back and forth, it was OK going to the pub, the return journey after a gallon or more of ale was a different tale, Mutt took great delight in setting off fast leaving his inebriated pillion sat in the road waiting for him to return, needless to say, everyone relying on him for a lift, was polite to him most of that evening.

Two of the lads attending the rally got a lift to the pub in the organisers land rover on the Saturday, unfortunately on the trip back, one of them suffered with incontinence badly, he was seen washing his pants in the canal which was partially frozen.

The Land Rover spent many hours that weekend ferrying everyone back and forth from the camp site, it was a welcome sight after waiting in the freezing cold for your turn, but with no heating in the back, it was not a comfortable ride by any means, just above walking in my opinion after a few runs over the weekend.

At one point, a lot of motorcyclists had formed a circle in the field and were cheering, having a look over to see at what was happening, one guy was taking photographs of his mate getting a blow job from his girlfriend, classy. I wondered how he would get the film developed.

It's only the dirty ones we don't want - Philip Wilkinson

Moon rally badge © Author

ACU Moon Rally

Location Rising Moon Pub, Hyde, Manchester, May 1978, Stalybridge MCC

All I can recall of the Moon Rally is a few sketchy details, I recall Mutt on Saturday morning staggering about coughing his guts out, blowing his nose and washing his face in the stream, Spawny commented, does he always take this much getting started in a morning. Worse for wear he returned to his tent for some more sleep, but this was a bike rally, no time for sleeping we thought, so Frodo, backed his bike up to the tent, poking the exhaust through the slightly open zip, he started the engine and revved the bike a few times, this did not work however, so Spawny tried another tactic, tying his bike to Mutt's sleeping bag, then starting his bike, he took Mutt for a drag around the field. I don't know about you, but I reckon waking with a severe hangover was one thing, but with friends like these, who needed enemies.

By this stage of rally going, it was required that each biker had their own tankards, this eliminated issues such as glasses shortages, or worse plastic festival glasses. In the main they were made of pewter, glass bottomed tankards, originally introduced to prevent the unsuspecting from accidentally accepting the Kings shilling dropped into their drinks, were a poor choice as they tended to crack when the soft pewter tankard got distorted or dropped, however, like most engineers, we had developed a wheeze, un-soldering the bottom of the tankard and resoldering it flush with the base, meant that each now hold about one and a quarter pints.

I recently came across a film of the 1979 Moon Rally, the link page says "At the Moon Rally, organised by Stalybridge Motorcycle Club, 900 bikers meet up at the Rising Moon pub in Hyde, Greater Manchester, for a weekend of riding and talking bikes, rock music and drinking. And, of course, the sport of piston-flinging, the joys of the muddy campsite, the flimsy canvas portaloos, and a hearty fried breakfast to ease the hangover, which all make for a memorable weekend." You can view the 25-minute film at the link below, it really is a blast from the past

https://player.bfi.org.uk/free/film/watch-the-moon-rally-1979-online

212

It's only the dirty ones we don't want - Philip Wilkinson

Penny Farthing rally badge © Author

Penny Farthing Rally

Sorry location unknown, Penny Farthing MCC and The Lynton Flyers MCC, 1978

This was the first, and last Penny Farthing Rally, held in 1978, only 200 badges were made, 600 turned up to the rally, and I was one of the lucky few who got a badge.

All the members of both clubs were in the RAF at Linton on Ouse near York, the rally featured a rock and roll disco that ran continuously through the weekend, the site had been prepared with a covered area made from about 20 parachutes supported with poles, innovative in its time.

Several of the Are Valley MCC attended, as usual we drank a lot of beer, and even a few shorts and cocktails, this was about the time when Baileys Irish liquor was available, the original recipe had a high level of real cream in its make-up, this meant that once opened, the bottle must be consumed in three weeks, it was not uncommon for pubs to decline the sale of a glass of Baileys, due to its short shelf life, on this occasion, there was no hesitation to open the bottle, serving it as a chaser with beers, we cleared the whole bottle in just two rounds.

It's only the dirty ones we don't want - Philip Wilkinson

Thursday's in Whitelock's © Author

Our Thursday meetings for a period started out with a pint of Youngers No.3 in Whitelock's, the oldest and most renowned pub in Leeds, holds a special place in the city's history. Originally established as the Turks Head in 1715, it came under the ownership of the Whitelock's family in the 1880s. Tucked away in Turks Head Yard off Briggate, stepping into Whitelock's feels like stepping back in time.

As you enter the yard, you are greeted by benches and barrels serving as makeshift tables. However, the true time-travel experience begins when you cross the pub's threshold. Described by John Betjeman as "the very heart of Leeds," Whitelock's is one of the few remaining old-style luncheon bars found in select cities.

According to CAMRA's pub heritage website, the pub has been licensed since 1715 and was taken over by John Lupton Whitelock in 1867. Whitelock initiated its transformation in the 1880s, and in 1895, local architects Waite & Sons carried out a significant remodelling. In 1897, electric lighting was installed, and a revolving searchlight at the Briggate entrance advertised the establishment. During the 1890s, it became known as Whitelock's First City Luncheon Bar and earned a reputation as an up-market venue.

The interior of Whitlock's showcases a unique combination of a long, narrow layout that reflects the plot's medieval origins and a splendid late-Victorian design featuring dark wood panelling, dazzling copper and brass work, and a remarkable collection of antique mirrors. This exceptional environment has remained largely unchanged for over a century. The tile-fronted bar counter itself is a rarity.

Whitelock's continues to thrive today, serving as a bustling pub and dining establishment. While the rear section no longer functions as a separate dining area, it still retains its charm. The Turks Head Bar, located at the top of the yard, reopened in January 2016 after undergoing refurbishment and now offers craft keg beers.

It's only the dirty ones we don't want - Philip Wilkinson

Many memorable nights out have started with a determined effort to reach the bar and order a pint. Finding a seat is often a challenge due to the pub's enduring popularity. Instead, patrons often find themselves standing in the yard, savouring their drinks, and embracing the lively atmosphere. Whitelock's remains a beloved institution, treasured for its rich history, character, and unwavering popularity among locals and visitors alike.

© Author

Just looking at the photo of the bar, it makes me want to order a Youngers No.3 which was the tipple of choice whenever we visited, as I recall, you were very lucky to get a seat as it was always packed out especially on a Thursday and weekend, eventually they opened another bar further up Turks Head Yard, but it was a pastiche of the real thing, far preferable to be in this bar.

© Author

Picture of the Aire Valley MCC campsite, Much Wenlock   © Bilbo

Air Valley MCC trip to The George & Dragon Inn Much Wenlock

Beer in this era was moving rapidly over to keg as it could be set up without any training, did not go sour and was less wasteful, however we all preferred draft and went to the ends of the earth to enjoy as much of this as possible, hearing that the George & Dragon inn, Much Wenlock had started a micro brewery we decided this was cause for an expedition, a large contingent of the Aire Valley MCC set off to camp nearby and endeavour to drink the pub dry in a weekend.

On arrival we had warned the inn of our planned trip, and they were more than accommodating of us, providing access to a local field for our camping area, laying on a food service and brewing extra beer.

Drinking went on for most of the weekend, and the inn even sold its ale in stoneware quart bottles which we purchased for late night revelry on the campsite, I even managed to bring one home, I think the bottle is still somewhere in the loft.

I mentioned earlier that the engineers from Rose Forgroves had purchased a Wendy house for a joke tent, and many of you readers would be forgiven for not believing we camped in it, Much Wenlock was it's first outing.

It's only the dirty ones we don't want - Philip Wilkinson

Image of the Wendy house at the George & Dragon inn © Bilbo

Image of myself with my girlfriend at the George & Dragon inn © Bilbo

It's only the dirty ones we don't want - Philip Wilkinson

Getting a bit worse for wear now © Bilbo

Don't spill any lads © Bilbo

It's only the dirty ones we don't want - Philip Wilkinson

Bottoms up – using a pewter tankard ensured you always had a decent 'glass'   © Bilbo

That's me again on the right   © Bilbo

It's only the dirty ones we don't want - Philip Wilkinson

Watermill rally badge © Author

Watermill Rally second year

The Watermill Inn, near Pateley Bridge, October 1978, Pudsey MCC

© Author

October had arrived, the final rally of the year was an unforgettable one the highly anticipated second Pudsey MCC Watermill Inn rally. The folks at Pudsey MCC had quite the struggle convincing the landlord to host another rally after the chaos caused during the first one in the village of Pateley Bridge. Eventually, they struck a deal for a limited number, invite-only event with a maximum of 600 lucky souls. Invitations were sent to the clubs who had attended the previous year's rally, and the Aire Valley MCC eagerly awaited their four precious tickets.

But then, something unexpected happened. The landlord accepted an offer to sell the pub and leave town just a few weeks after the event. And what did he decide? Well, he proclaimed that this would be his grand finale, a last hurrah, and that the rally should now be open to all. Oh boy, little did he know what he was getting himself into.

It's only the dirty ones we don't want - Philip Wilkinson

As we arrived on that Friday, the sight that greeted us was jaw-dropping. There were approximately 2,500 motorcycles parked in the car park and adjacent field. Bikes were zooming back and forth between Pateley Bridge and Stean, taking advantage of the twisty roads perfectly suited for motorcycling. This weekend, the rally drew in nearly 4,000 bikers, and let me tell you, the poor old watermill pub was not prepared for such an influx. It was like trying to fit an elephant into a phone booth!

When it came to beer, there were only two options available, a crate of 12 bottles of Newcastle Brown Ale or a 6-pint jug of Theakston's Old Peculiar. And boy, were those jugs being continuously pulled to meet the unquenchable demand. We decided to go big and bought a dozen crates of Newcastle and the same number of jugs of Old P. We perched ourselves on the crates, swigging from the jugs and replenishing them as needed from the bottles. Classy, I know.

Just like last year, a live band rocked the evening, accompanied by a screening of an old sepia-toned film from the 1930s, "The Dance of the Seven Veils," set to the resounding anthem of Queen's "Fat Bottomed Girls." Well, let's just say it caused quite a ruckus. Fireworks were once again set off inside the pub, joining the cacophony of airhorns and football rattles. The place was absolute mayhem!

Now, picture this. There we were, queuing for the gents, and to our dismay, there were only three urinals. Desperate times call for desperate measures, right? So, we had a stroke of genius and started using the sinks to speed up the queue. Picture four motorcyclists at a time, relieving themselves in each of the sinks like it was a perfectly normal thing to do. Well, when the landlord himself walked in, peeing into one of the sinks, he took one look and quipped, "I guess I need to install more sinks in here."

Meanwhile, poor Pateley Bridge had completely shut down. The shops had even gone to the extreme of boarding up their windows in anticipation of the madness. The lone police officer in town had his hands full, and even the greasy spoon café had locked up tight. The town was in survival mode!

In the dark hours of the night, as we walked back from Pateley Bridge to the pub, we heard a peculiar sound. Lo and behold, it was the unmistakable rumble of a dump truck starting up. And what did we see? A dumper truck filled with a dozen or so daring motorcyclists, cruising down the road without a care in the world and without any lights on. Talk about living life on the edge!

And then, as the rally ended on that Sunday lunchtime, something bizarre happened on the maintenance bridge that linked the mill ponds with the overshot mill wheel. About twenty motorcyclists at a time decided to gather there. What were they doing, you ask? Well, most of them were taking a piss, turning the bridge into an impromptu waterfall. But, to our shock, on one occasion, we witnessed a dozen daredevils taking things a step further. Let's just say it wasn't a pretty sight to behold.

Oh, and let's not forget the delightful surprise I found in the morning. It seemed that some anonymous partygoer had decided to use my helmet as their personal vomit receptacle. Nice, right? Naturally, I did what any sensible person would do, I rinsed it in the stream. But no matter what I tried; I just couldn't get rid of that lovely scent of regurgitation. After a few weeks of futile attempts, I finally gave in and bought a brand-new helmet. Ah, the things we do for a fresh-smelling head!

So, there you have it, the outrageous and unforgettable tale of the second Pudsey MCC Watermill Inn rally. It was a weekend filled with wild revelry, questionable bathroom choices, and unexpected surprises. Sometimes, you just must embrace the madness and let the good times roll!

Getting into trouble, Manx Grand Pris 1981   © Bilbo

Regrettably, Pansy, a member of our group, developed a misguided sense of security in our company, particularly because of Teddy's formidable presence. He believed that he could deliberately provoke confrontations, knowing that we would come to his aid and help him fight his way out of trouble. This led to several incidents, including one memorable encounter involving a group of twenty scooter riders wearing parkas.

After enduring numerous situations of this nature, we collectively reached a decision. The next time Pansy found himself in trouble, we would refrain from intervening and allow him to face the consequences of his actions on his own. It didn't take long for this resolution to be tested. One evening, as we were gathered at the Adelphi pub, the pub quiz began, an annoyance we typically endured due to its intrusive volume and lack of interest to us. Frustrated by the noise, Pansy reached up and severed the cable to the speaker, abruptly cutting off the quizmaster's voice for half the pub.

It's only the dirty ones we don't want - Philip Wilkinson

Immediately, the bouncers were alerted to the disturbance and apprehended Pansy with the wire cutters still in his possession. They promptly escorted him outside, and the full extent of what transpired afterward remains somewhat unclear to us. However, Pansy later revealed that during the altercation, one of the bouncers had repeatedly jumped on his head, resulting in him sustaining severe injuries. Therefore, he lost 90% of his vision in one eye and had to be hospitalised for a brain injury. Remarkably, this traumatic event seemed to have a transformative effect on Pansy's demeanour. He became a much more agreeable person to drink with, and the incident appeared to have brought about a change in his character.

© https://www.yorkshireeveningpost.co.uk/heritage-and-retro/retro/the-whip-memories-of-a-men-only-leeds-pub-3611522

An encounter with the Leeds Ted's and Satan's slaves

The Whip pub on Duncan Street Leeds was a pub you did not go to alone, the favoured location for the Teddy boys meets, and the Satan's slaves.

One Saturday morning, I received a request from Teddy to give him a ride into town. Teddy had suffered a motorcycle accident that resulted in both of his legs being broken, and his lower body was encased in plaster from his ankles up to his groin. It was no easy task, but we managed to get him onto the pillion seat with his

crutches, and we embarked on our journey. It was interesting to note that Teddy had never ridden a bike with an engine larger than 125CC before. As we started our

ride, I accelerated quicky to impress Teddy with the performance of my bike, at 70MPH. Suddenly, a cat darted across the road, narrowly escaping the wheels of our motorcycle. It was nothing short of a miracle that the feline managed to survive. It appeared as if the cat

had exhausted nearly all its nine lives in just a single day. The incident left us momentarily stunned before we continued our way.

It's only the dirty ones we don't want - Philip Wilkinson

Our destination was the Whip pub in Leeds, where we eventually arrived and found a spot to park in the back alley. As we entered the pub, we were greeted by the sight of a dozen heavily modified motorcycles, affectionately known as "hogs," commonly associated with Hell's Angels. These bikes were stripped down, lacking proper exhaust systems, and emblazoned with additions such as Germanic cross shaped taillights and mirrors. Making our way to the back room of the pub, we noticed a clear divide among the occupants. One half of the room was occupied by Teddy's friends and their girlfriends, while the other half housed members of a group (chapter) called The Satan's Slaves.

The Leeds Teddy Boys in the Whip pub
© https://www.edwardianteddyboy.com/page39.html

© Pixababy

The Leeds Teddy Boys in the Whip pub

To my surprise, I noticed that there were several double-barrelled shotguns propped against the tables that were reserved for the angels.

It was a disconcerting sight, a stark reminder that these were individuals not to be taken lightly, you would not want to find yourself alone in the confines of a pub restroom with any of this crowd. However, I was relieved to discover that the atmosphere remained peaceful and devoid of any tensions that day. Both groups coexisted without incident, demonstrating a temporary harmony within the walls of the pub.

225

It's only the dirty ones we don't want - Philip Wilkinson

After spending some time inside, I stepped out into the open air. From the vantage point outside the pub, I witnessed a spectacle that caught me off guard. The members of Satan's Slaves were mounting their hogs, with the pillion riders gripping their shotguns tightly, pointing them skyward. They embarked on their journey, defying the traffic norms by riding up New Market Street in the opposite direction of the one-way system. It was evident that none of them bothered to wear helmets, and it was highly unlikely that their bikes were properly insured, tested, or taxed. Strangely enough, the police were present, yet they opted to observe the proceedings and turn a blind eye to these flagrant violations.

Teddy's 18ᵗʰ birthday   © Author

On the momentous occasion of Teddy's 18th birthday, we decided to kick off the celebrations at one of our cherished local pubs, the Old White Hart in Beeston. As our group arrived, we eagerly gathered at the bar and placed a substantial order for pints of our favourite beverages. The friendly barman, intrigued by our jovial spirits, couldn't help but inquire about the reason for our festivities.

With a mischievous grin, one of us replied, "It's Teddy's birthday today!" The barman, who happened to be the pub's landlord, extended his congratulations to Teddy, and proceeded to ask. "Which birthday is this for you?" he inquired. Teddy, without missing a beat, proudly responded, "My 18th."

To our surprise, the landlord's face lit up with recognition and a touch of amusement. "You little bugger," he exclaimed, "you've been a regular in here for over 4 years!" It turned out that Teddy had frequented the Old White Heart even before he had reached the legal drinking age. The revelation sparked laughter and playful banter among us, as we realised that Teddy had been a familiar face in the pub long before he officially came of age.

The notorious 148 club   © Pixababy

Ah, the legendary 148 club on Chapeltown Road in Leeds. It was a venue shrouded in infamy, and for some reason, I had never even heard of it. But fate had other plans, and there we were, squeezed into the back of a transit van as it pulled up outside this notorious establishment. Disembarking from the van, we paid our entrance fees and received our tickets, clueless about what awaited us inside.

Stepping into the club, we were greeted by a small stage with rows of chairs facing it. Naturally, our first stop was the bar, where we ordered a round of pints. I vividly remember that on this evening, our group consisted of about a dozen lads and two girls, and to our surprise, we seemed to be the only patrons in the entire club. Taking our seats, I happened to glance at our entry tickets and noticed a rather unexpected inclusion - pie and peas! One of the lads, ever vigilant, brought this to the attention of the perplexed bar staff. They exchanged bewildered looks, clearly unaware of such an offer. Eventually, the management was called over, and they confirmed that the offer was indeed valid. However, there was a catch - they only had eight pies left in stock. The rest of us would have to settle for sausage rolls and peas. Talk about an unconventional dining experience!

© Pixababy

So, there we were, munching on our pie and peas during a strip club, watching the mesmerizing performances on stage (some of which even ended up on my mates' laps), all the while trying to avoid spilling our beers and sitting uncomfortably close to my girlfriend.

Meanwhile, one of the lads was nowhere to be found. He and his girlfriend had sought the privacy of the trusty transit van parked outside the club. When they finally re-joined us inside, I jokingly told him to ask for their portion of pie and peas, as per his ticket. Little did I know, the club management had already dealt with this matter. Their tickets had been unceremoniously modified with an indelible felt-tip pen, and the offer was swiftly taken off the table.

Ah, the absurdity of it all! It was a night filled with unexpected twists, peculiar dining arrangements, raucous entertainment, and an unforgettable blend of laughter and disbelief. The 148 club had certainly left its mark on our memories, ensuring that we would forever recall the time we dined on pie and peas during a strip club escapade.

It's only the dirty ones we don't want - Philip Wilkinson

The Tan Hill Inn   © Shutterstock

On the previous Thursday, our group had planned an exciting trip up to the Tan Hill Inn, known as Britain's highest pub. We arrived at the pub after dark and decided to warm up with a few drinks before setting up our tents for the night.

The Tan Hill Inn takes pride in its continuous fire in the main bar, which offered a comforting and welcoming sight after our long ride through various towns and scenic routes. We started our journey in Otley, then made our way through Pateley Bridge, Grassington, Kilnsey Crag, Buckden, Yockenthwaite, Hawes, and finally crossed the Buttertubs pass to Thwaite. The road continued as a switchback over the moors until we reached the inn.

Neil and Sue Hanson had just taken over management the pub and in doing so, rescued it from the rat-infested run-down place into the pub most of us remember, Neil has published a book about this adventure which I highly recommend, The Inn at the Top, they made us welcome on arrival, and even said we were welcome to camp, and it was free.

After enjoying a few beers and grabbing a bite to eat from the pub's walker's fare, I can highly recommend Sue's giant Yorkshire pudding filled with lamb and gravy, we set up our tents and returned inside. Fuelled by the jovial atmosphere, we engaged in singing some rather cheeky and humorous songs, including classics like "Dinah Dinah." It was all in good fun and added to the vibrant ambiance.

Shortly thereafter, a group of Americans arrived at the pub. They had been out shooting in the area. Oblivious to the cold, they left the door open, prompting the landlord to call out, "Please shut the door to keep the sheep out." Intrigued by the comment, one of the Americans, emboldened by his newfound courage, asked if sheep really came inside if the door was left open. The landlord, ever the witty host, suggested that he open the door to find out. To everyone's surprise, three sheep casually strolled into the pub. Amused by the spectacle, the landlord provided the Americans with small biscuits from the coffee-making

It's only the dirty ones we don't want - Philip Wilkinson

Background image – the bar at Tan Hill copyright
https://kensbeerblog.blogspot.com/2015/08/nostalgia-at-tan-hill-inn.html Sheep head © Pixababy

stand. Holding the treats high, the sheep stood on their back legs, reaching up to enjoy the snacks, clearly accustomed to such gestures.

Shortly thereafter, a group of Americans arrived at the pub. They had been out shooting in the area. Oblivious to the cold, they left the door open, prompting the landlord to call out, "Please shut the door to keep the sheep out." Intrigued by the comment, one of the Americans, emboldened by his newfound courage, asked if sheep really came inside if the door was left open. The landlord, ever the witty host, suggested that he open the door to find out. To everyone's surprise, three sheep casually strolled into the pub. Amused by the spectacle, the landlord provided the Americans with small biscuits from the coffee-making stand. Holding the treats high, the sheep stood on their back legs, reaching up to enjoy the snacks, clearly accustomed to such gestures.

As the night wore on and the clock struck 1AM, one of the Americans inquired about the closing time of the pub. The landlord, Neil, considering his response, glanced at the floor, then the clock behind the bar, and finally his watch. With a mischievous smile, he pointed to the calendar on the wall and replied, "About October." It was a light-hearted exchange that added to the memorable experience.

The pub back in that time, as I recollect, had many curiosities pinned to the wooden beams, bank notes from around the world, postcards from well-wishers, silly items customers had donated to the collection, and a large black plastic spider on a fishing line controlled from the bar which Neil would, without warning, allow to drop a foot or so from time to time, the resounding screams of fear could be heard throughout the pub.

It's only the dirty ones we don't want - Philip Wilkinson

At 4AM, we decided to call it a night and retired to our tents. Along the way, one of our friends stumbled upon an unexpected discovery. He called out, "Has anyone lost a sock?"

As he examined it more closely, he realised it was a long, pink sock adorned with silk bows. The curiosity among us grew, and someone jokingly asked, "Who wears long pink socks with bows?" To our amusement, my girlfriend chimed in and replied, "It's mine." Laughter filled the air as we marvelled at the unexpected fashion find.

© Pixababy

The following morning, nursing our headaches, we forced ourselves to eat bacon sandwiches provided by Sue in the pub. One of the lads decided to try the "hair of

the dog" remedy and ordered a pint of beer alongside his breakfast. Curious about the pub's policy, my girlfriend approached the landlord, Neil, and asked, "Do you

charge for water?" With a smirk, he replied, "Not unless you're American." It was a playful exchange that lightened the mood.

In another room, two of the American visitors sat having breakfast. One of them appeared worse for wear. It turned out that a local regular, a plain and skinny woman with not many teeth and face you would describe as "lived in" estimated to be in her mid-60s, who often collected glasses in the pub without being on the staff, had a peculiar habit. She would use the spare keys for the rooms and sneak into unsuspecting visitors' quarters for late-night encounters. Unfortunately, it seemed that she had found another victim during the night.

It's only the dirty ones we don't want - Philip Wilkinson

The Tan Hill Inn how it looked in this era, July 1977   © Clint Mann

The Tan Hill Inn March 2010 winter still holding   © Mathew Hatton

Chapter 17

The superbike era

Suzuki GS750 circa 1978/9   © Author & Pixababy

My Suzuki GS750

In 1978, a close friend of mine, Spawny made an exciting purchase, a brand new red and black Suzuki GS750, now a classic Japanese motorcycle. Little did he know that this motorcycle would play a significant role in my adventures for years to come. It was during one of these escapades that Spawny found himself engaged in a high-speed chase with our friend Stu, who was riding his Honda CX500 on the motorway. They reached a blistering 115 mph when their adrenaline-fueled race was abruptly interrupted by the intervention of the police.

As Spawny and Stuart pulled over, it became evident that fate had intervened in the nick of time. The front tire of Spawny's bike was emitting smoke from the front tire, a result of a stone becoming lodged under the chrome front lip of the closely fitted front mudguard. This unfortunate circumstance had caused the stone to rub against the new tire, exposing the cords. It was a ticking time bomb, and had the police not intervened when they did, a catastrophic front wheel blowout would have been imminent.

In the aftermath of this thrilling encounter, Spawny faced the consequences of his actions. He received a six-month driving ban because of the offence. It was during this time that he made a decision that would impact both our lives. Spawny chose to sell me the GS750, an opportunity I gladly seized. The bike was nothing short of awe-inspiring, boasting incredible power and speed. However, its sheer acceleration from a standstill posed a challenge for passengers. Many times, they found themselves left behind, sitting on the road at traffic lights due to the bike's relentless surge forward. As I intended to carry my girlfriend as my pillion passenger, to address this issue, I installed a stylish chrome rear carrier on the bike.

The addition of the rear carrier not only provided a practical solution but also enhanced the overall aesthetic appeal of the GS750. It allowed me to secure my toolbox when I needed it for work or attach a tent and sleeping bag for camping trips and rallies. Little did I know that this modification would mark the beginning of a remarkable adventure.

Over the next five years, the GS750 became my trusted companion both travelling for work and on countless camping trips and memorable journeys. It took me on thrilling rides through scenic landscapes, covering an astonishing 60,000 miles in total. Each camping trip brought new experiences, creating a tapestry of memories that would stay with me forever. The freedom and exhilaration of the open road, combined with the practicality and versatility of the bike, made every journey a true adventure.

Those five years were a time of discovery and exploration, where the road became my guide and the bike my faithful companion. The Suzuki GS750 became more than just a mode of transportation; it became a symbol of freedom, excitement, and the joy of embarking on new experiences.

By this point, many had moved on the much bigger and better motorcycles, over the next few pages are a few examples.

Bilbo had a Honda CX500 V twin, but used the tractor in winter © Author & Pixababy

It's only the dirty ones we don't want - Philip Wilkinson

Frodo had moved up to the awesome Honda CBX1000 © Author & Pixababy

Mutt now owned a GS750 1978 model with wire wheels ©Author & Pixababy

It's only the dirty ones we don't want - Philip Wilkinson

Spawny at Elvington around 1987 his Kawasaki now had a 1260cc engine fitted, but
no quicker than the older 1054cc motor © AVMCC

Drag racing motorcycles.

Spawny's venture into hand-built, street-legal drag racing was nothing short of impressive.
Using a stock Kawasaki Z1000 as his canvas, he transformed it into an award-winning
machine. With modifications such as a box section rear swinging arm, a skimming of the
head, port polishing, over boring, and the addition of high compression titanium pistons,
the bike boasted incredible power. To enhance its performance further, Spawny installed a
custom hand-built exhaust system with a turbocharger sourced from a 1600cc car. This
amalgamation of upgrades propelled him to become the second fastest in his class in the
UK for several years.

The bike's power was awe-inspiring, capable of pulling acceleration wheelies in top gear
at a blazing 150mph. Just starting the engine in the car park would result in the
first six inches of the exhaust pipes glowing a fiery cherry red, a testament to the intense
heat generated by its immense performance.

However, despite his success and the undeniable prowess of his drag racing machine,
Spawny always harboured a sense of regret for selling me the GS750. He made numerous
attempts to find another that ran as impressively, even acquiring a GS550, GS850, GS1000,
two GS750s, and a GS1100 along the way. Despite his efforts, he never managed to find
another bike that captured his heart quite like the one he sold to me.

236

Secret Combinations

Come with us to a land where all is not as it first appears....

There must be something funny in the air up in the Crossgates area of Leeds that makes bikers try to hide what they ride. Odd chaps. Take Shaun Shovelin's bike for example: at first glance it looks like a CB900 Honda. None too interesting really. At second glance it looks like a Honda chassis with a big Kawa motor, but only a good long inspection can take in a combination of parts that involves the kitchen sink and a shopping trolley. This sounds like the sort of ingenuity that takes more time and money than using original parts, but let's have a peek.

The chassis started life wrapped round a standard CB750 F1, but has been well hacked about, with the top loop replaced by 14 gauge, and the rest of the frame supported by cross bracing. The home-made swinging arm runs on Timken taper roller bearings and the spindle comes from a Tesco shopping trolley. Umm. Tesco ones are notably strong of course, as you'll know if you've ever hit the serried rows of baked beans with one. The forks are at least from a bike — a CBX — while the wheels and brakes are off a 750 F2. A Kawasaki steering damper firms up the chassis, which Shaun reckons handles really well, particularly at speed. He claims a top whack of around

Article from Superbike magazine with photos copyright John Goodman

Spawny featured in the press at the time

It's only the dirty ones we don't want - Philip Wilkinson

Spawny on Rickman Suzuki at Shakespeare County Raceway © AVMCC

This photo is not really in the timeline for the book, but I decided to include it as it seemed a shame not to.

Chapter 18 – 1979

A time of change

My rally badge from the event © Author

The Ides of March Rally

The Moorcock Inn, March 1979, Salford Centurion's MCC

The Moorcock Inn   © Christine Johnson

Our next adventure took us to the Ides of March rally, an esteemed event organised by the Salford Centurion's MCC. At the Moorcock inn, this rally was reputed to be the oldest continuously run rally in England. However, this rally posed a unique challenge as severe weather was forecasted. my girlfriend, deciding to err on the side of caution, opted to stay behind this time

Actual photo of the Ides of March rally – before ten feet of snow fell.   © Bilbo

The Ides of March rally – Bikes parked on the road   © Bilbo

It's only the dirty ones we don't want - Philip Wilkinson

As we embarked on our journey, we encountered an unexpected obstacle. Approaching the M62 in Leeds, we noticed that the police had closed the motorway despite previous claims that weather would never hinder its operation. Disregarding the closure signs, we pressed on, joining the M62 via the slip road. Riding through freshly fallen snow, we cautiously made our way to the rally site.

Upon arrival, the snowfall intensified, accompanied by strong gusts of wind that caused drifting. Determined to ensure the safety of our bikes, we carefully parked them just off the road and quickly set up our tents before conditions worsened. Seeking refuge from the elements, we spent a few hours in the pub, seeking warmth and lots of good ale.

Camping at the Ides of March Rally   © Bilbo

To our astonishment, one rally attendee unintentionally discovered the full force of the weather when opening the pub door, only to be buried beneath a cascade of snow that poured into the establishment. Concerned about the conditions outside, a group of bikers ventured out to assess the situation. Only the occasional motorcycle mirror poking out from a snowdrift served as evidence of where the bikes were parked. To provide a marker for any passing snowploughs, we placed cones on the protruding mirrors.

Parts of the campsite were now buried under ten feet of snow, making it challenging to locate tents. Some bikers resorted to sleeping in the partially intact garage adjacent to the pub, seeking shelter from the harsh elements. Additionally, the first-time rally goers were subjected to a traditional initiation, involving stripping them of their clothes, dousing them

241

in beer, and compelling them to drink while naked, and having their nipples pulled by all they passed, a rite of passage in the biker community.

Adding a touch of humour to the experience, several members of the Aire Valley MCC had recently purchased a whimsical Wendy house from a catalogue. Complete with plastic windows, printed curtains, and even an owl on the chimney, it became the talk of the rally. Three of us, including myself, decided to spend the night in the cosy confines of the Wendy house, but soon realised it was too small to accommodate us comfortably, or at all. We reluctantly abandoned the idea and returned to the more conventional option of traditional tents. However, the next morning, we playfully resumed our stint in the Wendy house, with our boots and legs sticking out, much to the amusement of passing bikers.

Time to dig out the bikes to go home © Bilbo

Weeks later, while installing an alarm system at a bank in Leeds, I found myself seated in the staff canteen during my lunch break. Across from me sat a young clerk engrossed in a motorcycle magazine. Out of the blue, he looked up and exclaimed, "You're a biker, aren't you?" I confirmed his assumption, and he promptly turned the magazine around, revealing a centrefold photo.

To my surprise, it was a snapshot of the Wendy house at the Ides of March rally, unmistakably capturing our boots sticking out into the snow. In disbelief, he exclaimed, "Have you seen this lot camping in a Wendy house in the snow?" I proudly revealed that it was indeed myself and my mates in the photograph, with my motorcycle serving as proof of my presence. The young clerk was taken aback by the revelation, his astonishment bridging the gap between our chance encounter in the canteen and the memorable rally experience we shared.

It's only the dirty ones we don't want - Philip Wilkinson

Rally badge from the event © Author

Monkey Hanger Rally second year

Monkey Hanger Rally, Trimdon, March 1979, Monkey Hanger MCC

This time, rather than calling the rally by its former name, it became the Monkey Hanger Rally, once again set in Trimdon. Travelling to the rally with my girlfriend as pillion this year was a long, arduous drive as there were constant roadworks and it was cold, dark, and wet, we got a bit confused as there are two similar named places signposted off the dual carriageway, Crimdon and Trimdon, fortunately someone from the Monkey Hangers MCC had put up a sign on the right turn off.

The rally was again a raucous affair, beer flowed freely, and the pub, having learned its lesson from the previous year, had overstocked on beer, and brought in extra staff to cope, much better.

Friday's session was lively as usual for these events, singing of bawdy songs was de-rigour and we all had a great time, and a skin full.

Now, let me share a couple of mishaps that happened to my girlfriend and me at the start. As we parked our bike in the pub's car park to use the toilets, believe it or not, someone pilfered our beloved tankards! Heartbroken but undeterred, we hopped back on the bike to cross the road and set up our tent in the camping field. Well, let's just say my judgment of the embankment angle was a tad off, and we ended up toppling over sideways. It was quite a sight, but we managed to pick ourselves up, with my girlfriend still sitting pillion, and rode on to the field.

Thankfully, we had a spacious 4-man tent, affectionately dubbed "the marquee," which we had purchased to ensure my girlfriend's comfort. It was a far cry from my friends cramped 2-man tents. With its clever design and ample space for storage and cooking, it became a hub for food, beer, and merry gatherings.

This year there was no disco at a club with busses, the event would be limited to the pub and associated camp site, but this was fine and what we expected of a rally.

243

It's only the dirty ones we don't want - Philip Wilkinson

The following day, hundreds of motorcyclists fell in with the doors for a mid-day session, typically a gallon each would suffice, this time however, the pub had obtained a licence allowing them to stay open from 12 noon until midnight, there would be some bad heads the next day.

That afternoon, the atmosphere at the bike rally took a dark turn with the arrival of the Satan's Slaves. Their presence brought a sense of unease as they began to instigate trouble and disturb the otherwise joyful event. Among their disruptive antics, three of them decided to roll a portaloo around the field, causing chaos and distress.

© iStock

In a surprising turn of events, several rally goers decided to confront the situation head-on. Unaware of what awaited them inside the rolling portaloo, they opened it only to discover one of their rally colleague's unconscious and covered in the unpleasant contents of the toilet. It was clear that immediate medical attention was required, so an ambulance was called to transport him to the nearest hospital.

The rally goers, fuelled by a mix of concern for their safety and frustration with the Slaves' behaviour, decided to take matters into their own hands. Spotting a nearby lorry loaded with scaffolding poles, they made a daring choice to appropriate them for their cause. With a newfound determination, they confronted the Satan's Slaves, aiming to teach them a lesson they would not soon forget.

Using the scaffolding poles as makeshift weapons, the rally goers defended themselves and the spirit of the event against the troublemakers. While resorting to such measures was regrettable, their actions served as a strong deterrent and a reminder that their collective enjoyment should not be marred by the unruly behaviour of a few.

It's only the dirty ones we don't want - Philip Wilkinson

Rally badge from the event – note the spelling error.

Dwyle Funkers Rally

The Hostry Inn, Llantilio Crossenny, 1979, MC Dwylefunkers

Image capture: Jun 2011 © 2023 Google

We were now full-fledged bike rally aficionados, having indulged in several of these wild events throughout the year. But one rally stood out—the inaugural Dwyle Funkers rally held at the Hostry Inn, nestled in the scenic countryside of Llantilio Crossenny, perfectly positioned between Monmouth and Abergavenny. It was a riotously good time, albeit with its fair share of hilarity and mishaps.

On the way to the rally, the motorcycles naturally formed groups based on their maximum speeds. The larger bikes, with engines 750cc and above, roared ahead at an exhilarating

It's only the dirty ones we don't want - Philip Wilkinson

120mph on the motorway. Following closely behind were a group of riders on 350 to 400cc bikes, maintaining a steady pace of around 100mph. A few stragglers brought up the rear, enjoying a more leisurely ride.

A Honda 400 four like the one Flaps rode   © Author & Pixbaby

However, amidst the rush of excitement, an unexpected incident occurred. Flaps, one of the girls known for her adventurous spirit and playful nature, was riding her Honda 400 four when disaster struck. Without warning, her front wheel suffered a blowout, causing her bike to veer across all three lanes of the motorway. It was a moment of panic for all who witnessed it.

By some stroke of luck, the grass banking adjacent to the motorway was tall enough to halt her unplanned trajectory. Flaps skidded to a stop, shaken but thankfully unharmed. In the aftermath, we couldn't help but jest about the incident, using humour to cope with the shock. We playfully remarked, "She must have opened up her flaps to stop the bike," an inside joke that lightened the tension and brought a smile to our faces.

In the years that followed, the story of Flaps and her unexpected detour became a legendary tale among our group. It served as a reminder of the unpredictability of life on the road and the importance of staying vigilant.

To get between the pub and the campsite, we had to rely on a minibus shuttle, which added a comical twist to our biker escapades. As for the rally's name, it was an eye-catching Welsh phrase that, when translated, had something to do with sheep shaggers. But here's the kicker: the badge maker made a typo on the badges, leaving us all in suspense about what the translation might imply. I have a badge from that fateful first year and can confirm that it is an oblong mahogany coloured enamel badge the words M.C. at the top, Rally at the bottom, and DYLE FUNKERS down the left and right sides, in the centre, in polished silver relief, there is a pigs head over a beer tankard

It's only the dirty ones we don't want - Philip Wilkinson

Image of myself eating a bean sandwich Dwyle Funkers rally   ©Bilbo

The rally was a buzzing hub of activity, just as you'd expect. There was an impressive beer consumption record, reckless motorcycle rides that could rival any daredevil stunt show, an eating competition that could make an elephant blush, and live music that rocked the socks off our boots. And then there was Melvin's legendary snack van, a place where culinary adventures mingled with a touch of peril. Melvin, a character whose name may or may not have been his real one (but hey, it was plastered on his van, so we rolled with it), had a van equipped with a serving hatch, complete with a stove and all the essentials. He also had a trusty trailer where he stored all the raw meat and food. Now, let's just say that refrigeration and proper storage weren't high on Melvin's priority list. You got what you were given, and it was like playing Russian roulette with your taste buds.

A snack van, Melvin's was not as posh as this, it also had a trailer for storage of meat and bread etc. the trailer had no chiller or fridge, which was OK for winter rallies, but in summer after 3 – 4 days the contents must have started to smell bad.

I'll never forget the sight of Melvin exiting the van, sauntering over to the trailer, and nonchalantly opening the door. With trays of hot dogs and raw beefburgers as his obstacles, he made his way to the bread, all the while coughing with a cigarette hanging precariously from his mouth. And just when you thought it couldn't get any better, he paused to pet his dog before strolling back to the van to continue his culinary extravaganza, all without a care in the world about washing his hands. It was a hygiene adventure like no other.

As the evening progressed, fires began to dot the vicinity of the tents. A cosy warmth embraced the frozen bikers huddled around the flames. But alas, their moment of tranquillity was swiftly interrupted by the farmer himself, striding through the field with a mix of authority and mischief.

It's only the dirty ones we don't want - Philip Wilkinson

© Pixababy

© Pixababy

© Pixababy

As the evening progressed, fires began to dot the vicinity of the tents. A cosy warmth embraced the frozen bikers huddled around the flames. But alas, their moment of tranquillity was swiftly interrupted by the farmer himself, striding through the field with a mix of authority and mischief.

He sauntered over to one of the fires, casting an appraising glance at the shivering bikers, and uttered those fateful words, "That's a nice fire." Grateful for the compliment, they responded with heartfelt gratitude. And then, in an act of bewildering audacity, the farmer delivered a swift kick to the base of the fire, igniting a frenzy of sparks and flaming logs that showered over the unsuspecting bikers. "Fires are not permitted," he declared, leaving them stunned and singed, before marching off to tackle another group.

Later that night, on our way back from the pub, crossing the field under a moonlit sky, Mutt, one of our merry gang, couldn't help but vent his frustration about the farmer's tyrannical treatment of the fires. "It's freezing out here, we need those fires to stay warm!" he grumbled. We all nodded in solidarity, commiserating over the injustice. And then, seizing a moment of pure inspiration, I chimed in with a mathematical flourish, "Listen, guys, I've done the calculations. There can't be more than 0.001% of this vast field that would be damaged by fires, even if we all lit one!" With that profound proclamation, I sealed my fate as the one and only Prof, a title that would forever echo through the annals of rally history.

The Lake District National Park ©Author

Two men and a Datsun Cherry

It was summer and time to take stock, a holiday was on the cards and after the success of our trip two years earlier, Richie and I determined we would repeat the experience, the Datsun Cherry by now had been upgraded and sported the Sunny 1200cc top end allied to the Cherry's original gearbox, acceleration off the line was much improved but top speed remained unchanged as the gearbox was originally designed for the smaller engine block.

The black paintwork was immaculate now, passers-by would comment on just how shiny it was, and how the reflections were totally free of ripples of bobbles usually found on vehicle paint finishes, this was unsurprising as Richie worked professionally repairing vehicles and was a highly skilled painter.

Travelling from Leeds, we arrived without event at Windermere, stopping at the main town on the lake, Bowness, we enjoyed lunch be the lakeside as the weather was perfect. We then travelled around the top of the lake and turned off to follow the notorious Hardknott and Wrynose passes referred to in equal measure as "Britain's two most dangerous roads" and "Britain's most scenic drive".

A quick search on the internet reveals a review by the BBC – extracts from the article reproduced below.

The review says, built by the Romans and considered one of Britain's most "outrageous" roads, it's filled with sharp hairpin turns and is the width of a bridleway.

249

It's only the dirty ones we don't want - Philip Wilkinson

If I'd steered hard around the hairpin bend, I'd have driven straight into a frightening gradient of crumbling road, rearing up like a tidal wave in front of me. Rainwater poured down the middle of the rough carriageway like a mountain stream. I reached to change gear and realised I was already in first. Just then, a nonchalant sheep strolled out in front of me, causing me to slam on the brakes.

Hardknott Pass in England's north-west Lake District is, technically, the most direct route from the central Lake District to West Cumbria, but it is so steep and difficult that outsiders are often warned to take hour-long detours to avoid braving its twisting, single-track slalom up a mountainside. It was described as one of Britain's "most outrageous roads" by The Guardian,

Image capture: Sept 2011 © 2023 Google

Image capture: Oct 2021 © 2023 Google

Hardknott Pass, The Lake District National Park

and locals are full of tales of cars suffering brake failures, drivers freezing with the challenge and of skids and misjudgements causing cars to plunge off the narrow carriageway.

It's only the dirty ones we don't want - Philip Wilkinson

This leaves some asking: should this extraordinary 13-mile stretch between the towns of Boot and Ambleside be closed to traffic – or celebrated as a national treasure?

Each year, visitors set off westwards from genteel tearooms in the tourist hub of Ambleside, hoping for a pretty potter through the England's largest national park, the UNESCO-inscribed Lake District. Instead, they run straight into the most challenging stretch of road available to British drivers; a sequence of steep switchbacks climbing a bleak mountainside. Appropriately you'll find this "most outrageous" of roads snaking around England's highest peak (Scafell Pike) and deepest lake (Wastwater) in the mountainous wild west of the Lake District. Many consider Hardknott a hazard. "We put guests off from coming over Hardknott Pass," said local holiday-home owner Greg Poole, matter-of-factly.

The Institute of Advanced Motorists' spokeswoman Heather Butcher said: "Depending on the rider or driver's experience, it could be one to avoid. We don't recommend putting yourself or others in danger… You can read reviews online from various sources confirming that it's a challenging road, a thrill, etcetera, but we would advise all riders and drivers to approach roads like this with caution." And Neil Graham, a communications officer for the Cumbria Police added, "People shouldn't seek out the road to challenge themselves."

And yet, to others, this daunting route is a landmark to be celebrated; a challenge to be attempted. Extract from https://www.bbc.com/travel/article/20211213-the-hardknott-pass-britains-wildest-road

This is what we had signed up for, the Datsun Cherry with its oversized engine and lower ratio gearbox, along with its small size, light weight and the modified ultra-wide wheels and tyres was the perfect vehicle for the challenge.

One of the issues of the passes is their extreme gradients, turns and incredibly narrow track width, at one point, going uphill at 12mph in second, the left turn is so severe you need to slow down and select first to negotiate it, on another bend, this time on the downhill section, you simply cannot see which way the rod goes and have to trust to your instincts and judgement to continue.

Eskdale to Ravenglass light railway, reached by the pass © Author

It's only the dirty ones we don't want - Philip Wilkinson

One of the main issues is in Summer, when car, motorcycles etc. are in larger numbers, the main ascent can be seen in all its glory from the bottom where fortunately the road widens slightly meaning cars etc. can wait until there is no other vehicle coming down before starting their run, as it is simply impossible to pass another vehicle on the uphill section of the pass. Whilst we waited our turn, an unfortunate lady driver decided to make her run at the hill, unfortunately as she reached the top, she missed a gear change on one of the hairpin turns and rolled backwards down the hill at some speed, fortunately she ran off onto the grass, but in most places this luxury is not available and rocky crags to both sides of the track make it treacherous. To add to the issues, the road surface is liable to flooding and very worn, patched, and uneven.

Wastwater, the deepest lake in England   © Author

Pitching our tent in the picturesque Wasdale, we embarked on the lakeside round trip walk, blissfully unaware of the impending adventure that awaited us. Halfway through our jaunt, just as the scree on the far side of the lake turned into massive boulders resembling oversized cars, the sky decided to throw a tantrum. The heavens turned black, and a thunderstorm loomed overhead. Rain cascaded down upon us with such intensity that it felt like the clouds were playing a cruel game of "how wet can you get?" And to add a touch of drama, heavy hailstones joined the party, making us question our sanity.

Seeking shelter, we huddled beneath the protective embrace of one of the larger boulders on the scree face, peering out at the spectacle unfolding over the dark and ominous Wastwater. The lake, always mysterious, took on a whole new aura during the thunderstorm. Lightning danced across the sky, striking the lake and surrounding trees with electric fury. It

252

was a show that Mother Nature herself had choreographed for our amusement, a spectacle that left us in awe and drenched to the bone.

Undeterred by the forces of nature, we soldiered on with our walk, albeit resembling drowned rats in need of a good hairdryer. As luck would have it, kindness found us in the form of a caretaker at the YHA Wasdale Hall. Taking pity on our bedraggled state, they granted us access to the washroom, allowing us to tame our rebellious hair and served us a steaming hot drink to warm our souls. Their generosity was a ray of sunshine after the storm.

Ah, the infamous Datsun and its mischievous "whoopee whistle." Yes, even during nature's tantrums, our trusty car's unconventional accessory managed to bring a hint of amusement to our journey. Hidden discreetly under the steering column, the cable to activate the whistle never failed to elicit a silly, high-pitched sound powered by the engine's vacuum. Unfortunately, the local sheep population, notorious for obstructing roads, remained unimpressed by our whimsical attempts to clear the way.

© Author

Now, let's talk about Lion ales, brewed by Mathew Brown, Blackburn, Lancashire, a staple in nearly every pub in the region. Alas, their quality had not seen any remarkable improvements. Our survival strategy was to order a half-pint of Lion ale and pair it with either a bottle of brown ale or Guinness, creating a mixology experiment that aimed to make their beers somewhat palatable. It was a daring endeavour, a battle against mediocrity in the realm of brews.

After our escapades in Wasdale, we embarked on a journey that mirrored our previous trip, this time heading over the to the enchanting Honister pass on route to Buttermere. A world apart from Wastwater. Here, the hills embraced us with gentleness, the scree taking a backseat to allow the beauty of the landscape to shine. Trees, dry stone walls, and, of course, the ever-present short, hardy Herdwick sheep adorned the scenery, painting a picture of serenity and charm.

But erecting a tent in the Lake District posed its own unique challenge. The ground, notorious for its rocky layer lurking just beneath the grass, tested our tent-pitching skills. In fair weather, we could drive the pegs at an acute angle into the thin layer of topsoil, creating a sturdy foundation. However, fate had a different plan this year. An unexpected storm brewed, catching us off guard.

It's only the dirty ones we don't want - Philip Wilkinson

Buttermere lake, the Lake District © Pixababy

By 1 AM, extreme winds and freezing rain assaulted our campsite, rendering our tent peg trick futile. We had to take desperate measures. During lulls in the tempest, we dashed around the tent, resetting pegs and even pilfering top stones from the nearby wall to secure any part of the tent we could grasp. And when the winds howled with their mightiest roar, we found ourselves sitting in the darkness, each gripping a tent pole as if it were a lifeline.

Campsite destroyed by wind © Pixababy

Finally, at around 9 AM, the storm surrendered to the sun's warmth, and we emerged from our shelter to a campsite that resembled a ghost town. We were the lone survivors in a sea of abandoned tents. Cold and ravenous, we scoured our supplies and discovered a treasure, a large tin of Heinz tomato soup meant for a family feast and a loaf of bread. Igniting the stove inside the tent, we heated the soup and, in turn, warmed our shivering bodies. That bowl of steaming hot soup, accompanied by humble slices of bread, became an unexpected feast, a meal that will forever hold a special place in our memories.

As the day unfolded, news reports trickled in, revealing the havoc wreaked by the storm. The Fastnet race, once teeming with 303 yachts, had fallen victim to nature's fury. Twenty-four vessels were abandoned, and fifteen sailors tragically lost their lives. A massive rescue operation involving the Royal Navy, RAF Nimrod Jets, helicopters, lifeboats, and even a Dutch warship saved 125 yachtsmen. It was a sobering reminder that the sea could indeed be an unforgiving mistress, validating the age-old saying that things are always worse at sea.

In the end, our escapades in the Lake District were filled with unpredictable weather, remarkable encounters, and moments that tested our resilience. Through thunderstorms, mishaps, and the comforting warmth of a simple bowl of soup, we discovered that nature's fury only served to enhance the beauty and wonder of our journey.

A red Ford Escort MK2 like Erotic's car © Author & Pixababy

Erotic buys a car.

During this time, Erotic took a leap of faith and acquired a MK2 Ford Escort 1.6. Now, Erotic was no stranger to danger, mostly involving bicycles and motorbikes. But this new set of wheels took his antics to a whole new level. I'll spare you the endless tales, but rest assured, they extended well beyond the confines of this volume.

It's only the dirty ones we don't want - Philip Wilkinson

One fateful night, as we gathered at the Travellers Rest in Halton, our appetites were craving Chinese food. I hopped on my trusty GS750 and Erotic followed suit in his

Escort. Little did we know, our culinary quest would take an unexpected turn just a few hundred yards down the road. Erotic, in his eternal quest for speed, attempted an audacious overtaking manoeuvre on a treacherous S bend. Worried about the slippery road, I let him pass. But alas, his ambitions exceeded his skills, and he lost control, spinning the car into a dry-stone wall. The Escort and the wall suffered significant damage, leaving us pondering the wisdom of our dinner choices.

Then there was the infamous incident with Erotic's girlfriend onboard. They were searching for a secluded spot to indulge in some amorous activities. Naturally, Erotic ventured down a country lane, only to discover it was a dead end. Caught up in the moment, his girlfriend's distractions caused Erotic to attempt a speedy 3-point turn in the narrow lane. Unfortunately, his manoeuvring skills fell short, and the car ended up rolling over onto its roof. Talk about a passionate tumble!

On another occasion, as I strolled with my girlfriend along Beeston Town Street en-route to our regular haunt, The Old White Hear pub, disaster struck again. Out of nowhere, screeching tires and billowing smoke heralded the arrival of Erotic's car. The window rolled

down, and with a mischievous grin, Erotic offered us a lift. Foolishly, we accepted, not knowing what awaited us. With the rear tires spinning in excitement, we embarked on an adrenaline-fueled adventure. As we neared our destination, Erotic, at approximately 50mph, executed a daring 90-degree turn into the Co-op car park. And just when we thought the show was over, he finished it off with a grand handbrake turn, neatly sliding into a parking spot between two unsuspecting cars. We stumbled out of the car, questioning our life choices while Erotic beamed with pride.

© Pixababy

The following week, when Erotic screeched to a halt, eager to "give us a lift" again, we politely declined. The poor Escort spent more time in Richie's repair shop than on the road. Welding, painting, and reshaping became routine, turning Erotic's car into the poster child for rust-free Escorts of its age. But trust me, you wouldn't want to be the unlucky owner following Erotic's unique brand of abuse.

© Pixababy

In the annals of automotive history, Erotic and his Ford Escort will forever be remembered as a spectacular display of driving prowess gone hilariously wrong.

It's only the dirty ones we don't want - Philip Wilkinson

Me again, second from the left with my orange tent 'the marquee'   © Bilbo

Camping most weekends

My girlfriend and I were true camping enthusiasts, embarking on weekend adventures that were nothing short of legendary. Whether it was joining the bike club, hanging out with the Thursday club, or simply venturing out on our own, we found ourselves pitching tents and embracing the great outdoors with unwavering enthusiasm. Motorbike rallies were a favourite destination, where the atmosphere was electric and the company infectious. On Sundays when we returned home, the bike covered in a layer of dirt, and my girlfriend, with her trusty diary in hand, looked up at me from the comfort of the couch. There was a spark in her eyes as she made a startling realization. "Do you know," she exclaimed, "that we've been camping for the last 46 weekends in a row?" I paused for a moment, absorbing the magnitude of our camping streak, before mustering a response. With a mischievous grin, I replied, "Well, I have no intention of putting the brakes on our camping escapades just yet."

Week after week, we would pack our gear, mount the bike, and venture into the wilderness. We would immerse ourselves in the beauty of nature, laugh under starlit skies, and savour the simple pleasures of campfire conversations and toasted marshmallows. Our camping weekends became a sacred ritual, a chance to recharge our spirits and reconnect with the world around us.

It's only the dirty ones we don't want - Philip Wilkinson

Still image from the film Life of Brian   © Handmade Films

The Leeds watch committee

In the 1970s, a lesser-known group in Leeds operated a second level of censorship that aimed to prevent what they deemed as inappropriate films from being screened in the city. This group consisted of well-intentioned individuals, including Christians and councillors, who believed they had the authority to control the content shown in cinemas.

Being intimately connected to the workings of this committee through my parents, I gained insight into their decision-making processes. I discovered that films like "The Exorcist" and "Equus" were subject to their scrutiny. While it might be somewhat understandable that "The Exorcist" was considered controversial, it was puzzling that "Equus," which had been performed live in Leeds from April to July 1976, was later banned as a film upon its release in October 1977. Apparently, the committee members believed it was acceptable to witness the nudity and content on stage but not on the silver screen. It's worth noting that their jurisdiction only extended to films, not plays.

When "Life of Brian" came into their purview, the decision to ban screenings was unanimous. This film was deemed blasphemous and contradictory to the principles of religion. However, their efforts were not entirely successful, as only Kirklees council declared a ban on the film in the Leeds area. Interestingly, it was later revealed that none of the committee members had watched the film before making their decision.

I recall a personal experience when I went to watch "Life of Brian" with my girlfriend at the Lounge cinema in Headingley in 1979. We were met with a peculiar sight. The committee had gathered there, distributing leaflets, and using megaphones to dissuade people from watching the film. To shield our identities, we felt compelled to cover our faces while waiting in line. Among the committee members, my mother and father were just as vocal in their opposition.

Ironically, many years later, my father visited my house one evening to apologize for an incident earlier that day. At that moment, I happened to be enjoying a beer and watching "Life of Brian." After accepting his apology, we continued watching the film together,

259

starting from the iconic scene where the characters purchase stones. Unbeknownst to him, he found the humour in the subsequent jokes uproarious, laughing wholeheartedly.

Reflecting on this situation, I couldn't help but ponder the extent of hypocrisy exhibited by the committee members. Their initial strong opposition to the film contrasted sharply with my father's eventual enjoyment of it. It served as a reminder of the subjective nature of censorship and the unpredictability of personal perspectives.

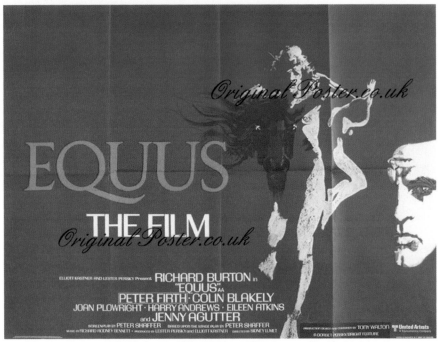

Poster for the film version of Equus at the time

It's only the dirty ones we don't want - Philip Wilkinson

Image The Old Hill Inn, Chapel le Dale, Ingleton ©Andrew Curtis

It's only the dirty ones we don't want.

Our next weekend camping escapade at the Hill Inn in Chapel Le Dale, Ingleborough, turned out to be quite the adventure. It all began with a downpour of rain as we embarked on our journey, leaving us thoroughly drenched by the time we reached the inn. With visions of a cosy fireplace dancing in our minds, we trudged towards the field designated for camping. But alas, due to some complaints about excessive camping from the inn's neighbours, (their neighbours comprise a few farms in the area and are a considerable distance from the inn) the camping area had been reduced, leaving us with a mud-soaked mess. As we surveyed the scene, a JCB stood proudly in the corner of the field, its work of levelling the land unfinished. A slippery ramp created by its bucket beckoned me to ride our bike onto the grassy section above. However, in the treacherously wet conditions, our bike slid sideways, sending us crashing into the mud beneath. my girlfriend 's helmet became a mud magnet, smearing her hair and face in the process. After a few choice words and a good laugh at our muddy misfortune, we finally managed to lift the bike back up and park it on the grass.

It's only the dirty ones we don't want - Philip Wilkinson

To our dismay, as we approached the inn's front door, we noticed a new sign that read "no motorcyclists allowed." Disheartened and voicing our grievances about our previous visits and patronage, we turned to walk away. But just as we were about to leave, the inn's door swung open, and the landlord called us back with a welcoming gesture. "You two are alright," he said, holding the door open. "It's only the dirty ones we don't want."

Relieved and grateful, we settled into the inn, shedding our wet gear, and placing everything near the open fire to dry. After setting up our tent, we returned to find our table joined by a group of cavers. The inn had these fascinating cartwheels serving as dividers between alcoves, and cavers had a tradition of climbing through them. It was quite the sight to behold, with handmade wheels and uneven spokes requiring careful selection before attempting the climb.

As the evening unfolded, we indulged in Theakston's Old Peculiar, a strong brew that I approached with caution. Sipping my pint slowly, time seemed to slip away unnoticed. Suddenly, I glanced at the clock and realised it was a staggering 4 AM. We knew it was time to call it a night. However, as soon as I stepped outside into the fresh air, the alcohol took hold, and I collapsed unconscious on the inn's doorstep. my girlfriend, initially thinking I was joking around, soon realised the seriousness of the situation. Desperate for help, she rushed back inside and enlisted the cavers from our shared table to carry me to our tent and tuck me into the sleeping bag. They were bewildered, as just moments before, I had been engaged in conversation, perfectly coherent.

The next morning arrived with a pounding headache it struck me that I must have consumed around 15 pints of Old Peculiar last evening. We decided that a hearty meal was in order and set off to Ingleton for breakfast. As we rode along the straight road, seemingly plucked from Roman times, my girlfriend began to worry. The bike was gradually slowing down, and she feared I had dozed off. Nervously anticipating the first corner, she held her breath. To her immense relief, I managed the turn smoothly, steering us into the town unscathed. We found solace in a cosy café, where scrambled eggs on toast provided the perfect remedy for our morning woes.

And so, our adventure continued unabated. We were a pair of camping enthusiasts, forever in search of new landscapes, fresh air, and the liberating feeling of pitching our trusty tent.

Whether it was setting up camp amidst a sea of fellow bikers or finding solace in the solitude of nature, we revelled in the freedom and joy that camping brought us. There was a thrill in embracing the unknown, discovering hidden gems, and creating memories that would last a lifetime.

Hill Inn camp site 2010   ©Chris Heaton

Ironically the Old Hill Inn campsite has been restored and now, looks like the photo above. On our fateful visit, some 80% of the lower section had been removed for a car park and was a sea of mud.

This story stayed with me over the years, and when I realised the significance of what the landlord had said it struck me that this was one of the shaping factors of my life, my school uniform and the taunts, bullying and segregation I was forced to endure, writing this autobiography I decided this phrase was so significant, it should be used as the title.

It's only the dirty ones we don't want - Philip Wilkinson

A frozen adventure
© Author & Pixbaby

Despite it being February and had been snowing all week we decided to embark on another adventure to the Watermill Inn near Pateley Bridge. Unlike a bike rally, this outing attracted people from our regular Thursday group, with some arriving on motorcycles, others in cars, and a few using public transport. The weather forecast predicted extreme frost following the snowfall that occurred during the previous week.

As the group gathered at the pub, the twins Frodo and Bilbo, accompanied by Mutt and Spawny, were the first to arrive. Since the pub hadn't opened yet, they knocked on the landlord's residence and made a request. They asked if we could camp behind the pub as we planned to have a weekend session there. After a moment, filled with laughter behind the closed door, the landlord gave us permission. We ascended the steps built into the banking behind the pub and set up our tents. The ground appeared to have a light dusting of snow but was frozen solid. We had to borrow top stones from a nearby dry-stone wall to secure the tent pegs into the ground. I arrived later in the day, primarily intending to mock the lads for camping in extreme weather conditions once again and with no intention to stay. As I drove to the pub, descending Greenhow Hill, I encountered snowdrifts up to 12 feet deep. The road had only been cleared a few hours earlier by a snowplough equipped with a blower attachment. The plough had created a 12-foot-wide passage down the hill, depositing the snow into the surrounding fields. Riding cautiously on the ice left behind by the plough, I couldn't help but entertain the thought that if I slipped off the road, I might remain undiscovered for several days. However, upon arrival, I was offered a spot in one of the tents and a spare sleeping bag, tempting me to spend the night.

The evening at the pub was rowdy, with our group being the primary patrons for the weekend. The landlord taught us a trick to heat our tankards of beer using a red-hot poker from the fire. The effectiveness of this method in combating the extreme weather conditions remains debatable. As the night progressed, Frodo and Julie Belstaff engaged in a drinking competition. By around 2 AM, they had reached their twelfth pint of Theakston's Old

Peculiar, a strong brew with a 6.4% alcohol content. Julie eventually collapsed under the table, and Frodo triumphantly finished his and her last pint, securing his victory. On the way to the tents however, Frodo decided he needed to pee, so several lads helped him, but when Julie Belstaff said she needed the same, suddenly everyone had disappeared, and she was on her own.

Watermill Inn 1978   © Bilbo

With the pub nearing closing time, we decided to purchase beer for takeaway to enjoy in the tents. We bought 20 bottles of Theakston's bitter, which came in new wide-mouthed bottles with tear-off foil tops. We carefully placed the bottles inside the tents for safekeeping while we attempted to light a fire. Despite our efforts, the fire sank twelve inches into the snow, extinguishing itself due to the excess water. Frustrated, we retrieved the beer only to discover that the bottles had frozen solid, causing the foil tops to pop off. The beer was undrinkable.

Defeated by the elements, we called it a night and crawled into our tents. Some of the group, who had arrived by car or public transport, were ill-prepared for the weather, wearing shirts, denim jackets, or light jackets without proper boots or waterproof gear. Those sleeping in tents without doors or groundsheets didn't fare much better. As for myself, despite being promised a sleeping bag, I was only given a small blanket measuring about four feet square. I kept my motorcycle clothing on, including my helmet, in a futile attempt to stay warm. The bitter cold penetrated to my core.

It's only the dirty ones we don't want - Philip Wilkinson

Image of tents in similar conditions to those we endured © Pixababy

Our fire simply sank into the frozen snow and extinguished itself © Pixababy

That night, the guards at the nearby Menwith Hill listening station suffered from frostbite, and the temperature recorded was minus seventeen Celsius. As dawn broke the following morning around 6 AM, we decided to abandon the idea of sleeping and focused on warming ourselves up.

It's only the dirty ones we don't want - Philip Wilkinson

Those who arrived by car were fortunate enough to have a heater. Some of the motorcyclists tried to warm themselves using their bikes' hot exhaust pipes, but they were too hot to touch and provided little relief. Frodo, who had chosen to sleep in a military-style divvy bag in the field, woke up to find his hair frozen to the ground. He called for our assistance, and in the circumstances, the best we could offer was to urinate on his hair to thaw it so he could get up.

We stumbled into the greasy spoon café in Pateley Bridge around 7 AM, cold, dishevelled, and nursing hangovers. The owner couldn't believe his luck, having a full café so early in the morning, and he found great amusement in our tales from the previous evening.

© Pixababy

The dawn that day was something to behold, as the sun finally crawled into the sky, the sunrise was truly spectacular against the frozen backdrop of Nidderdale. What did we decide to do, well you guessed correctly, we stayed another night of course.

It's only the dirty ones we don't want - Philip Wilkinson

© Shutterstock

A trip to London Sporting Motorcycle Show at Earls Court

My badge from the show © Author

The adventures of the Aire Valley MCC continued as they embarked on a coach trip to the Racing and Sporting Motorcycle Show at Earls Court in London 1979. Picture about fifty members of the club, filled with excitement and crates of ale, speeding down the motorway from Leeds towards the bustling capital. Surprisingly, the coach made excellent time, outpacing their expectations. As they cruised along, another coach, undoubtedly carrying fellow motorcyclists headed to the same event, gradually overtook their coach. But that's when the mischief began.

Like mischievous schoolchildren, everyone on board the coach climbed onto their seats and gleefully mooned at the passing motorcyclists on the other coach. In a delightful display of bottoms, the motorcyclists from the other coach reciprocated the mooning and even snapped a few photographs of this memorable moment.

Finally arriving at Alexandra Palace, the two coach loads merged, and one of the other group members had the brilliant idea of using a Polaroid camera. We eagerly begged for copies of the photos taken earlier, eager to relive the hilarity of our impromptu mooning spectacle. After spending a decent amount of time at the car show, the group decided it was time to explore the vibrant city of London. The lads, driven by curiosity, insisted on venturing into Soho, the notorious district known for its seedy reputation. While my girlfriend wasn't particularly enthusiastic about the idea, I agreed to a brief visit.

Image Soho, London   Pixababy

And oh boy, Soho certainly lived up to its reputation. Strip shows, pornographic magazine shops, and sex toy emporiums lined the streets. During it all, a handful of daring lads from the group decided to experience one of the infamous live shows. They paid their entry fee, expecting an intriguing spectacle. Little did they know what awaited them.

Led through a maze of corridors and down a labyrinth of stairs, they were eventually ushered out into a dimly lit back alley through an old fire door.

Pixababy

Seizing the opportunity for more hilarity, the lads attempted to squeeze as many motorcyclists as they could into a telephone box before parting ways.

269

It's only the dirty ones we don't want - Philip Wilkinson

The Albert Hall © Author

As for my girlfriend and I, we opted to explore other parts of London, completely unfamiliar with the city and having done no prior research. We stumbled upon sights that were far from typical tourist hotspots. The triangular rotating sign of New Scotland Yard caught our attention, followed by the imposing presence of the post office tower. A visit to Speaker's Corner in Hyde Park added a touch of eccentricity to our day. Finally, we marvelled at the grandeur of the palace, the Houses of Parliament, and the serene beauty of the Thames embankment.

Buckingham Palace, The Mall © Pixababy

It's only the dirty ones we don't want - Philip Wilkinson

© Pixababy

Home brew

Home brewing became a prominent feature once again, as I decided to resurrect my brewing skills in a valiant effort to save some money. I invested in a fancy 40-pint plastic tub and two "plastic pigs" pressure vessels to ensure a continuous supply of brew. The brewing process commenced in the tub, and after about five days, it was time to transfer the concoction to one of the pigs, where sugar would be added to complete the fermentation.

To my surprise, the beer cleared up rather swiftly, thanks to the clever float mechanism in the pigs that ensured the tap always drew beer from just below the liquid level, guaranteeing a steady supply of crystal-clear beer.

On several occasions, the Thursday group found themselves back at my house, eagerly partaking in the homemade brew. It turned out that the economic aspect of brewing was overshadowed by the sheer enjoyment we derived from the process.

However, my girlfriend, bless her soul, wasn't always as thrilled. Imagine her dismay when she woke up in the morning to find a dozen or more hungover guys sprawled all over the house like a scene from a college frat party. And the cherry on top was the time she innocently walked into the bathroom, only to discover one of the lads peacefully dozing off on the bathroom floor. Oh, the joys of home brewing and its aftermath!

Then came the birth of my first child (1985 - out of the timescale but included for fun), having left my wife in the care of the midwives after delivery, and thinking I had a few days to myself, I went out for a beer with the Thursday club, of course when the pub declared last orders, we had never had enough, so it was round to mine to empty the home brew casks, after we passed out, there was a familiar noise I could not fully place, as it continued I started to realise it was the phone, limping over the bodies in the lounge, I picked it up, it was my wife saying I should come and collect here now, it was 07:00am, I tried to stall, but she had no sympathy at all, and I got the mother of all rollockings when I arrived back with her, and the baby, to half a dozen snoring bodies draped all over the house.

Image copyright https://www.allmusic.com/artist/the-tourists-mn0000921200/biography

The Tourists

During that period, my little brother found himself deeply involved in the music scene as the keyboard player for a successful band named Hooker. Their talent and energetic performances had propelled them to play at various large venues, including regular gigs at Leeds University and Menston Psychiatric Unit. Interestingly, my brother noticed a peculiar phenomenon during their performances at the psychiatric unit—the patients, despite the loud volume, would eagerly place their heads inside the bass bins. He speculated that this unusual behaviour might have served as a temporary respite from the overwhelming noises and voices they experienced, providing them with a sense of relief.

Amidst the exhilaration and chaos of one of these gigs, the soundboard technician encountered a challenge in achieving the perfect mix. Frustrated, he found himself approached by a man who struck up a conversation. Initially, the interaction seemed friendly, but as time went on, the man's presence became increasingly bothersome. Finally, the technician had reached his limit and firmly instructed the man to leave him to his work, telling him to "go and do one." Accepting the dismissal, the man redirected his attention toward the warm-up act for the evening, a band called The Tourists. Little did anyone know at that moment, the persistent man who had been dismissed by the soundboard technician was Dave Stewart himself, a talented musician and visionary. Undeterred by the technician's rebuff, Dave approached the members of The Tourists and engaged them in conversation. Recognizing their potential and impressed by their performance, he saw an opportunity and decided to sign them. This pivotal encounter with Dave Stewart marked the beginning of a new chapter for The Tourists, as well as for two of its members, Annie Lennox, and Dave Stewart.

Over time, the band evolved and transformed, taking on a new name and direction. Annie Lennox's mesmerizing and soulful vocals, combined with Dave Stewart's innovative musical arrangements, formed the core of the newly formed duo known as The Eurythmics. From their humble beginnings as The Tourists, The Eurythmics would go on to achieve tremendous success and become one of the most influential and iconic musical acts of their time.

Looking back on those days, my little brother's involvement in Hooker not only provided him with incredible experiences and the thrill of performing in front of enthusiastic crowds, but it also connected him to a remarkable story deeply intertwined with the legacy of The Eurythmics. The journey from being regulars at Leeds Uni and the Menston psychiatric unit to witnessing the rise of Annie Lennox and Dave Stewart's musical career serves as a testament to the unpredictable nature of the music industry and the profound impact chance encounters can have on shaping destinies...

I am still in contact with Annie Lennox from back in her Tourist's days and recently we chatted about those times, she was sorry to hear of the lead singer and my brothers demise and I hold her to a promise of tickets and pre concert drinks next time she is touring in my region, a classic lady indeed.

Chapter 19 – 1980

Moving Forward

Dragon Rally Badge © Author

Dragon Rally

Campsite Betws Garmon, Wales Conway and District Motorcycle Club, 1980

Our next event was the legendary Dragon rally in the beautiful Snowdonia region of North Wales. This rally has been going on since 1962, making it one of the oldest and most iconic motorcycle gatherings in the UK. Now, let me take you back to the year of our tale, where the rally was set to take place in a pub with a vast field for camping. As expected, the place was teeming with bikers from all corners, and the beer was flowing well. The field was a colourful spectacle, adorned with hundreds of tents, ready to shelter the adventurous souls who dared to face the wintry elements.

On the way, Mutt, and his peculiar fear of overpaying for fuel was an issue again. It seems his frugality knew no bounds, even when it came to his beloved bike.

Whenever we embarked on camping trips or joined rallies, a stop at the filling station was inevitable. Most of us would dutifully fill our tanks to the brim, ensuring we had enough fuel for the journey ahead. But not Mutt.

Oh no, Mutt had a routine of his own. He would march up and down the forecourt, grumbling about the exorbitant prices and refusing to part with his hard-earned cash. The rest of us would drive off, thinking he'd come to his senses and catch up later. However, like clockwork, Mutt would find the next filling station, resume his complaints, and begrudgingly pump in a measly half a gallon of fuel. This bizarre ritual repeated itself until, inevitably, he found himself stranded on the road, running on fumes.

Now, here's where it gets interesting. Mutt, in his infinite frugality, relied on the kindness (or exasperation) of his fellow riders. We became his fuel saviours, scrounging around for any container we could find—a disposable plastic cup, perhaps—to siphon some precious fuel from our own tanks. We'd reluctantly oblige, knowing it was the only way to keep the group moving forward. But even then, Mutt would hesitate, reluctant to partake in this act of financial surrender.

Well, on this occasion, a few of us had had enough. We made a pact, silently agreeing that if Mutt ran out of fuel again, we would leave him behind. Harsh, yes, but after countless episodes of his penny-pinching antics, we felt it was time to teach him a lesson.

As Mutt's bike sputtered to a halt, abandoned by the fuel that he had stubbornly refused to purchase, we continued our merry way, leaving him in the rear-view mirror. Whether he learned his lesson or not, we can only speculate. But one thing was certain: Mutt's days of relying on the generosity of his fellow riders were numbered.

It was an unusual situation, Mutt would spend a fortune maintaining his bike, new shiny bits almost every week, new tires when the old were half used, replacement chrome hex key bolt sets for the engine casings that were not shiny enough, so he sold the set to me, and bought another, change the oil every 500 miles and more. He just drew the line at petrol. Mutt still has the black GS750 to this day.

Sometimes, the road teaches us its own lessons, and Mutt's journey was certainly one for the books. Perhaps his next camping trip would involve a crash course in fuel management and a newfound appreciation for the value of a full tank. But until then, he was left to ponder the consequences of his thrifty ways, hoping for a knight in shining armour with a spare cup of petrol to come to his rescue.

Betws Inn Betws Garmon, Wales   Image capture: Oct 2021 © 2023 Google

Now, picture this: the Friday night was in full swing, the rally-goers were revelling, and the air was filled with laughter and excitement. Suddenly, out of nowhere, two peculiar gentlemen strolled into the pub. But here's the twist, they were wearing nothing but a bowler hat, a tie, carried a briefcase, an umbrella, and completed their ensemble with black leather shoes, socks, and garters. Yep, you heard it right, they were strutting their stuff in their birthday suits, except for those odd accessories. Their audacious entrance sliced through the crowd, leaving jaws dropped and eyes wide open. They made their way to the bar, completely unfazed by the spectacle they were causing, and nonchalantly ordered two pints of beer.

Well, as you can imagine, the sight was too much for the poor landlady to handle. She burst into uncontrollable fits of laughter and had to excuse herself to go lie down, trying to regain her composure. Those two gents, with their unique fashion sense (or lack thereof), leisurely sipped their pints and then disappeared into the night, leaving everyone in awe and disbelief. No one seemed to know who they were or what prompted them to grace the rally with their outrageous presence. They must have hatched a plan to surprise the whole event, and boy, did they succeed!

Rally badge from the event © Author

Ides Of March Rally my second year

The Moorcock Inn, Halifax Rd, Littleborough, March 1980, Salford Centurion's MCC

The Moorcock Inn © Bill Boaden

It's only the dirty ones we don't want - Philip Wilkinson

Following the blizzards that plagues last year's Ides of March, we hoped for slightly better weather this time around, whilst cold and wet, we were spared the snow. The Moorcock Inn is one of those pubs that is just unforgettable, it is now a country pub, & restaurant, but in the day, it was not so pretentious, and even let a motorcycle club hold a rally or two.

The previous year, the police had closed the M62 due to sever snow and ice, the news footage showed police running and sliding down the middle carriage with Jac knifed lorries around them after their rolling lorry clearance solution had failed.

As I recall, beer was in plentiful supply, the pub was warm and welcoming, if a tad over filled, the rally had been required to reduce the numbers this year and so this was an invite only rally.

I recollect seeing two late sleepers about 11AM on the Saturday getting the wake-up call, rally style, their tent was opened quietly so as not to disturb the sleeping inside, bikes had been tied to their sleeping bags and with a sudden start of engines, they were being dragged round the field. After a few seconds, they were awake, and I could not help but think why not just let go of the sleeping bags rather than bounce/drag round the whole camp site, turned out, they both slept in the buff and wanted to protect their modesty, or the little they had left, and it was very cold.

© Pixababy

Milestones

The year marked a significant milestone in my life as my apprenticeship reached its conclusion. my girlfriend and I had taken our relationship to the next level and were now engaged.

It's only the dirty ones we don't want - Philip Wilkinson

During our camping adventures, we made the decision to embark on another exciting journey together, to purchase our first home. We scoured various properties, but none seemed to capture our hearts until we stumbled upon a charming three-bedroom townhouse in Kirkstall, boasting a picturesque view of the abbey.

The house checked all the boxes we had envisioned, a spacious layout with well-proportioned bedrooms, a cosy living/dining area, a functional galley kitchen, and a remarkably large back garden. Enamoured by its potential, we eagerly agreed to purchase the property for £16,000.

To make our dream a reality, we secured a mortgage of £11,400 at an interest rate of 15.75%.

Initially, our new neighbours, a retired couple, welcomed us with open arms. They were acquainted with my girlfriend's mother and were delighted to have us as their new neighbours. However, as we began making improvements to our home, including installing new central heating, double-glazed windows, and transforming the coal and tool sheds near the front door into a stylish glazed porch, the dynamics changed. The couple's initial delight turned into envy, and tensions began to rise.

Within a year of moving in, our once-friendly neighbours ceased all communication with us. We were met with icy silence, and any attempts at conversation were met with cold indifference. As time went on, their hostility intensified to the point where they solely communicated with us through solicitor's letters. It was a distressing turn of events that left us bewildered and saddened by the deterioration of what could have been a harmonious neighbourhood relationship.

© iStock

One Christmas day, after having travelled to my girlfriend's parents for dinner, we arrived home about 2pm to find that the driveway was blocked with a visiting relatives car, as the property was on a cul-de-sac, parking in the turning circle was not permitted, yet they had chosen to park and deliberately blocked my driveway, ignoring this stupidity, I parked in the only space left open, right behind their car. At 4am the following day the police arrived and woke us to move our car, the police gave me a verbal warning for parking in the cul-de-sac blocking a car from leaving. By this time, the car had been parked blocking my driveway for over 15 hours, at any time during this period, a reasonable person could have called around, wished us a merry Christmas and we could have swapped places with the cars, but these were not reasonable people.

Despite the strain caused by our neighbours' actions, my girlfriend and I remained resilient. We focused on turning our house into a warm and inviting home, cherishing the memories we created within its walls. Our determination to create a comfortable and welcoming space for ourselves became a testament to our perseverance and love for each other.

© Pixababy

During another eventful period, we had a group of friends who were expert builders, their wedding present was to transform the area behind our house into a beautiful stone patio. The project involved levelling the sloping ground and creating raised stone flowerbeds, resulting in an impressive and visually stunning patio. Simultaneously, we were also replacing the old cracked and broken concrete path around the property with new York stone flags.

However, amidst the construction process, we encountered an unexpected and unpleasant incident with our neighbour. They took it upon themselves to open the gate that connected our gardens and proceeded to cut all the builders' tapes that crossed the pathway. This act of interference and vandalism caused unnecessary disruption and frustration.

To our surprise, we received a solicitor's letter shortly after, accusing us of removing the pathway that provided our neighbours with a right of way for emergency access.

The letter from their solicitor contained various threats, highlighting potential legal actions and the associated costs. It even insinuated that I had violated the law by removing the pathway.

However, by the time the letter arrived, the path had already been reinstated and made safe. The entire process, from removing the old path to installing the new one, had taken a mere four days to complete. It was an efficient and swift resolution to the situation.

It's only the dirty ones we don't want - Philip Wilkinson

Reflecting on the incident, it was truly a tale that seemed almost unbelievable. The clash with our neighbour, their interference with the construction process, and the subsequent legal threats all created a narrative that one would find hard to fabricate.

In the end, the challenges we faced with our neighbours served as a reminder of the importance of finding solace within our own sanctuary. We learned to rely on each other, cherishing the joy and tranquillity our home provided. The house in Kirkstall, overlooking the abbey, became a symbol of our commitment and the beginning of a new chapter in our lives together.

In due course we would marry in our local church Saint Mary's C of E at Hawksworth and hold the reception in the Vesper Gate pub at the bottom of the street, then in the evening, we and several of our friends got changed, rode out to Grassington where most camped in Grass Woods for the night whilst we took a room at the Black Horse Hotel.

Moving on

Ides of March would not be my last rally, I attended the Pennine and Monkey Hangers and the now infamous Northern Venturer rally along with the second Dwyle Funkers Rally (badge a bit small but correctly spelled this time. but pressures were mounting, and changes were happening, the house needed work and I spent five months that year working away from home based out of Sheffield branch, covering the Peak district and even parts of Manchester. I still went camping a few times a year with my girlfriend and a wedding was now planned.

My badges for Pennine, Monkey Hangers, Northern Venturer and Dwyle Funkers 1980

Closing thoughts

As the years passed, the memories of youthful adventures and misadventures became cherished anecdotes among our group of friends. We had grown older and wiser, our paths diverging in various directions, but the bonds forged in those formative years remained unbreakable. The experiences we had shared, whether joyous or challenging, had shaped us into the individuals we had become.

It's only the dirty ones we don't want - Philip Wilkinson

Looking back, it was evident that our youthful escapades had taught us valuable lessons. We had learned the importance of friendship, the thrill of discovery, and the resilience needed to overcome obstacles. Our shared passion for tinkering, exploring, and pushing boundaries had ignited a curiosity within us that continued to burn brightly.

Bilbo and Frodo had pursued their scientific interests and found success in the fields of electronic and satellite engineering. They never lost their fascination for gadgets and inventions, continuously seeking new challenges to conquer.

As for Erotic, his mischievous spirit had found a more constructive outlet. He had developed a keen interest in automotive engineering and had become an accomplished engineer. Surprisingly, his reckless tendencies had transformed into excellence in the workplace, where his skills and determination earned him recognition and respect.

Our adventures on two wheels had left an indelible mark on us, even if some of those memories were tinged with pain and mishaps. We had discovered the limits of our physical abilities, the importance of safety, and the need to appreciate the simple pleasures in life. Our love for cycling, motorcycles and camping had evolved into a shared appreciation for the great outdoors, which we continued to explore in different ways.

With the passing of time, we had gained a deeper understanding of ourselves and the world around us. Our collective experiences had shaped our values, instilling in us a sense of responsibility and a desire to make a positive impact. We recognised that the friendships forged in our youth were not just about shared adventures but also about supporting one another through the ups and downs of life.

And so, we set forth into the world, ready to make our mark, armed with the lessons learned from our shared past and the unwavering support of lifelong friends. The road ahead was uncertain, but we faced it with courage and the knowledge that our youthful escapades had prepared us for whatever lay ahead.

The story of our extraordinary adventures may have reached its final chapter, but our individual narratives were far from complete. The echoes of our laughter and the spirit of camaraderie would forever resonate in our hearts, reminding us of a time when the world was our playground, and anything seemed possible.

As the book closed on this chapter of our lives, we eagerly turned the page, ready to embrace the next great adventure that awaited us. The journey was not without its challenges, but with the memories of our shared escapades fuelling our spirits, we were determined to seize the opportunities that lay ahead.

The end of this tale marked the beginning of countless new stories, each filled with its own unique blend of triumphs and tribulations. And so, we bid farewell to the past and set our sights on the horizon, ready to create a future filled with laughter, discovery, and the enduring bonds of friendship.

The end.

PS.

Despite a difficult start in my early school years, marked by discouraging comments from Mr. Slack (Headmaster, Abbey Grange CofE), I chose to view those challenges as motivation.

From the third year of school onwards, my teenage years significantly improved as I formed strong, lifelong friendships, took a keen interest in science and maths, ultimately succeeded in my GCE examinations and this interest paved the way for a successful future.

I seized the opportunity to receive an apprenticeship with Chubb Alarms, which eventually led me to establish and manage my own approved intruder/CCTV company for 15 years in the role of technical director.

I then served as both technical director and managing director of Xtag Limited, I spearheaded the development of innovative ultra long-range RFID tagging solutions for asset monitoring. These solutions were successfully implemented in various contexts, including monitoring newborn babies in postnatal wards—an important application that contributed to the safety and well-being of infants, I successfully applied for two grants for development from Yorkshire Forward and led a small team to success.

Furthermore, I managed a £2.7 million project in collaboration with Depuy (Johnson & Johnson) to advance orthopaedic technology.

Presently, I am the proud owner and Managing Director of a successful business, Online Security Products Limited. This achievement further underscores my dedication and entrepreneurial spirit.

Additionally, in 2020, I fulfilled a lifelong personal aspiration by becoming a published author, now with five books to my credit.

This journey demonstrates the power of perseverance and the ability to overcome adversity. It serves as a reminder that one should never let others' negative opinions define their potential. So, in response to Mr. Slack, I can confidently say that I have achieved remarkable success and accomplishments throughout my career and personal life.

It's only the dirty ones we don't want - Philip Wilkinson

Photo gallery of bike club meets and rallies taken at the time.

Reproduced with kind permission, these are photographs taken at the time of the Aire Valley bike club meets and a few rallies between 1977 and 1980, those featured may recognise themselves, however I have not named any individuals save for myself, There are a few photos not attributed, if you know where they were taken, please let me know

Copyright remains with the photographer/s Bilbo and Aire Valley MCC for all images reproduced in this section.

Photo of me, centre, wearing some of the rally badges from the day, probably about 1978 as both the Watermill Rally badges are present

Another of me, left, on the same day.

A few of the lads, estimated 1978

It's only the dirty ones we don't want - Philip Wilkinson

Camping, Isle of Man 1979

Antics on a CB125 bike estimated 1978.

It's only the dirty ones we don't want - Philip Wilkinson

Camping again, estimated 1978

Aire Valley MCC trip to Isle of Man, note the bikes from this era estimated 1979.

It's only the dirty ones we don't want - Philip Wilkinson

Drinking more beer

I am third from the left here

It's only the dirty ones we don't want - Philip Wilkinson

Not sure where this was taken.

Isle of Man 1978

It's only the dirty ones we don't want - Philip Wilkinson

In the Old Hill Inn barn 1978.

Creg-Ny-Bar Hotel Isle of Man 1979

It's only the dirty ones we don't want - Philip Wilkinson

Just setting off – Templegate Rise Halton

The Tankard Rally, Leeds 1978   ©Bilbo

It's only the dirty ones we don't want - Philip Wilkinson

A selection of my motorcycle rally badges 1977 – 1980   © Author

It's only the dirty ones we don't want - Philip Wilkinson

Copyrights –

Images, I have tried to acknowledge copyright for any images used, please advise if you disagree/or own the copyright and I will remove the image, or provide correct attribution as required.

Text, where any text has been utilised from an article or other publication, I have credited the author or publication with the copyright adjacent.

Author

Bilbo

Spawny

Members of the Aire Valley MCC with kind permission

Shutterstock

iStock

Pixbaby

It's only the dirty ones we don't want - Philip Wilkinson

Other publications by the author

Alarming Stories
Tales of an apprentice intruder alarm engineer

https://www.alarming-stories.co.uk

A series of short stories detailing the highs and lows of an apprentice in the late 1970's. This autobiography provides an insight into many rude, funny, annoying, and sometimes downright dangerous situations I encountered during my formative teenage years. It also provides an understanding of early high security intruder alarm systems, which were surprisingly crude by modern standards.

The tales of a famous Yorkshire vet published when I was eleven in 1970, televised in 1978 and the re-run in 2020 had a lifelong influence on me. Driving through Yorkshire to service and repair security systems in all weathers and at all times of the day, I felt an affinity with him and often visited remote locations all over Yorkshire, always and in all weathers. I have often mused if it would be possible to write a similar fact-based story about my own unique experiences within the intruder alarm industry.

Alarming Stories II
Tales of a security engineer

During my period as a security engineer, I witnessed many interesting situations. The following tales give a flavour of what it was like in the industry in the early 1980's.

It also provides an insight into many rude, funny, and sometimes downright dangerous situations I encountered during the early years of career.

The stories that follow were mainly witnessed by myself first-hand, a few were related to me in detail by the engineers I worked with. Care has been taken to conceal the names of the people I worked with to protect their identity; however, I suspect many will be able to recognise themselves when the read the book.

Alarming Stories III
Tales of a security company director

In this captivating book, we are invited into a world of incredible stories, poignant reflections, and transformative experiences of a director tasked with the running of a small security company in the North of England.

Through the author's words, we gain insight into the challenges faced, the lessons learned, and the growth that emerges from navigating life's twists and turns. Whether you are seeking solace in the face of adversity, seeking guidance in times of uncertainty, or simply craving a deeper understanding of the human experience, this book will resonate with you. It is a testament to the power of conversation, the beauty of vulnerability, and the limitless potential for growth and transformation that lies within us all.

Prepare to be moved, uplifted, and inspired as you dive into the pages of this extraordinary book. Let the author's words resonate within you and embark on a journey of self-discovery and connection that will leave an indelible mark on your soul.

Fireworks
Tales of a pyromaniac

https://fireworks.me.uk/

Dive into the kaleidoscopic world of fireworks through the pages of this captivating memoir. From the cobblestone streets of Headingley to the pinnacle of retirement, the author's passion for pyrotechnics has set a lifetime ablaze. Organizing private and professional displays, running a successful retail business, and crisscrossing Europe for the grandest spectacles—every chapter is a burst of vibrant experiences.

Relive the charm of communal bonfire parties, the aroma of plot toffee, and the crackle of roaring flames that fuelled the author's lifelong enchantment. A precocious ten-year-old orchestrating penny-for-the-guy collections, meticulously curating firework lists that impressed even the most discerning neighbours—each anecdote is a testament to the enduring magic of the craft.

As adolescence ushered in the freedom of a motorcycle, the author traversed the UK to witness and partake in myriad fiery displays. Settling down brought forth the resurgence of home firework displays, evolving from family selections to orchestrating elaborate showcases that culminated in a millennium celebration utilising electronically fired professional fireworks set to music with 60 neighbours.

Venturing further into the fiery realm, a business partnership led to the establishment of a prominent fireworks retail franchise, offering access to awe-inspiring displays, and professional fireworks from mortar shells to thunderous 1000-shot wonders. Today, the competition for the most colossal single firework in the neighbourhood remains a vibrant tradition, with the author proudly showcasing a Klasek King of Fireworks F4.

But the excitement doesn't end at home. In a departure from tradition, this year unfolds a unique adventure as the author travels to Reykjavik to witness the explosive spectacle of Icelandic New Year's Eve fireworks. In a land where pyrotechnic exuberance knows no bounds, eye protection is not just recommended—it's a necessity.

This memoir is a celebration of a lifelong love affair with the dazzling world of fireworks, a journey marked by passion, competition, and the enduring magic that continues to light up the author's world.

Printed in Great Britain
by Amazon